SPACESHIP IN THE DESERT

EXPERIMENTAL FUTURES

Technological Lives, Scientific Arts, Anthropological Voices

A series edited by Michael M. J. Fischer and Joseph Dumit

Spaceship in the Desert

ENERGY, CLIMATE CHANGE,

and URBAN DESIGN *in* ABU DHABI

GÖKÇE GÜNEL

DUKE UNIVERSITY PRESS · *Durham and London* · 2019

Printed in the United States of America on acid-free paper ∞
Designed by Matthew Tauch
Typeset in Minion Pro by Graphic Composition, Inc., Bogart, Georgia

Library of Congress Cataloging-in-Publication Data
Names: Günel, Gökçe, [date] author.
Title: Spaceship in the desert : energy, climate change, and urban design in Abu Dhabi / Gökçe Günel.
Description: Durham : Duke University Press, 2019. | Series: Experimental futures | Includes bibliographical references and index.
Identifiers: LCCN 2018031276 (print) | LCCN 2018041898 (ebook)
ISBN 9781478002406 (ebook)
ISBN 9781478000723 (hardcover : alk. paper)
ISBN 9781478000914 (pbk. : alk. paper)
Subjects: LCSH: Sustainable urban development--United Arab Emirates—Abu Zaby (Emirate) | City planning—Environmental aspects—United Arab Emirates—Abu Zaby (Emirate) | Technological innovations—Environmental aspects—United Arab Emirates—Abu Zaby (Emirate) | Urban ecology (Sociology) —United Arab Emirates—Abu Zaby (Emirate)
Classification: LCC HT243.U52 (ebook) | LCC HT243.U52 A28 2019 (print)
DDC 307.1/16095357—dc23
LC record available at https://lccn.loc.gov/2018031276

Cover art: Innovation Centre, Masdar City, United Arab Emirates, 2014. Photo by Hufton and Crow / VIEW / Getty Images.

Contents

Acknowledgments

This book project began more than ten years ago in Ithaca, and carried me to Cambridge, Damascus, Dubai, Abu Dhabi, Bonn, Durban, Split, Doha, Houston, New York, Tucson, and every now and then, Istanbul. In each city, I met thoughtful interlocutors who gave me important feedback on this work and shaped its priorities. As W. G. Sebald says in *Austerlitz*, "We take almost all the decisive steps in our lives as a result of slight inner adjustments of which we are barely conscious." I thank everyone who engaged with this project for facilitating these slight inner adjustments, and for letting me learn from them.

In Ithaca, I learned how to collaborate with others on seemingly solitary projects. I thank Hiro Miyazaki, Mike Fischer, Chuck Geisler, and Karen Pinkus for encouraging me to write about energy, climate change, and urbanism, and for leaving their imprint on the early stages of this work. I thank Aftab Jassal, Melissa Rosario, Saiba Varma, Chika Watanabe, and Courtney Work for reading the first versions of my chapters in our writing group, and for making constructive comments. Saiba and Chika have remained careful readers of the work and have seen its transformations over many years. Anindita Banerjee, Dominic Boyer, Susan Buck-Morss, Jeremy Foster, Webb Keane, Dominick LaCapra, Stacey Langwick, and

Barry Maxwell supported the project during my years at Cornell. I also thank Rishad Choudhury, Ali Çakır, Can Dalyan, Berk Esen, and Chris Levesque for their friendship. Khaled Malas gave me inspiration. I thank him for his care and support.

The relationships I established in Houston while I was a postdoctoral researcher at Rice University have been transformative in professional and personal ways. My thanks to the participants of the Cultures of Energy Seminar at Rice, who met regularly to discuss questions of significance to this book. My engagement with Dominic Boyer and Cymene Howe on energy issues started during my year as a Cultures of Energy fellow. Andrea Ballestero, Shirine Hamadeh, Cyrus Mody, Seda Karslıoğlu, and Aynne Kokas supported me during that fellowship year. George Hirasaki and Eugene Levy met with me to talk about carbon capture and storage technologies. Albert Pope offered thoughts about many aspects of urbanism and climate change. Jim Faubion and W. R. Dull not only helped me during periods of indecision and uncertainty, but were also there to mark moments of conviction and certitude. I wrote most of this book in the Houston office of SCHAUM/SHIEH Architects. I thank all the designers in the office for sharing their days with me, and for reminding me how difficult it is to make a building. Most of all, I thank Troy Schaum, who made Houston a home.

In New York City, I found a very rich intellectual environment. Cassie Fennell, Brian Larkin, Brink Messick, Beth Povinelli, Mick Taussig, and Paige West were important interlocutors at Columbia and provided productive and precise feedback on my work. I especially thank Brian Larkin for reading the introduction to this book at a critical turning point and giving me useful advice. I was lucky to share my experience at Columbia as a postdoctoral scholar with Brian Goldstone, Sarah Muir, Chelsey Kivland, and Zoë Wool. They each supported the project in their own ways. I also thank the organizers and participants of the four workshops and reading groups I attended regularly during my time in New York and where I shared work: the Ecology and Culture Seminar at Columbia, organized by Paige West; and the Animal Studies Workshop at Columbia, organized by Brian Boyd; the Science and Society Workshop at NYU, organized by Rayna Rapp and Emily Martin; and finally the G-Line Seminar, organized by Mick Taussig.

During my time at Columbia and beyond, I received comments on my work from colleagues who work on infrastructure and urbanism, including Nikhil Anand, Jonathan Bach, Keller Easterling, Michael Goldman, Max Hirsh, Orit Halpern, James Holston, Eric Kleinenberg, Shannon Mattern, Bettina Stoetzer, and Austin Zeiderman. I received support from scholars who work on these issues in the Middle East, especially Jessie Barnes, Steve Caton, Julia Elyachar, Arang Keshavarzian, Laleh Khalili, Mandana Limbert, and Joanne Nucho. I also had opportunities to learn from colleagues who work on different aspects of science, technology, and the environment, including David McDermott Hughes, Karen Pinkus, Kaushik Sunder Rajan, Jennifer Wenzel, Jerome Whitington, Jerry Zee, and Tyler Zoanni. My friends Saygun Gökarıksel, Karen Holmberg, and Aslı Zengin have read parts of the work. Over the years, I have been in writing groups with Sarah El Kazaz, Bridget Guarasci, Toby Craig Jones, Aynne Kokas, Anne Rademacher, and Sophia Stamatopoulou-Robbins. This project has been shaped by their attentive questions.

I finished revising this book in Tucson. The School of Middle Eastern and North African Studies at the University of Arizona has been very generous, giving me the space and time to sharpen the book's final drafts. I thank Ben Fortna for showing his support for me in most critical times. Brian Silverstein and Anne Betteridge provided me with guidance. Many thanks to my colleagues at Arizona for their engagement with the project in different forms. I also thank Kris Hogeboom, Jennifer Paine, and Eldon Vita for helping me with university bureaucracy. My students have read drafts of the manuscript in graduate seminars and shared their comments.

Most of the preparation and fieldwork for this project took place between 2008 and 2012. I especially thank Mike Fischer for hosting me at MIT, and for visiting me in the UAE. Canay Özden-Schilling, Tom Özden-Schilling, Bhavin Patel, and Bernardo Zacka shared my initial fieldwork experiences in Cambridge. I thank David Rojas and Jessie Barnes for time spent at the Climate Summits in Durban and Doha. In Damascus, I thank Gülay Türkmen and Katharina Grüneisl who attended Arabic classes with me. Khaled Malas and his family irrevocably shaped my relationship to Damascus. In Dubai and Abu Dhabi, many people whose identities I cannot reveal assisted me and taught me about the spaces we inhabited together. I thank them for making time for my questions and for sharing their thoughts and experiences on energy and climate change. I met Daniel Haberly, Daniel Cardoso Llach, and Nida Rehman in Dubai as fellow fieldworkers. I am thankful to Arda Doğan, who navigated, among many other places, the Arab Gulf with me, and made this project possible.

I presented sections of this book at Boğaziçi University, Columbia, Cornell, Durham University, FIU, Harvard, Haverford College, Hong Kong University, Humboldt-Universität zu Berlin, Koç University, LSE, MIT, New York Academy of Sciences, Northern Arizona University, NYU, NYU-Abu Dhabi, Oberlin College, Ohio State, Princeton, Rice, Sabancı University, The New School, University of Arizona, University of Chicago, University of Oslo, Washington University in St. Louis, and Yale. I workshopped the manuscript with audiences at Rutgers University and the University of Texas in Austin. I thank my hosts in all of these institutions, especially Tim Allen, Gianpaolo Baiocchi, Ayfer Bartu-Candan, Anne Betteridge, Brian Boyd, Steve Caton, Young Rae Choi, Jason Cons, Sarah El Kazaz, Cassie Fennell, Mike Fischer, Curt Gambetta, Fatoş Gökşen, Natalia Gutkowski, Erik Harms, Max Hirsh, David McDermott Hughes, Eric Kleinenberg, Sheila Jasanoff, Andrew Alan Johnson, Toby Craig Jones, Joe Masco, Brink Messick, Jörg Niewöhner, Knut Gunnar Nustad, Rayna Rapp, Scott Reese, Jesse Shipley, Bob Simpson, Genese Sodikoff, Justin Stearns, Glenn Davis Stone, Paige West, Max Woodworth, Zoë Wool, and Deniz Yükseker, for making these presentations happen. Many thanks to audience members in all of these forums for their careful engagement with the text.

Many colleagues helped me with arduous visa and permanent residency applications, allowing me to stay in the United States as a foreigner. I thank Dominic Boyer, Joe Dumit, Julia Elyachar, Mike Fischer, Chuck Geisler, Erik Harms, Joe Masco, Hiro Miyazaki, Jörg Niewöhner, Karen Pinkus, Beth Povinelli, Bob Simpson, Jerome Whitington, Deniz Yükseker, and Austin Zeiderman for assisting me at different stages of my immigration process with their letters. Their support has been invaluable. I also thank Ben Fortna for being so understanding about these issues.

I would like to thank the Wenner Gren Foundation and the ACLS Foundation for their financial support for the project. I also received financial assistance from Cornell University, Rice University, Columbia University, and the University of Arizona. Earlier versions of some of the text presented in the chapters appeared in the following journals: *Anthropological Quarterly*, *Limn*, *The Fibreculture Journal*, *The ARPA Journal*, *The Yearbook of Comparative Literature*, and *Anthropology News*. I have also contributed to the following edited volumes: *Climates: Architecture and the Planetary Imaginary*, *Anthropocene Unseen: A Lexicon*, *The New Arab Urban*, and *Frontier Assemblages*. I thank the reviewers and editors, especially Dominic Boyer, Stephen Collier, Jason Cons, Michael Eilenberg, James Graham, Cymene Howe, Janette Kim, Chris Mizes, Harvey Molotch, Gustav Peebles, Anand Pandian, Davide Ponzini, and Antina von Schnitzler, who helped sharpen my arguments, and improved the text.

Many thanks to Ken Wissoker, Elizabeth Ault, Mary Hoch, and Susan Albury at Duke University Press. Ken's insights were key in making vital decisions about the project. I also thank the anonymous reviewers for their incisive suggestions. Deirdre O'Dwyer edited the manuscript and gave detailed and attentive comments on each sentence. I have learned so much from her careful work. I would also like to acknowledge Don Larson and Paula Robbins for their work on maps and illustrations, and Eileen Quam for her work on the index.

Most of all, I thank friends and family members who have heard about this book during its decade-long evolution. Hayal Pozantı, Başak Aydın, Arda Doğan, Zeynep Güzel, Seda Karslıoğlu, Baki Kantaşı, Zeynep Kayhan, Emil Keyder, and Erdem Taşdelen witnessed its various ups and downs. Many thanks to Ayşin and İbrahim Demirtaş and my cousins Aylin and Ada. My parents Melek and Sabit Günel had confidence in my work. I thank my sister Cansu Günel for her curiosity. My grandmother Güler Demirtaş was my first teacher. I dedicate this book to her. Finally, I thank Troy Schaum for the pleasures of our shared life.

Introduction: The Soul of Carbon Dioxide

In May 2011, shortly before I left the United Arab Emirates, I took a long cab ride with Marco from Masdar City to Dubai. Marco was an Ecuadorian man in his late thirties and had been working with Abu Dhabi's Masdar Carbon as an environmental consultant for about two years, focusing on climate change policy. I had been researching Abu Dhabi's emergent renewable energy and clean technology infrastructures, spending my days on the same floor as Marco for almost a year, but we had never exchanged words before taking this ride. My cubicle was a few feet away from his office, which, despite its glass partition wall, afforded him relative privacy. He also specialized in a project that I did not know much about and did not collaborate very often with my group. But on this afternoon, for reasons purely coincidental, we were headed to our apartments in Dubai, sharing the back seat of a heavily air-conditioned Toyota.

Masdar, where Marco worked and I conducted research, had officially been founded in May 2006 as a multifaceted renewable energy and clean technology company. Abu Dhabi–owned Mubadala, an investment company that seeks to facilitate economic diversification in the emirate, provided funding for the project. The word *masdar* means "source" in Arabic, an origin from which something comes or can be obtained. The company was widely known for Masdar City, the "futuristic" eco-city that had been master-planned by the London-based architecture firm Foster + Partners to rely entirely on renewable energy. Prior to being selected as the planners for Masdar City, Foster + Partners had designed famous projects such as the Gherkin in London and the Reichstag in Berlin, and were also working on a building in Abu Dhabi called the Souk, Abu Dhabi Central Market.[1] Their Masdar City master plan would offer living and working space to fifty thousand residents and forty thousand commuters in a 640-hectare area neighboring the Abu Dhabi International Airport, the Yas Marina Formula 1 Circuit, and the Al Ghazal Golf Course.[2] Strategically located to facilitate transportation for the renewable energy and clean technology professionals who would live on site, Masdar would be linked to the airport by existing roads. A twenty-minute drive from Abu Dhabi proper and about an hour's drive from Dubai, the site was situated to serve as a hub for the UAE's renewable energy and clean technology sector.

While the eco-city and its multiple infrastructure facilities were central to Masdar's development, Masdar had also been investing in renewable energy via its other operations—Masdar Power, Masdar Carbon, and Masdar Capital—in an attempt to ensure that Abu Dhabi would remain a significant player in the energy industry well after its oil reserves run dry or become less valuable. Masdar Institute, the energy-focused research center that was set up and supervised by the Massachusetts Institute of Technology's Technology and Development Program, operated on a growing campus amid the fledgling eco-city.

During 2010 and 2011, the period of focus for my research into renewable energy and clean technology infrastructures in Abu Dhabi, the Foster-designed Masdar Institute campus was the only operational structure at the Masdar City site (though other buildings such as the Siemens headquarters were under construction). The campus had officially been inaugurated in November 2010 (see chapter 1). It provided classrooms, laboratories, office space, and dormitories for Masdar Institute students and faculty, and housed a cafeteria, a sushi restaurant, a coffee shop, a small gym, a library, and an organic grocery store. Yet most of the professionals working with Masdar, such as Marco, spent their days in a simple makeshift compound next to the Masdar City parking lot that was intended to be dismantled upon the construction of the Masdar headquarters building. The compound had a separate cafeteria, but occasionally Masdar employees walked, took a shuttle bus, or rode the personal rapid transit pods

FIGURE I.1 · Masdar City

to the Masdar Institute campus to have lunch at the sushi restaurant or take a coffee break at the Caribou Café branch. Some Masdar employees also frequented the Institute building to collaborate on research projects or supervise the construction process. Depending on my daily research schedule, I divided my time between the Masdar Institute campus and the compound and took rides back to Dubai in the evenings.

For about a thirty-mile stretch, the eighty-mile road from Abu Dhabi to Dubai was ornamented with date palms, green grass, and at times wildflowers. While there were no clear estimates of how much water was required for these landscaping practices, it was widely believed that the Abu Dhabi government expended an extraordinary amount of resources to keep these roads verdant, nearly as much as the military budget for the emirate. They used desalinated water to take care of the imported plants. When these plants died, they quickly replaced them with new ones, within a matter of hours. The vegetation was even more manicured around the Masdar City site due to the construction of a VIP airport for members of Abu Dhabi's ruling family.

Looking out the window, Marco began drawing on his knowledge of ethnobotany to suggest that the plants were actively rejecting their new location. They did not want to be here. He recounted to me that at the age

FIGURE I.2 · Imported flowers on the road from Masdar City to Dubai, as seen from inside a car, 2014. Photo by the author.

FIGURE I.3 · Date palms on the road from Masdar City to Dubai, as seen from inside a car, 2014. Photo by the author.

of ten, in the jungle together with his parents, he had tried *yage*, a hallucinogenic drug obtained from an Amazonian vine known as *ayahuasca* and used in ceremonies among the indigenous peoples of the Amazon basin. This experience had served as the beginning of his cosmological education. The jungle had become alive, demonstrating its interiority in a way that had astonished Marco. In further developing his ontological theories, Marco had been influenced by Carlos Castañeda, Richard Evan Schultes, Fritjof Capra, Albert Hoffman, and Ken Wilber—writers interested in hallucinogenic experiences and in seeking to combine spirituality with scientific findings. And now he was reading *Return of the Children of the Light: Incan and Mayan Prophecies for a New World* (2001), by Judith Bluestone Polich, which proposed that all matter was made of light: "The new worldview will make it evident that the world we live in is part of a larger whole. We will be able to perceive that all matter is energy, that we are wave-like, that we are in constant communication with the whole. Through this shift in consciousness, we will begin to function as multi-dimensional beings, and we will realize we have potentials beyond anything yet dreamed of, adding our heightened light vibration to the Earth's own."[3]

I had read Carlos Castañeda's *The Teachings of Don Juan: A Yaqui Way of Knowledge* (1968) some years before moving to the UAE, and knew a little about the other authors Marco mentioned.[4] In *The Teachings of Don Juan*, Castañeda experiments with peyote, jimson weed, and magic mushrooms on the path to becoming "a man of knowledge" (under the strict guidance of his mentor Don Juan). It was surprising to hear this writer's name in association with the plants on Abu Dhabi's medians. I analyzed my experiences there differently. Before I had arrived in Abu Dhabi in the summer of 2010, when I was still preparing for my time there, Jack, an American faculty member at Masdar Institute who held a PhD in engineering science, had asked me over the phone if my research would result in a book like Bruno Latour's *Aramis, or the Love of Technology* (1993). In that book, Latour embarks on a sociological investigation of the failure of Aramis, a high-tech automated personal rapid transit (PRT) system that was developed in France during the 1980s; he seeks to convince his readers "that the machines by which they are surrounded are cultural objects worthy of their attention and respect."[5] Given the presence of a similar PRT system in Masdar City, the association was perhaps understandable. Glad to share a common vocabulary, I conveyed to Jack that the reference to

Aramis accurately reflected some of the goals of my research. But Marco's allusions to writers like Castañeda were a bit difficult to fathom in this context of high-tech renewable energy projects.

Marco was quick to explain that his ontological theories fit the market-based technological projects of Masdar. He imagined humans would soon awaken to a new understanding of how animals and plants, but most importantly carbon dioxide, have souls. Over the past few years, Marco had been developing some practical tools to acknowledge the soul of carbon dioxide. He believed that a market-based system would be an effective mechanism for suspending the differences among humans, animals, plants, and carbon dioxide: all beings would be redeemable in cash, made equivalent under a common denominator. Before he was recruited by Masdar Carbon, Marco had worked with a number of climate change consultancies around the world. He explained that he had started out at a critical moment, just as the global governance of climate change was becoming more urgent. Unlike many of the consultants he worked with, he had faith that global governance could sort out the climate change problem, and he reminded me that we were still at the very beginning of the Kyoto Protocol—that the treaty had been adopted in 1997 but entered into force only in 2005. The Kyoto Protocol was an international agreement that bound its signatories to certain carbon dioxide emission reduction goals. It acknowledged that developed countries were responsible for the high levels of greenhouse gas emissions due to more than 150 years of industrial activity, and it placed a heavier burden on these nations in mitigating climate change. Marco perceived the Kyoto Protocol as a significant first step toward a global emission reduction regime that would eventually allow humans to control emission levels, providing the groundwork for future international collaboration on climate change. The climate change regime would improve, but it would take time. Carbon markets, created as part of the Kyoto Protocol, were small (roughly the size of the flat-screen TV market), but they helped everyone understand that the air was not free. Through carbon markets, we could recognize carbon dioxide as a spiritual being.

As we approached Dubai, the plants disappeared, the quality of the asphalt changed, and the road became bumpier. Abu Dhabi could invest in iconic projects like Masdar City, but Dubai had been shaken significantly by the economic crisis of late 2008, an event that made the differences between the emirates more evident. Once a small fishing and pearling community, Dubai grew as a trading center in the early twentieth century. The oil revenues of the 1960s facilitated a frenzy of consumerism and helped accelerate the early development of the city in the 1970s and 1980s. The city invested in aviation, financial services, tourism, and real estate, managing to diversify away from fossil fuels and attract foreign white-collar and blue-collar labor. As of the mid-1990s, non-oil revenues constituted about 90 percent of Dubai's economy. Because Dubai was more susceptible to the booms and busts of the global financial markets than its oil-rich neighbor Abu Dhabi, it had felt the impact of the 2008 crisis more forcefully. Many argued that the real estate bubble that had propelled Dubai's expansion—enabling some of the city's more fantastical projects, such as the construction of an archipelago of small, artificial islands in the shape of the world map, situated 2.5 miles off Dubai's coast—had finally burst. In late 2008 and early 2009, the international media reported on white-collar workers abandoning their cars with the keys in the ignition at the airport parking lot, leaving the city for good.[6] Blue-collar workers were losing their jobs in the construction sector and looking for ways to return to their home countries. More than two years after the crash, the impact of the financial crisis still remained visible. We drove past billboards advertising recently shelved real estate development projects. One billboard promised that Dubai's coastline could be doubled, while others promoted theme parks. There had also been plans to import a blue whale, which would live inside an aquarium in the largest shopping mall in the world, but no one really talked about this prospect any more. Dubai had planned to re-create nature for itself through bold gestures; after the crisis, the city was transformed, marred by abandoned construction sites.

When I stepped out of the taxi outside my apartment building in Dubai, Marco pleaded, "Please don't think I've gone crazy."

Technical Adjustments

This book has three aims. First, it seeks to understand how cosmopolitan, innovative actors in Abu Dhabi, such as Marco or Jack, set about the task of building a renewable energy and clean technology sector. Second, it attempts to show that these actors shared the common yet heterogeneous goal of constructing what I call "technical adjustments" as central components of the renewable energy and clean technology industry, aspiring to mitigate climate change and future energy scarcity through new business models, technological innovations, and design solutions. I see Marco's proposal of acknowledging the soul of carbon dioxide through carbon markets as one such technical adjustment. Third, it documents and analyzes the discursive and technical means by which these actors deferred the question of success or failure in reflecting on their work, thereby generating the material and conceptual indeterminacy described in the following chapters.

Articles on Masdar had been appearing in the international press since the official launch of the project in 2006. "Abu Dhabi, the capital of the United Arab Emirates, the fourth largest OPEC oil producer with about 10 percent of the known reserves, is seeking to become a center for the development and implementation of clean-energy technology," a *New York Times* article announced in 2007.[7] Masdar City, the proposed "zero-carbon" district, would cost $22 billion and eventually accommodate 1,500 businesses. The proposed automated personal rapid transport (PRT) network would allow the city to completely prohibit car entry. The effort to start a graduate research institution focused on renewable energy at the center of the city by bringing in MIT was also publicized by Masdar's marketing department, with the promise that it would transform Abu Dhabi in the same way that MIT had transformed the Boston area into a start-up haven (chapter 2). Together with other satellite campuses, including New York University in Abu Dhabi (NYU-AD) and the Sorbonne, Masdar Institute would play a significant role in instituting a knowledge-based economy in Abu Dhabi.

Some commentators appreciated the fact that an oil-rich emirate was investing in renewable energy resources and acknowledging that the energy portfolio of the future would not consist of fossil fuels only. Others mocked the Masdar City project for being located in a country where the carbon footprint per capita was the highest in the world. Many drew attention to the fact that the Abu Dhabi government was starting a massive renewable energy and clean technology project that would be funded by oil revenues. To these commentators, the project seemed rather paradoxical.

In response, the project's proponents argued that the oil-based infrastructure could be gutted because Masdar could provide a whole new circulatory system for Abu Dhabi. In a 2013 documentary on the project, Sultan Al Jaber, then CEO of Masdar, extended his earlier arguments on the main goals of their initiative: "Masdar is a strategic, holistic, comprehensive approach to renewable energy, to seriously and in a meaningful way contribute to the advancement of clean technologies. We believe this is a logical step for a major oil-producing nation to venture into. Who knows energy better than us? We are trying to create the home for renewable energy, which is Masdar City. . . . There has never been a single attempt by anybody in the whole world as aggressive and as ambitious as Masdar City."[8]

This book is about the ways in which Abu Dhabi might prepare for a post-oil future. In exploring this imagined transition, it investigates the construction of a renewable energy and clean technology sector and pays specific attention to the Masdar project as it unfolded in the years 2010 and 2011. The book draws on ethnographic research at MIT in Cambridge, Massachusetts (between January 2010 and May 2010), in Abu Dhabi (between September 2010 and June 2011), and at the United Nations Framework Convention on Climate Change (UNFCCC) office in Bonn (in March and April 2012). After completing this fieldwork, I continued to follow the project's developments, met my interlocutors in various places around the world, attended conferences on energy and climate change where I had the opportunity to sharpen some of my questions, and took short trips back to the UAE. Yet given the high turnover of foreign workers in the region, many of the people whose perspectives I discuss here no longer work with Masdar; they have mostly left Abu Dhabi. In this book, I do not claim to provide a comprehensive overview of the project's present condition. Instead, this book describes and analyzes how cosmopolitan actors shaped the field of renewable energy and clean technology in Abu Dhabi in the years 2010 and 2011. This period is particularly important as it saw the opening of the eco-friendly Masdar Institute campus in November 2010, enabling Masdar Institute students, the first residents of Masdar City, to start living in student residences on campus. This period also set the stage for the cancellation of the Foster-designed Masdar City master plan and its associated transportation infrastructure in late 2010. Masdar City eventually transformed from what its developers had called "a zero-carbon eco-city" to what later marketing campaigns labeled "a city of possibilities," in other words, a special economic zone for renewable energy and clean technology companies. This book studies the occasions when Masdar's renewable energy and clean technology projects failed, succeeded, or were reformulated in response to everyday hindrances.[9]

By providing an in-depth analysis of developments in Abu Dhabi's Masdar in 2010 and 2011, the book demonstrates that the Masdar project was capacious and heterogeneous enough to involve actors with various contradictory agendas. Thus, Masdar was not one thing but rather an amalgam of widely varying ambitions and demands for the future; the believers, the utopians, the cynics who contributed to this project all acted upon this future in unique ways. Interrogating how imaginaries of renewable energy and clean technology are articulated and experienced both at a personal level and at the level of project management, this book provides gateways to understanding the emergence of novel infrastructures of knowledge, technology, and governance in Abu Dhabi.

Yet, however varied the visions of the actors who built Masdar, there are certain fundamental inclinations and preferences that they held in common and reproduced. In order to explain how innovative actors shape energy and climate futures in Abu Dhabi, and to foreground these shared qualities, I have found it useful to focus on a central idea that I label "technical adjustments." Abu Dhabi's renewable energy and clean technology projects, such as Masdar City, have aimed to generate technical adjustments as a means for vaulting ahead to a future where humans will continue to enjoy technological complexity without interrogating existing social, political, and economic relations. In effect, I understand technical adjustments as imaginative and wide-ranging responses to global climate change and energy scarcity, which open up certain interventions (such as extending technological complexity) while foreclosing others (such as asking larger-scale moral, ethical, and political questions regarding how to live). Invested in an image of the future drawn from science fiction, the technical adjustments that the producers of Masdar implemented served as methods for concentrating on modifications that bring forth promissory capital, enabling a multiplicity of actions and nonactions to be taken in the face of global environmental collapse. While producing innovative (and at times fun) artifacts, technical adjustments eventually obfuscate and efface the simple realization that humans cannot continue to live and consume as they do.

The idea of "technical adjustments" offers a mode of response for dealing with climate change independent of ethical, moral, and political entailments.[10] According to this perspective, climate change is a management problem that experts may resolve, rather than an ethical and moral problem that humans around the world should recognize, discuss, and address as political agents. This approach indicates that solutions to climate change are not centrally about ethics, morality, or politics. Instead, they involve market-oriented technical fixes—such as green buildings (chapter 1), research into renewable energy and clean technology (chapter 2), novel ways of imagining exchange (chapter 3), innovative designs for vehicles (chapter 4), and new global governance mechanisms (chapter 5)—that promote a belief in the possibility of sustaining the status quo and even improving life for certain segments of society through technology. Technical adjustments, which are intended to maintain existing values while inventing new technology to address climate change and energy scarcity, operate in opposition to environmentalism. The hope is that technical adjustments will allow humans to extend their beliefs and perspectives into the future without requiring them to ask new moral and ethical questions and without developing new virtues.[11]

To illustrate this approach, let's turn to Sam, a Lebanese executive in his late forties who was critical in starting the Masdar project in 2006. Sam had been working in Dubai as a consultant for about a decade when he came up with the idea of founding an eco-city. He partnered with two other consultants and presented his idea to ruling elites in Qatar, but he was not given the green light. Eventually, he contacted the Abu Dhabi government, presented the same idea, and found more support from the ruling elites there. "Abu Dhabi has always been the most visionary of the Gulf states," he explained to me. "It's not unusual that they liked the idea and pursued it immediately." After the project took off, Sam was hired as an executive, managing Masdar Carbon, the climate change policy wing.

During one of our meetings in his office in the temporary buildings of Masdar Carbon, Sam explained to me that in the long run humanity needed something that altered capitalism by reformulating consumerism. "There are projections, like, in seventy years a bottle of water will cost $500," Sam said. "We shouldn't let that happen." He believed that humans needed to stop making insatiable demands on the planet for short-term benefits. "But of course, these are only long-term goals," he continued, "and this is not how or why we started Masdar." Sam knew that Masdar did not have the capacity to overcome the workings of capitalism: it could only operate in conjunction with the status quo. While he was aware of the multiple challenges of the climate change problem, he could not attend to them. According to Sam, instead of seeking to challenge capitalism, the Masdar project attempted to rechannel consumerism through resource management—through the efficient and effective deployment of the earth's resources, not necessarily to be framed as environmentalism. That's why, Sam said, it was not extraordinary to see hundreds of SUVs in the eco-city's parking lots. The technical adjustments endorsed inside Masdar City through innovative vehicle designs such as automated pod cars also embraced the SUV.

In Abu Dhabi, climate change and future energy scarcity emerged as business opportunities. When defining their understandings of renewable energy and clean technology, many of my interlocutors, who came to Abu Dhabi from all over the world, explained that they did not advocate closing down businesses and stopping production. Just the opposite: they imagined Masdar as a test bed that would create more business potential for Abu Dhabi. They did not aspire to surrender or challenge capitalist consumerism, which is often seen as the reason for dwindling resources and climate vulnerability, but instead attempted to generate a strategic, holistic, comprehensive approach to renewable energy. In addition to admitting that not many of them would self-identify as "environmentalists,"[12] renewable energy and clean technology professionals in different sectors found it significant to highlight how "the environment was a sexy part of the economy," and therefore could be integrated into existing models of social and political life seamlessly. Like many businesses around the world, they could supply environmentally friendly products that would perhaps supplant the demand for nongreen products, such as fossil fuels.

Yet because the drive for technical adjustments was varied at Masdar, the professionals there not only advocated market-oriented technological solutions for climate change, but also consistently crafted justifications for their projects in light of various contradictions that they recognized as existing in such a perspective. For instance, Marco suggested that market-based solutions would in fact allow humans and nonhumans to be redeemable in cash over an egalitarian platform, producing a new world order. Sam used market mechanisms, specifically price, as signifiers for future destitution, and expressed his worries about the planet by talking about his preoccupation with the cost of water. He knew that humans needed to rethink capitalism, but he didn't know exactly how. In engaging with planetary-scale conditions as well as everyday realities, the people at Masdar experienced dislocations, about which many of them spoke with passion, anxiety, and confusion. In thinking through their challenges, they went back and forth between abstract conceptions of the planet and the everyday realities of social and professional life, consistently inhabiting sets of unanswered (or perhaps unanswerable) questions and conflicts.

The tensions between domains that inevitably gave rise to inconsistencies was evident in the results of a survey conducted by Elif, a Turkish master's student in engineering systems design at Masdar Institute, for a term project on transportation and the environment. Almost all of her one hundred respondents (most of them students, postdocs, faculty members, and employees of Masdar) self-identified as caring about the environment.[13] However, in answering another critical question on the survey, they had expressed that they would "never" use public transportation, regardless of their dedication to the environment and their sensitivity toward planetary-scale problems. In Elif's analysis, while "caring about the environment" was embraced as an abstract value that demonstrated thoughtfulness regarding planetary-scale problems, the immediate practices associated with this sentiment were not socially desirable—in the emirates, public transportation was denigrated as a mode of travel for low-wage immigrant workers.

Rather than examining or resolving such tensions, the producers of Masdar responded by suggesting that their initiative was "not environmentalism," and that the project did not seek to be located outside the present social, political, and economic conditions. Instead, Masdar City would build and promote technical adjustments and thereby produce and offer a status quo utopia, creating technological innovations with the goal of preserving the present during a time of ecological destruction. Simply put, the future was a thinly disguised version of the present.

People at Masdar—for example, Elif, Sam, and Marco—interrogated the market-based and technologically complex aspirations of the project, and often called for reformulations based on the problems they perceived on site on an everyday basis. Articulating their understandings of the project through the use of metaphor and metonymy, they referred to Masdar as "spaceship in the desert" (chapter 1), "a technocratic dictatorship" (chapter 3), or "an expensive toy" (chapter 4). In this way, they managed to keep the project not only materially but also conceptually incomplete. By creating new language to talk about the project, they demonstrated how—despite its willingness to remain within the confines of the status quo—Masdar was proposing rather strange new material conditions for them.

Oil Futures

This book is the first full-length ethnography of contemporary Abu Dhabi. The Arab Gulf has long been marginalized in the social sciences and humanities, and it received little attention in older ethnographies. At times, the Arab Gulf has been considered culture-less and history-less, a misconception that has slowly been corrected through important contemporary research projects on immigration patterns, legal structures of citizenship, transnational connections, and the built environments of the region.[14] Yet there remain major thematic lacunae in studies of the Gulf. Anthropologists working in the Middle East more broadly have not taken a deep interest in environmental issues, a situation that is now changing through emergent research.[15] At the same time, while some significant works have started looking into the ways in which global technologies transform social relations and become vernacularized,[16] science and technology studies do not inform studies of the region adequately.[17] By investigating the ways in which the Abu Dhabi government prepares for a future with less oil, this book demonstrates the increasing importance of environmental issues and technological projects in thinking about this part of the world.

Through projects like Masdar, a marketing department representative at the company explained to me, Abu Dhabi managed to preserve the legacy of Sheikh Zayed, the founding father of the United Arab Emirates, and to follow his perceived commitment to a green environment. Zayed was known for having a special interest in wildlife and hunting, which led him to build environmental organizations. For instance, he announced a public afforestation policy in 1969, and founded the emirate's first "artificial forest."[18] In the late 1970s, he established the National Avian Research Center to protect falcons and houbara bustards. A faculty member at Masdar

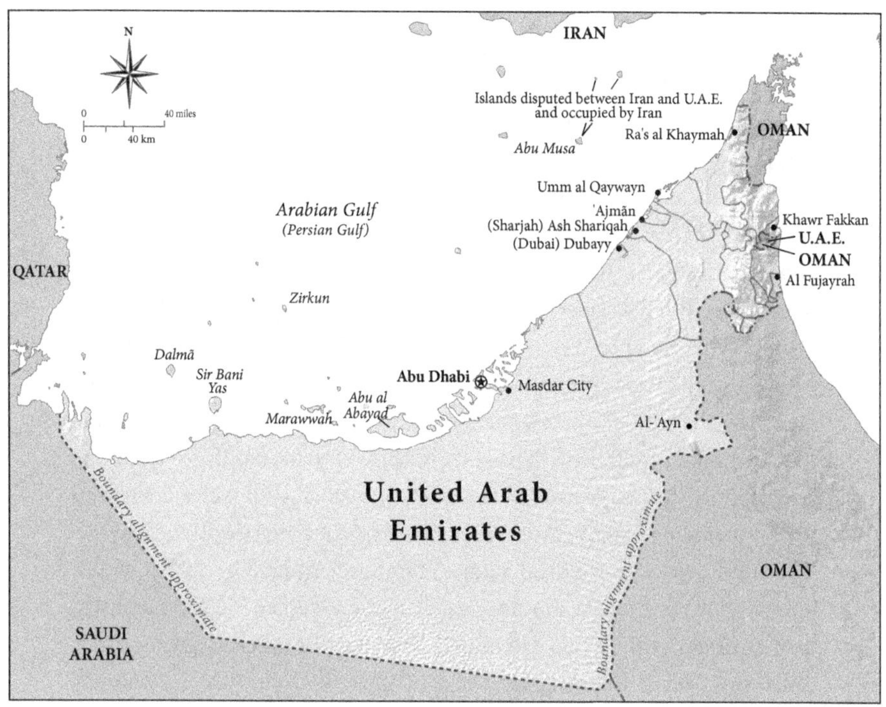

MAP I.1 · United Arab Emirates map.

Institute suggested that the Sheikh Zayed legacy, and any romanticized notion of being "at one with nature," were actually an impediment for the adoption of environmentally friendly practices in the UAE. "It's as if when you mention the Sheikh Zayed legacy, you automatically become green, so you don't really have to do anything about it, you don't have to change your behavior," she underlined. While for the marketing department "the Sheikh Zayed legacy" appeared to be an incentive to engage with environmental projects, for others at Masdar it was almost a setback, through which Abu Dhabi residents legitimized their often wasteful preferences. But perhaps at the representational scale the argument about Sheikh Zayed's legacy did work, for it framed Abu Dhabi's investments in initiatives like Masdar as having reverence for the founding father of the United Arab Emirates.

In the early 1960s, while still under British control, Abu Dhabi commanded around 10 percent of the world's proven hydrocarbon deposits. However, under the rule of Sheikh Shakhbut, often remembered for not fully complying with British interests, Abu Dhabi refused development interventions.[19] From 1946 to 1966, Zayed, Sheikh Shakhbut's youngest brother, was the governor of Al-Ayn, Abu Dhabi's second-largest town, an oasis where many would spend the summer (before the arrival of air-conditioning); Zayed developed his power base there. Christopher Davidson, a political scientist who has written extensively about the UAE, suggests that "Zayed had no fear of the future and the changes it might bring," and explains that he demonstrated his entrepreneurial spirit by transforming Al-Ayn into the region's economic hub, surpassing the capital city Abu Dhabi.[20] For example, Zayed built a modern hospital in Al-Ayn six years before a hospital was built in Abu Dhabi. Such transformations were welcomed by the elites in the region. Sheikh Zayed replaced Sheikh Shakhbut in 1966, not only with British backing but also with his family's recognition and support. As promised, he drastically transformed policies during his rule, prioritizing oil concessions and contracts until his death in 2004.[21]

Sheik Zayed was a critical actor in founding, in late 1971, what is now known as the United Arab Emirates, bringing together the seven constituent emirates (which had previously been part of a British protectorate called the Trucial States): Abu Dhabi, Dubai, Sharjah, Ras al-Khaimah, Fujairah, Ajman, and Umm al-Qawain. Given its great oil wealth, and therefore its capacity to finance a federal state, Abu Dhabi was named the capital of the newly established union under President Zayed. The emirates transferred key issues, such as control of the military, foreign policy, and immigration, to the central federal government, but retained power over their natural resources and their economic development strategies. Since the founding of the UAE, Abu Dhabi and Dubai have dominated the central government, with their rulers taking the positions of president and prime minister, and have held veto power over the decisions of the Supreme Council, which is the highest authority in the federal state.

Of all the emirates, Dubai has been known globally as the Gulf's cosmopolitan center and business hub. Its large shopping malls, tall towers, and luxury hotels are often in the news. (So are the failures of these projects.) Given its physical proximity to Dubai, Sharjah has also become a recognized node (known for the American University of Sharjah and the Sharjah Biennial, an international art exhibit), and comes after Dubai in terms of wealth. Relatively inconspicuous, Abu Dhabi has, since the founding of the UAE, been what Davidson terms a "capstone" emirate: fundamental to the union, critical for Europe's and Japan's oil supply, and much wealthier than the other six.[22]

By the 1990s, twenty years after the formation of the federation, Abu Dhabi accounted for over 90 percent of the UAE's oil exports, with the capacity to pump 2.5 million barrels per day. Sheikh Zayed's successor, Sheikh Khalifa, took charge in 2004, and began to mold a more globally competitive image for Abu Dhabi, specifically by investing in high-profile development projects in the fields of tourism, urban transformation, and technology transfer, importing new technology from other countries in an attempt to boost the emirate's economy.[23] UAE-based architect and writer Yasser Elsheshtawy explains that while Sheikh Zayed had transformed Abu Dhabi from "a provincial backwater to a modern city," he had been reluctant to make it readily available for international investments, thereby precluding it from becoming a crossroads comparable to Dubai. This was expected to change under Sheikh Khalifa, with the construction of globally significant cultural projects such as NYU-Abu Dhabi, the Guggenheim Abu Dhabi, and the Louvre Abu Dhabi.[24]

Strikingly, foreign labor has designed, built, and managed these projects. Of the 9 million people who live and work in the UAE, almost 8 million are not Emirati citizens. These immigrants come to the UAE on temporary renewable work contracts sponsored by their employers—a system known as *kafala*. Although the work contracts can be renewed indefinitely, the temporary nature of these contracts makes it difficult for immigrants to form communities, or to feel a sense of belonging in the UAE. The contracts ensure that they will remain perpetual outsiders, with no prospect of cultural assimilation or naturalization as Emirati citizens; indeed, they often expect they will be forced to leave.[25]

In the UAE, some of these immigrants hold white-collar jobs in sectors such as tourism, finance, and construction, while many of them are low-wage male workers from South and Southeast Asia. For white-collar workers, the UAE is an attractive location, especially because of its high salaries, low taxes, and convenient and cosmopolitan environment. Conditions are very different for blue-collar workers, who come to the UAE mostly from Pakistan, India, Bangladesh, Nepal, and the Philippines, and receive on average salaries between 500 and 750 dirhams (US$135–$190) per month. Many of these workers live in decrepit all-male labor camps far away from city centers, such as Dubai's infamous camp Sonapur, literally meaning "land of gold" in Hindi and Urdu, and often travel to their work sites on non-air-conditioned Tata buses. The violation of workers' rights by the UAE, especially on construction sites of large projects such as the Guggenheim and NYU-Abu Dhabi, has been well documented by international institutions as well as the media.[26]

Meanwhile, in publicizing the aspiration to diversify the economy away from oil exports, the Abu Dhabi Economic Council published a key document in November 2008 titled "Abu Dhabi Economic Vision 2030." The document, a topic of conversation at Masdar during the time of my research, proposed: "Economic growth is currently coupled too closely with oil prices and the key to more sustainable development lies in stimulating non-oil sectors, diversifying the range and depth of economic activity taking place in the Emirate, and increasing productivity through a focused approach on Abu Dhabi's competitive advantages."[27] Practices of resource management were expected to protect Abu Dhabi from fluctuations in oil prices, to ensure consistent levels of welfare in an oil-less future.[28] In contextualizing these aspirations, Abu Dhabi officials made comparisons between the emirate and various oil-rich countries. For instance, Norway produced quantities of oil similar to Abu Dhabi, but its energy sector accounted for just 24 percent of its GDP, making it far less dominant.

In the literature on oil wealth and networks, it is often argued that conceptions of endless oil supplies enable progress to be conceived as infinitely expandable, without material constraints. In the mid-twentieth century, the cost of energy did not present a limit to economic growth, as oil prices continuously declined. Given how simple it was to ship oil across the world, this resource could easily be treated as inexhaustible. In his book *Carbon Democracy* (2012), Timothy Mitchell shows how this belief in the infinity of oil also played a key role in producing "the economy" as an object that could expand without limit.[29] We now know that the age of abundant fossil fuel supplies is ending, but we seem unable to abandon the ways of living and thinking that fossil fuels made possible. In preparing for a future without abundant oil, the Abu Dhabi government has attempted new strategies of resource management, hoping to generate a new type of infinity through technical adjustments.

In line with these developments, the UAE government announced a renewable energy policy in 2009 that set the goal that renewable energy sources would provide at least 7 percent of the emirate's power generation capacity by 2020.[30] Some have estimated that Abu Dhabi could rely on oil exports for another 150 years.[31] For the 2013 edition of *Campbell's Atlas of Oil and Gas Depletion*, a guide to the future of fossil fuels, the seasoned geologist Colin Campbell argued: "For the moment, the Emirates are enjoying the benefits of the high price of oil, whose revenues have allowed them to develop major industries, a world airline and an important regional financial centre. . . . It is thought that they can maintain their current level of oil production for another 20 years or so, meaning that they will continue to enjoy ever larger revenues, albeit subject to volatility in the face of global economic recessions."[32] According to Campbell, the oil will be gone by the end of the century.

Yet, as geologists often note, the study of oil depletion is an inexact science, which allows for variations in imagining and planning the future of fossil fuel resources (see chapter 5). This lack of precision is coupled with a lack of clarity regarding the value and the future price of oil.[33] Predictions about global peak oil differ based on methodologies, which are in turn based on a number of contentious assumptions regarding coping with uncertainties of supply, demand, and technology.[34] Whether there has been or will be a peak, and if so when, are ongoing matters of debate.

I asked oil executives in Abu Dhabi and at energy and climate change meetings around the world how much oil they think is left. They mostly responded to me with a question: "How much are you willing to pay?" They were referring to recent investments in new techniques for the production of petroleum. Due to the possibility of future oil scarcity, oil industries and governments internationally have been investing in unconventional oil sources, such as shale oil and oil sands, which has sparked environmental concerns regarding the impact of these new sources. As with conventional oil exploration, the production of unconventional petroleum is a frontier that remains obscure, uncertain, and widely debated.

The Abu Dhabi government might find a way out of these ambiguities by diversifying its economy and becoming less dependent on oil exports. It could build museums, universities, and industrial facilities, generating new types of returns. The construction of a renewable energy and clean technology industry in the emirate, specifically at Masdar City, could be perceived as an admission that the oil will one day run out or become less valuable—that someday oil would cease to serve as the bedrock of Abu Dhabi's economy.

As Douglas Rogers, an anthropologist who studies oil in Russia, proposes, "Oil as an item of anthropological knowledge has . . . been closely tied to cyclical perceptions of oil's scarcity (and associated soaring prices) in high-consuming metropolitan centers."[35] One example of this type of work is Mandana Limbert's *In the Time of Oil* (2010), which offers an analysis of the possible depletion of oil in Oman and foregrounds a different, more cyclical understanding of the future. Limbert explains how, for some of her interlocutors, oil depletion marks a return to the pre-oil past—a time when Omanis lived in palm-frond *barasti* huts rather than air-conditioned villas. As she points out, "the *now* in this logic is the temporary and anomalous state of wealth between eras of poverty." When the oil runs out, "Oman's recent past, its 'renaissance,' [will] have indeed been just a dream."[36] This sense of a "dream" is useful in understanding other locales that are enlivened by oil wealth, then troubled by its disappearance. For instance, Todd Reisz, an architect and writer who specializes in Gulf urbanism, describes how "Dubai's optimism was at its peak in 1968, when oil seemed to be what would vouchsafe its permanence." Toward the end of the 1980s, however, "Dubai began to segue from the promise of oil wealth to the alarm of oil's impending depletion. The period in between—a fat time of oil money—seemed to have ended before it had begun." Oil depletion forced Dubai to diversify its sources of income. Yet, according to Reisz, "Dubai has grown rich, but it has never achieved what it wanted from that wealth—a place whose existence was unquestionable."[37] Instead, the city is always on the verge of disappearance, dismayed by the possibility of becoming irrelevant.

Unlike Oman and Dubai, where progress became tainted by the inevitable disappearance of resources, Abu Dhabi has physically and socially constructed knowledge of renewable energy and clean technology as an alternative resource, a safeguard for the future. The Abu Dhabi government has done so to refute and challenge the idea that its energy resources are finite. In my fieldwork during 2010 and 2011, I observed that the practices adopted in promoting renewable energy and clean technology infrastructure—such as setting up a research institute, entering joint ventures with environmentally conscious utility companies, and generally investing in an eco-city—were aimed at transforming Abu Dhabi's "brand image" from oil producer to technology developer, rendering the emirate "more elite." Through projects like Masdar, Abu Dhabi hoped to induce a "perception shift" that would attract foreign investment. "In 2005,

Abu Dhabi was perceived to be a high polluter, and was heavily associated with hydrocarbon consumption and exports," a marketing department employee told me. But in 2010 and 2011, through Masdar and other initiatives like the World Future Energy Summit, an annual trade show dedicated to renewable energy and clean technologies, Abu Dhabi seemed to be at the forefront of the emergent renewable energy and clean technology development. Masdar constituted a renewable "source" for the growth of a knowledge-based economy (chapter 2), and facilitated the transformation of oil-based relations into knowledge-based ones. In this framework, "resource management" implied another direction toward which Abu Dhabi's economy could be steered by building new sites of production to extend economic diversification efforts.

In Abu Dhabi, an environment afflicted with climate change and energy deficiency problems, the proposed renewable energy and clean technology infrastructures served as spaces of hope.[38] Conceptions of the approaching end of the world were complemented with imaginaries of a utopian future, driven by a coming together of vernacular architecture and experimental technology. The on-site Foster + Partners architects I spoke with regularly during my research suggested that they borrowed from old Arab cities in thinking about Masdar and pointed to Shibam of Yemen as an example (chapter 1). Moreover, the city would be "smart"; it would have "a hidden brain," which, in the words of one architecture critic, "knows when you enter your building, so that your flat can be cooled before you arrive, while in public places flat screens broadcast uplifting news on the environmental performance of the complex" (chapter 3).[39] Framed as a utopian (or science fiction) project that might be completed, the renewable energy and clean technology infrastructure of the UAE needed the backdrop of a world being struck by climate change and energy deficiency. The marketing and communications campaigns put together by Masdar aimed at proving that the opposite was also true—that the world needed Masdar City.

The Luster of Potential

Laura, an American student in her mid-twenties, had relocated to Abu Dhabi from the United States with an ambition to learn about renewable energy and clean technology at the new Masdar Institute, having received her bachelor's degree from a private engineering college in Massachusetts. "The first night of living in a Masdar apartment was hilarious. I didn't understand how anything worked: the stove, the lights, the bathroom faucet, the cabinets, and I couldn't figure out how to turn off the AC," she wrote on her blog in September 2010, right after moving onto the campus of the Masdar Institute. Her studio apartment was situated at the center of the Masdar City site, inside a student dormitory. "The Masdar Institute is the first part of [Masdar City] to be completed, it includes the library, laboratory buildings, and the student residences," Laura continued. "And all these buildings fit together in a cube. And this cube is located in the middle of what is still a giant, flat, dusty, deserty construction site as progress on other phases of the city continues. It's quite a mind flip to be in such a strangely beautiful environment, then look [*sic*] a window and see flat dusty landscape stretching out to the horizon." She titled the blog post "I live in a spaceship in the middle of the desert."[40]

On her blog, Laura defined herself as an "engineer and eco-geek," and added that she "has fanatic obsession with social entrepreneurship as a tool for solving poverty."[41] She was planning on moving to Ghana after graduation to start an organization that would apply renewable energy technologies as a humanitarian tool. When she posted the entry "I live in a spaceship in the middle of the desert," she received unexpected attention from journalists and researchers around the world. Laura represented the hundred or so students who had moved onto the Masdar Institute campus: she was trying to make sense of her experience with Abu Dhabi's emergent renewable energy and clean technology infrastructures.

Laura's writings on her blog indicate that she struggled with the novel technical features of the Masdar City project. The stove, the lights, the bathroom faucet, the cabinets, and the AC became central to her understanding of her new apartment, and they gave her a hard time. These new materials, coupled with the unfamiliar dry land surrounding the campus, made her feel like she was in an exotic environment. It took Laura some time to get used to the occasionally uncontrollable trajectories of the materials she relied on. She felt like a test subject, and she also had a sense of the inherent potential of the half-working materials; the same could be said for many of her classmates at the Masdar Institute (chapter 1).

The fundamental difficulty of the materials Laura tinkered with wasn't that they were breaking down, but that they were never really coming to life. For instance, while the building management system of Masdar Institute attempted to stay outside the conscious awareness of its residents through an intelligent air-conditioning system, constant dysfunction prohibited such invisibility (chapter 3). Masdar Institute students like Laura could not help but always sense the building management system. They did not know whether it would ever function as intended, but they continuously talked about it and tried to resolve its problems. While emergent infrastructure seemed to define the project of building a renewable energy and clean technology sector in Abu Dhabi, it remained consistently out of reach. As harbingers of future technical adjustments, Abu Dhabi's renewable energy and clean technology infrastructures increasingly became laden with lustrous potential.

People like Laura who produced and used this emergent renewable energy and clean technology infrastructure came to reject the ideas and labels of success and failure, and instead imagined and believed that the projects they were part of had potential. Scholars have often written about success and failure, trying to analyze the lives of technological or developmental projects. The example Jack used in relating to my research—*Aramis*, wherein Bruno Latour shows the multiple steps that led to the cancellation of a personal rapid transit project in Paris—is one of these studies. Another important work that addresses this quandary is James Scott's *Seeing Like a State: How Certain Schemes to Improve the Human Condition Have Failed* (1998), which demonstrates how high-modernist projects that attempted to design society in accord with what are believed to be scientific laws have resulted in failure.[42] In his book *Anti-Politics Machine: Development, Depoliticization, and Bureaucratic Power in Lesotho* (1994), James Ferguson underscores how such failure may be productive, and looks at what he calls its "instrument effects." The subjects of Ferguson's study, development workers seeking to implement projects in Lesotho, admit that their projects have failed, or have not worked in the ways they had imagined, but Ferguson's ethnography shows that their projects had overarching effects nonetheless.[43] In each of these studies, there is an agreement over failure that I did not find at Masdar City, and this led me to ask a different set of questions.

How exactly do people feel potential, and feel that they can rely and act upon technical adjustments to confront climate change and energy scarcity? How is potential negotiated, realized, limited, or changed? I propose that potential becomes embedded and condensed around particular half-finished or half-working networks of things; I highlight the dynamic materiality of such imaginaries. It is not only words or images—in the form of unstructured everyday conversations on site, or of polished marketing and communications campaigns—that evoke a potential for technical adjustments, but also the inklings of the stove, the lights, the bathroom faucet, the cabinets, and the AC. Ingrained in these half-finished materials, the possibility of a technically adjusted future becomes a way of making the projects sensed, not only by the residents of Masdar but also by outsiders. Abu Dhabi's renewable energy and clean technology infrastructures become visible not because they break down, but because of the potential that they insistently radiate.[44]

Given that many of Masdar's projects, such as the Masdar City master plan or the full-scale implementation of automated personal rapid transit pods, were left permanently unfinished, in this study I consider the existence of such potential without any relationship to growth, expansion, or realization. In other words, by studying the potential in this permanently incomplete state, I wish to highlight the presences rather than the absences that Abu Dhabi's half-working projects carry. In turn, I seek to understand what this material and conceptual incompleteness generates through Masdar. I suggest that Masdar's technical adjustments, in their half-finished material state, were not going to change, as would a seed into a plant. On the contrary, they were going to remain permanently indeterminate, and therefore permanently incipient, indicating the possibility of technical adjustments in an unidentified space and time inside or outside Masdar City.

Critical theorist Giorgio Agamben's essay "On Potentiality" (2000) has been inspiring for me in this context, because Agamben argues against the idea that potential only exists in an act or through its realization.[45] In this Aristotelian description of potentiality, the poet keeps her ability to write or has the potential to compose poems even if she does not do so. Similarly, Italian philosopher Paolo Virno thinks of potential as an infinite incompleteness, and proposes that potential does not expire with the culmination of an act.[46] Karen Pinkus's work identifies this potentiality as a way to distinguish between fuel and energy.[47] But as anthropologist Gisa Weszkalnys notes, "To approach potentiality empirically and ethnographically differs quite markedly from contemplating it philosophically."[48] In the context of Masdar, my interlocutors saw potential in renewable energy and clean technology projects that did not and would not take off. For them, Masdar City could offer a new form of eco-friendly urbanism to the world even though it would never be built in the way it was planned. My goal is to focus on the ways in which my interlocutors summoned this potential, engendering particular perspectives toward their work.

It is important to note, however, that half-finished infrastructures do not always carry or convey the same effects. They oriented the producers of Masdar toward a future through practices of speculative forecasting, and they have given rise to different and at times contradictory versions of that future. For some, the future of Masdar is a ruin that operates as an amusement park. For others, the future is a special economic zone, perhaps devoid of the various half-finished technological artifacts, but still invested in a business plan around renewable energy and clean technology. In effect, potential does not necessarily induce a linear temporal movement toward the completion of projects in the way that was intended, but rather an assemblage of varying, overlapping, and contradictory trajectories.

As such, these trajectories allow people to change scales and mobilize various orders and dimensions in speaking about their actions and nonactions. They have warranted the producers of Masdar to think simultaneously about, say, carbon markets and the soul of carbon dioxide. As half-finished infrastructures, Masdar's technical adjustments have the potential to propose incentives toward one trajectory over another, enabling planetary-scale transformation. The people I spoke with at Masdar negotiated this potential through varying imaginaries, pushing them to their limits.

The infrastructures of technology, knowledge, and governance that make up the future renewable energy and clean technology sector in Abu Dhabi are still in the making. Bettina, a German environmental consultant who had been working with Masdar since 2007, concentrating most specifically on the making of carbon capture and storage policy, explained to me in December 2012 at the Climate Summit (COP 18) in Doha that despite the construction of some new buildings within Masdar City, Abu Dhabi authorities were frequently discussing the possibility of abandoning the project, because it did not generate satisfying economic returns. "We always criticized Masdar for investing so much into marketing and promotions," she noted, "but in 2012, when the company was almost closing due to a shortage of profits, we saw that marketing also works as a promise." Through widely circulating imaginaries of its future presence, Masdar had promised its audience that it would deliver, and the Abu Dhabi leadership could not break its promise so easily, Bettina clarified. Promissory words and images operated together with the physically and conceptually incomplete infrastructure in fueling novel imaginaries of the future.

Rather than taking failure versus success as a given, this book explores what each comes to mean in the context of various renewable energy and clean technology projects. In the following chapters, I try to answer this question by studying five different artifacts. The Masdar City project may be shelved, it may transform into a regular real estate development project, or it may eventually be completed as planned (chapter 1). Keep in mind that cities are by definition incomplete aggregates, which will never be "finished." In discussing the "completion" of Masdar, I refer to the realization of the master plan as originally designed by Foster + Partners. In thinking about half-finished artifacts, I refer to the completion of the projects in the ways they were planned by particular Masdar executives. Attempts at producing carbon capture and storage policy may add to Abu Dhabi's international prestige, regardless of the fact that they do not instigate the removal of excess carbon dioxide from the atmosphere (chapter 5); the personal rapid transit units may be considered to "work" depending on whom you ask, or how you conceptualize the project (chapter 4). In examining the different artifacts, I stay away from classifying the projects as successes or failures, and instead focus on their physical and conceptual indeterminacy, foregrounding the debates around their implementation.

Research Methods

"Masdar is about a commitment to trial and error," Anna, a former faculty member at Masdar Institute who grew up in Bulgaria, lived in the United States and the UAE, and finally moved to Germany, explained to me during a meeting in Bonn. After finishing her PhD at an American university, Anna had been hired as a full-time faculty member at Masdar Institute. She was among the first group of full-time faculty who came to Abu Dhabi to, in practical terms, set up the Institute. She had an intimate understanding of the project—she professed that during the three years she worked at the Institute she was more involved in its founding than in her research into the role of women in science and technology in Abu Dhabi. When her contract expired in 2011, she left the UAE for a position at a development agency in Bonn. We had initially met in 2008, during my preliminary research on Masdar, saw each other often in 2010 and 2011, and kept in touch after she left. We agreed to catch up in March 2012, when I was conducting research at the United Nations Framework Convention on Climate Change in Bonn.

For Anna, the potential of Masdar lay in its capacities as a test bed, where everything was in beta mode. The technical adjustments Masdar proposed could malfunction, but this would constitute only a temporary problem, and would encourage the next version of these adjustments. The everyday disruptions people faced at Masdar, Anna theorized, would help build a better smart city in Rio or New York or Shenzhen. Through trial and error, developers would prepare a next version, and engineers and planners would unearth a code for eco-friendly modes of living, facilitating the rapid construction of new test beds globally. As historian of science Orit Halpern (2015) shows in her work on the construction of South Korea's smart city Songdo, this trial and error would never end, especially because every limit would become a new engineering challenge, a new frontier to develop toward an ever-extendable horizon.[49] This mode of thinking allowed Anna and her colleagues to render questions regarding success or failure irrelevant.

"And a project that is about trial and error needs documentation. That's the most important way in which we can contribute to discussions on sustainability," Anna emphasized. "We need to know exactly why the concept of sustainability could not be implemented at Masdar in the way it was planned, or why it was such a great challenge." She told me how she had been part of an initiative some years before to document the everyday workings of Masdar in order to learn more about practices of trial and error, specifically by collaborating with ethnographers. Anna's proposed project had demanded the close cooperation of anthropologists and sociologists from universities in the UAE in producing a database regarding the seemingly mundane daily dynamics of the initiative. She imagined that having such a database at their disposal would elicit and encourage self-reflection, enabling the producers of Masdar to look back and understand what had gone wrong at what stage of the project, possibly to help them correct their mistakes in the future. Since someone who had direct stakes in the development of the project could not do this, they needed to bring in independent ethnographers. In this way, the project would also have global impact, Anna imagined, providing others with a thorough knowledge base that would clearly illustrate the potential tribulations of implementing such a large and complicated technological project.

But Anna's plan would be shelved, like so many other plans conceived for Masdar. She had been able to recruit two anthropologists interested in working at Masdar full-time, but she had not located sources for funding. She had contacted the company's sustainability department, explaining her need for funding. But the executives did not fully agree with her understanding of such knowledge-making practices. "Unfortunately," she explained, "this [anthropological] type of knowledge was argued to be too esoteric for a project like Masdar." After listening to her concerns and claiming to understand her rationale, the sustainability department had decided to hire a global management consulting company to conduct research within the organization for three months. This research culminated in a comprehensive report titled "The Masdar Experience," which concentrated on raising questions such as who should be residing at Masdar City upon its completion, rather than interrogating the on-site debates and queries in the way Anna had proposed.

Anna's attempt at bringing anthropological tools into the project had somehow been sidelined, demonstrating the tensions between two types of knowledge inside the institution. While anthropological knowledge was perceived to be marginal and commercially ineffective, the consultants' knowledge would be readily digestible and transferrable to capital. The consulting company promised to deliver a report in just three months, while Anna had hoped that the anthropologists would conduct fieldwork in the company for one or two years and be compensated accordingly. In the executives' analysis, the longer ethnographic study was somewhat impractical and unnecessary. When the consultants from the multinational company did complete their work, however, they had managed to produce new imaginaries for Masdar to implement, but had overlooked decision-making processes and potential conflicts within the organization while neglecting to document in detail the project's different stages.

While my ethnographic study did not benefit from the financial or organizational means that Anna had planned for, it started out with similar prospects, aspiring to investigate and examine the various trajectories of the renewable energy and clean technology projects at Masdar. After conversations with administrators at Masdar, I had come to believe that I would be able to live on the Masdar Institute campus. Accordingly, during the first two weeks of my stay in the UAE, I was hosted at a hotel together with the Masdar Institute students, and I expected to move into the dormitories with them. However, at the end of those two weeks, two administrators pulled me aside and explained that I needed a security clearance to be able to reside in the Masdar dorms. They estimated that the security clearance would materialize roughly two weeks after I submitted an application. That evening, I talked to a close college friend who lived in Dubai and asked if I could stay with her during those two weeks while I waited for the security clearance to be processed. Despite repeated efforts on my part, my application never received a response and I did not move out of my friend's apartment until the end of my fieldwork.

As a result, I lived in Dubai's Dubai Marina neighborhood from September 2010 to June 2011, carpooling to the Masdar City site every day along with a number of people who worked at Masdar's various departments. The trip back and forth was approximately 125 miles and took about two hours a day. Given the conversations that the enclosed space of the car and the relatively long trip facilitated, the people who gave me rides from Dubai to Masdar became my closest friends and research collaborators in the UAE. During our car rides, Eda, Michael, Anna, and Alexander, among others whose pseudonyms appear in this book, offered me feedback on my interviews, pointed to other potential sources of information, and introduced me to fellow employees; overall, these interlocutors had a drastic impact on the ways in which my fieldwork was formulated. It is fair to say that much of my ethnographic research on the production of renewable energy and clean technology infrastructures took place inside SUVs, driving on the Dubai–Abu Dhabi highway.

During the workday, which typically lasted from 9 AM to 5 PM, I collaborated with Masdar Institute faculty on an energy currency experiment; I worked with Masdar Carbon, assisting them with a policy proposal on carbon capture and storage; and I was asked to help present Masdar Institute's master's programs at Turkish universities in Ankara and Istanbul. Even though I had no formal attachment to Masdar, I had two cubicles in different parts of the company (one at the Masdar Carbon building and the other within Masdar Institute), which rooted me inside the organization and allowed for routine conversations and everyday engagements with neighboring students, faculty, and professionals. I shared my writing with some of my research collaborators at different stages of the project and received feedback from them, but I did not officially contribute to decision-making protocols on site.

Many of my interlocutors had come to the UAE with the belief that they would leave in two or three years. Some of them had contracts with limited durations. Others imagined that their work experience at Masdar would be beneficial for them elsewhere, and indeed, they were able to take up new positions in multinational corporations, nongovernmental organizations, and academic institutions in other countries. My acquaintances at Masdar held citizenship in countries including Algeria, Colombia, Egypt, Germany, Greece, Iceland, India, Iran, Lebanon, the Sudan, Romania, the United Kingdom, the United States, and Turkey.[50] While most of these professionals were men, there was also a constituency of Emirati and non-Emirati women in the organization, who were well trained and received relatively high salaries. They were all fluent in English, the language of conduct at Masdar (and many institutions in the UAE). I kept in touch with a number of these engineers, architects, researchers, and students after they left the region; through these longer-term relationships, I learned of my interlocutors' reflections on Masdar beyond their employment there.

At the end of my research, I agreed with Anna that this project required an ethnographer to track the multiple trajectories of Masdar's technical adjustments; this book presents the multiple challenges inherent in five Masdar projects. By following projects with different goals, I not only analyze the ways in which business models, economic returns, and technological complexity were celebrated at Masdar; I also foreground the social relations that have produced and sustained Masdar's aspirations.

Perhaps we can understand the Masdar project as an indicator of a general trend in climate change management. This book is grounded in the technical adjustments in Abu Dhabi's Masdar; however, it is easy to observe such adjustments in other parts of the world. Electric cars, biodegradable plastic bags, and energy-efficient light bulbs exemplify contemporary methodologies of engaging with energy scarcity and climate change, and they provide the piecemeal means through which humans seek to extend their lifestyles into the future while tackling climate change. Here "technical adjustment" emerges as an ethnographic category that finds various expressions in different contexts, and that guides living arrangements and shapes social possibilities in technocratic, typically anthropocentric, ways, along lines drawn by affluent nations. To see these innovations as mere continuations of an existing apparatus, however, is to underspecify the novel infrastructures of technology, knowledge, and governance, which elicit new tensions in the contexts in which they manifest themselves.

Our current era is marked by contingencies that force us to question dominant modes of thinking about the world, and to seek novel ways of attending to climate change and impending energy issues. In this book, I show how the production of technical adjustments—only one among many ways of responding to global environmental collapse—evoked potential in the UAE, where this potential was instrumental for economic diversification and generating a new brand image. The clean technology infrastructure of Masdar City fueled an aspiration for the manageability of ecological problems, where business models were thought to contain and resolve climate change and energy scarcity without surrendering hope for increasing productivity and technological complexity. But in fact, climate change and energy scarcity should propel humans to challenge such ideals of technological development and economic growth, to pay attention to the alternative futures rendered invisible by the drive for infinity, and to cultivate new modes of inhabiting the planet.

Outline of Chapters

This book tells the story of Masdar, at once a "utopia" sponsored by the emirate's government and a company involving different sorts of actors who participated in the project, each with their own agendas and desires. In this telling, as people with varying visions act upon the project, it emerges as not just one spectacle but many, all serving different ends. For those involved, the goal has not necessarily been to produce one totalizing object, but rather a whole host of things, some of which may be mutually incompatible. In reflecting this diversity of viewpoints, I follow a Rashomon-like structure, where each chapter focuses on a different artifact (such as personal rapid transit pods or policy documents) to present what Masdar is as well as different imaginings of what it can and should become.[51] This multifaceted perspective demonstrates the contradictory ways of thinking, knowing, and interpreting Masdar City, and is useful for understanding the complexities and the ambiguities of the project. Each chapter represents distinct visions of Masdar, foregrounding contested interpretations of developments in the company. While the chapters are peopled by multiple actors who had diverse responsibilities, each features central characters—among them Laura, Fred, Alexander, Elif, Salim, and Anand—whose perspectives are essential to the descriptions and analyses that follow. This book starts by asking what Masdar means and goes on to show that a univocal statement would miss the richness of the project.

I start by focusing on the construction of Masdar City, specifically concentrating on the imagery that was deployed in speaking about the eco-city in the years that followed the project's launch. One of the central characters in this chapter is Laura, the American student at Masdar Institute who coined the term *spaceship in the desert* to describe the project. This chapter explores the intellectual origins of Masdar City as an urban-scale test bed whose design and construction were widely discussed by its producers as well as the international media. Why and how did Masdar become conceptualized as a "spaceship," and what did it mean for the project to be located in an "other" time, in addition to being located within a bounded area in the desert, often conceptualized as an "other" space? What, or perhaps when, was the future imagined through Masdar City? While showing how, at Masdar City, the present was teeming with activity, I point to the ways in which the imagery used in framing Masdar City consistently formulated the present as a vacated category and located the city in a perpetual future. In addition to thinking through the imaginaries of the city, the chapter addresses the material reality of Masdar, and investigates the exclusions it enacts in its current state, keeping laborers, such as the "man with a brush," outside its confines. In this way, this chapter seeks to generate a sensibility of how technical adjustments produce space and time.

The second chapter tells us the story of Masdar from the perspective of Fred, an MIT faculty member in his early seventies, who was critical in building Masdar Institute as a renewable energy and clean technology research center. In June 2011, about eighty students from around the world completed MSc degrees at Masdar, which were aiming to replicate degree programs at MIT.[52] These first alumni often remarked that they had been test subjects in the experiment of building an eco-city.[53] On the other hand, the UAE government, which offered full scholarships to all enrolled students, expected they would stay in the country, contributing to a knowledge-based economy based on clean technology and renewable energy. In this chapter, I study Masdar Institute as a node that may transform the UAE by producing knowledge on renewable energy and clean technology. In doing so, I concentrate on "beautiful buildings" and "research contracts" as networking devices through which relationships might be established and preserved, facilitating—as technical adjustments for an oil-less future—the emergence of an economy of innovation.

Besides helping implement the UAE's economic vision, Masdar Institute attempted to engineer an economic vision of its own, specifically by planning a new energy currency. As a faculty member at Masdar Institute, Alexander worked with a research team on the "ergos" project, which imagined that future inhabitants of Masdar City could be issued a balance of energy credits as a means of defining and regulating an allocated energy budget. Through individual monitoring and regulation, ergos aimed at decreasing the energy consumption of Masdar City's residents. And yet Alexander, like many of his colleagues, occasionally mentioned that the ergos project had a "Big Brother side" to it, and that it could lead to a "technocratic dictatorship." In this chapter, I explore the paradoxes that emerged during the project and map out the stakes of this currency proposal for the actors involved.

Another artifact that attracted much attention to the construction site of Masdar City was the driverless electric personal rapid transit (PRT) pods, offering automated transportation for groups of up to six people between two points on a network. While the PRT was envisioned to connect the entire eco-city, such plans were dropped in late 2010 due to financial challenges. Still, there was one destination that the PRT pods stationed at Masdar Institute could travel to: the parking lot outside the building. The ten pilot PRT vehicles completed around 250 trips per day, and their futuristic design drew many visitors to the site. The PRT was the subject of a central debate on the Masdar City site, leading some to designate it a victory, while others were more skeptical regarding its capacities. Many who experienced the PRT wondered why one wouldn't bicycle or simply walk the short distance, and some called the experimental transportation device "an expensive toy." Recurrent breakdowns resulted in complaints, facilitating discussions on technoscientific experimentation. Masdar Institute students Elif (whose survey results I referred to above) and Salim gave me guided tours of the pod cars and helped me interrogate what failure or success meant for the PRT project. This chapter argues that the affective modalities of infrastructure may at times overcome expectations of functionality, demonstrating how, in the case of Masdar City, the experience of "fun" could override the debatable operational capacity of the pod cars.

In the fifth chapter, my ethnography descends underground, as I follow policy making on carbon capture and storage (CCS), a controversial climate change mitigation technology that operates by obtaining carbon dioxide from industrial compounds, carrying it to storage sites, and injecting it into the ground. By injecting carbon dioxide into fields and forcing oil out, oil producers could potentially extend the lifespan of the oilfields. Some policy makers and scientists have argued that CCS could cause the leakage of concentrated amounts of carbon dioxide, and that liability protocols related to such incidents remain lacking. By drawing on my experiences working with environmental consultant Anand and others at Masdar Carbon, I study the preparation of a CCS policy proposal for the United Nations Framework Convention on Climate Change (UNFCCC), and I focus primarily on how uncertainty and risk are defined by different groups of experts in realizing this technical adjustment. Providing insight into the backstage discussions of climate change governance, I lay out how participants translate across their zones of professional comfort, how business plans and government policy work at odds, and how national policies are crafted through negotiations with multinational oil companies.

In an epilogue, I look to the global horizons of Abu Dhabi's renewable energy and clean technology projects, which have moved forward and, indeed, have been disseminated globally regardless of their inherent problems and contradictions. This closing analysis of Masdar's attempts to produce an international carbon capture and storage policy, a new currency based on energy expenditure, a renewable energy and clean technology research institute, and, finally, an eco-city, provides an overview of how the actors producing Masdar participated in the constitution of constructive ambiguities for the contemporary renewable energy and clean technology sector.

I KNOWLEDGE

Inhabiting the Spaceship 1

An Enclosed Space

"Imagine—imagine a place where the challenge of living in an extreme climate is overcome at no cost to the environment," announced a Masdar City promotional video produced in early 2008. "Imagine a place of the future with all of the benefits of twenty-first-century living, yet none of the stresses of outdated twentieth-century cities." The video went on to explain how the new city's master plan drew inspiration from the vernacular forms of Arab architecture, relied on cutting-edge technology, and helped its residents minimize their energy consumption and carbon footprint. Densely populated narrow streets and shaded walkways would decrease the need for air-conditioning by reducing direct sunlight in a pedestrian environment. Rooftop photovoltaic panels would produce enough electricity for the whole city, powering driverless automated transit pods for public transportation. Through a wide variety of innovations, ranging from wind towers to personal automated transit pods, Masdar City's planners aimed from its start in 2006 to create a zero-carbon eco-city that would eventually fulfill its energy demands through renewable energy sources, emitting no carbon dioxide. The final message of Masdar's promotional campaign was ambitious and clear: "Masdar City is the city of the future and the role model for the world. Masdar City: one day all cities will be built like this."[1] This is how the future of Masdar City was marketed, initially.[2]

At the groundbreaking ceremony in 2008, Sultan Al Jaber, then CEO of Masdar, declared: "We are creating a city where residents and commuters will live the highest quality of life with the lowest environmental footprint. Masdar City will become the world's hub for future energy. By taking sustainable development and living to a new level, it will lead the world in understanding how all future cities should be built."[3]

According to the first digital renderings, a wall would surround the "desert utopia," or "high-tech oasis," insulating it from desert winds and sand. Inside, previously unimagined technologies would terraform the surrounding landscape as a space of experimentation. Fascinated with the proposed technologies, some critics extrapolated that human sweat and other ambient moistures would be "plucked out of the air" in Masdar City and recycled into drinking water.[4] A German engineering professor at MIT whom I spoke to in early 2010, and who was not officially affiliated with Masdar Institute, provocatively stated that Masdar was "the only utopia to emerge from the Middle East since Islam." According to him, Masdar was so revolutionary in its aspirations that it could reorganize social, political, and economic relations in the region—like a new religion.

Behind the scenes, many professionals who worked at Masdar's various departments argued that the company's marketing budget was its largest investment. Many saw the marketing and communications campaigns as portraying a "science fiction" project. In describing the city, many referred to films such as Luc Besson's *The Fifth Element* (1997), Paul Verhoeven's *Total Recall* (1990), or Ridley Scott's *Blade Runner* (1982); the latter was based on Philip K. Dick's novel *Do Androids Dream of Electric Sheep?* from 1968, and Margaret Atwood's recent novel *Oryx and Crake*, from 2003, was also considered a good analogue. Most of these works are set in bounded cityscapes where life is impossible outside technologically supported zones. Soon, Masdar's promoters forecast, life would need to be sequestered in enclosed and self-sufficient spaces due to climate change and energy deficiency.

As a city built from scratch, Masdar offered a vision of technologically complex, eco-friendly, and enjoyable modes of living, and aimed to serve as a potential engine for economic growth. But the future that animated interest in this complex was at times dark. By the logic of Masdar's

FIGURE 1.1 · Computer rendering of the Masdar City Master Plan, 2007. Image by Foster + Partners.

marketing campaign, the time and space of Masdar City was at once apocalyptic and utopian. Indeed, when executives working with Masdar City utilized analogies based in science fiction narratives, they received tongue-in-cheek criticism from reviewers. An environmental news website quipped, "Masdar City is bringing *Blade Runner* to the fore? No one wants to live in a city full of replicants, even if it's eco-friendly. Someone better call Deckard to fix this mess before it gets out of hand."[5] The news website pointed out that many works of science fiction are critiques of totalizing environments, where corporate power looms large, the police seem omnipresent, and large-scale social problems remain inevitable despite extensive rational planning. At the same time, *Blade Runner* signified a future that had already passed. Masdar City was relying on and reproducing an imaginary of the future dating back as far as the 1960s; it was not necessarily generating the fresh and innovative future its marketers promised.

This chapter focuses on the imagery employed in speaking about the "futuristic" Masdar City project in the years that followed its launch in 2006. Why and how did Masdar become conceptualized as a city of the future, and what did it mean for the project to be located at an "other" time, in addition to being located within a bounded area in the desert, often conceptualized as an "other" space? What, or perhaps when, was the future imagined through Masdar City? The chapter explores the spatial and temporal discourses and mechanisms that were put to use while planning and building the eco-city. How did the residents of Masdar City understand the labor involved in producing a green city in the middle of the desert in an oil-producing country? It examines how students, architects, and executives imagined a technologically enhanced space that did not yet exist, within a present in which they could not be held fully accountable for their projections. By pointing out how major renewable energy and clean technology companies shared and contributed to these spatial and temporal discourses, this chapter also contextualizes Masdar's strategies within a more general framework of renewable energy and clean technology innovation. Consequently, it shows how switching scales becomes a prevalent method, allowing renewable energy and clean technology professionals to use planetary-level concerns as justifications for their projects, and letting them depend on imaginaries of an abstract, idealized future.[6]

Spaceship in the Desert

The description, in September 2010, of the Masdar Institute as "a spaceship in the middle of the desert" on the blog of an American student named Laura, new to living there, was soon being cited by all manner of sources. The president of the Institute, and many other media like *The Guardian* newspaper,[7] or the ecology blog Green Prophet,[8] recalled Laura's blog when reporting on developments at Masdar. While Laura had used the description "spaceship in the desert" to refer to the Masdar Institute campus, located on the Masdar City site, her metaphor soon grew to stand for all of Masdar City. Laura had a studio apartment on the new campus, and had assumed her blog would reach a handful of friends and family members; she later searched for reasons as to why and how it had become so popular. Her post, like many other communications regarding the eco-city, was supplemented by computer renderings that ornamented the walls of Masdar Institute to articulate the promise that the futuristic city would one day be "finished."

In Laura's understanding, the Masdar Institute campus became an innovative technological model, proposing a means of survival based on rational scientific management. The spaceship would conserve life as it had long been known on earth, presenting a provisional solution to an uninhabitable environment outside. In this way, the spaceship would act as an ark: an artificial interior space expected to give birth to a next generation of resource pioneers. The spaceship would signify enclosure, archiving, selection, hierarchy, movement, and—most importantly—the maintenance of strict boundaries between interior and exterior spaces. The experimental hub (of another time and another space) would technologically maintain the lives and livelihoods of its residents indoors.

Since the 1960s, space travel technologies have inspired ecologically sensitive architecture, producing a blueprint for survival in a context of rising environmental concerns. As historians of science such as Peder Anker and Sabine Höhler have noted in their overviews of ecological design developments, the American space program of the 1960s had considerable impact on the ways in which designers imagined and planned eco-friendly life on earth.[9] Buildings would constitute self-regulating and decentralized systems with comfortable climatic conditions for humans, provide enclosed shelters for an impending ecological disaster, and serve as means of escape from possible destruction on earth. This is perhaps best symbolized by the well-known Biosphere 2 project, where in the fall of 1991 eight scientists entered a glass and steel complex in the Sonoran Desert in Oracle, Arizona, about an hour outside Tucson, to test whether they could sustain their lives in a sealed environment, with the hope that the model would someday be replicated to colonize outer space.[10] Occupying buildings inspired by space technologies, humanity would behave like astronauts with clear outer space missions.

In these histories, the spaceship is a finite, technically sophisticated, and insular habitat for an exclusive group of beings facing an outside world of crises. In his book *Shipwreck with Spectator* (1996), Hans Blumenberg explains how humans "prefer in their imagination, to represent their overall condition in the world in terms of a sea voyage."[11] The idea of the spaceship (much like the submarine that preceded it) then serves as an extension of the ark metaphor, demonstrating the inevitable boundaries of human activities, vilifying the space beyond human habitability, and producing the outside as a vacuum that should not be inhabited. As seas full of mythical monsters surround the livable environments on earth, the ship provides a safe interior space thanks to its strict boundaries, or as the German philosopher Peter Sloterdijk suggests, it acts as an "autonomous, absolute, context-free house, the building with no neighborhood."[12] In this way, the ship puts forward an alternative environment of peace and rationality, standing in opposition to the destructive and irrational crises of earth.

In prioritizing enclosure for some over collective survival—the tension that underpins most spacefaring movies—the spaceship also advances the principles of selection and endorses what Sloterdijk calls "exclusivity dressed up as universalism." Despite saving only a very small number of those who suffer a metaphorical shipwreck, the spaceship insists on addressing the planetary-scale questions of survival in the unknown, the sustenance of the species beyond ecological catastrophe, and the preservation of an existing civilization, albeit in highly limited and confined form. In fact, as anthropologist David Valentine shows, current space entrepreneurs also share this vision, intending to produce human communities in outer space, mainly with the purpose of ensuring species survival. Valentine adds that contemporary space advocates "see space settlement as beneficial in removing polluting resource extraction and manufacturing to space, enabling Earth to heal from human-induced damage," and touches upon the types of universalisms that these communities propagate.[13]

Masdar City was conceived to perform the role of "a spaceship in the desert"—to maintain the lives and livelihoods of its residents by relying on renewable energy and clean technologies. Architects working with Foster + Partners, based at the Masdar City site to monitor both the design of Masdar Institute and the implementation of the Masdar City master plan, suggested that the ecological mandate assisted Norman Foster, founder and chairman of Foster + Partners, as he produced his legacy, having himself been inspired by the history of ecological architecture in the 1960s and the 1970s. One of the on-site Foster + Partners architects told me, "Norman wants to be the Bucky Fuller of this century."

Buckminster Fuller was a multidimensional, somewhat eccentric twentieth-century inventor who attempted to resolve the global problems of housing, transport, education, and energy through his innovative design and writing projects.[14] He conceived of the earth as a beautifully designed spaceship that lacks comprehensible instructions, which he sought to provide in publishing, in 1969, *Operating Manual for Spaceship Earth*.[15] "We are all astronauts," in Fuller's assertion. "We have not been seeing our Spaceship Earth as an integrally designed machine which to be persistently successful must be comprehended and serviced in total."[16] In learning to successfully operate "Spaceship Earth" and "its complex life-supporting and regenerating systems," humankind was confronted with the challenge of self-instruction. Earth was an operable technological object, fully accessible to humankind. Fuller not only wrote about his technocratic understandings of earth, but also conceived many design and engineering projects to illustrate his philosophy, such as the geodesic dome, a lattice-thin shell structure that is able to withstand a very heavy load for its size, and that can be used for quick and lightweight housing projects around the world.

As a young architect, Norman Foster met Buckminster Fuller in 1971 to collaborate on the construction of the Samuel Beckett Theatre at Oxford. The theater—never built—marked the beginning of their twelve-year relationship (which involved several more collaborative endeavors that would never be materially realized). The theater would have been a

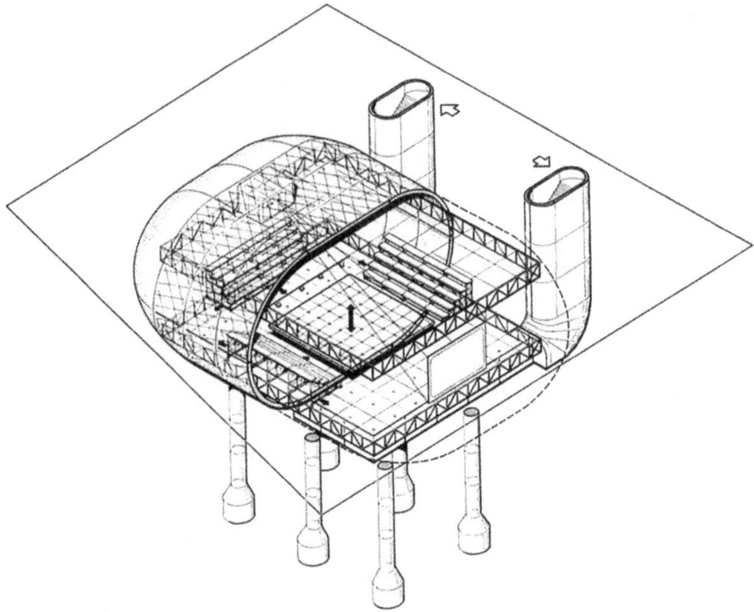

FIGURE 1.2 · Samuel Beckett Theatre at Oxford, 1971. Image by Foster + Partners.

subterranean building designed to house classrooms and exhibition spaces for St. Peter's College, and it would have utilized the geodesic, lightweight structures that had made Fuller famous by then. Foster claims this plan had a significant impact on the later stages of his own career: "I remember that Bucky made the comparison with a submarine because the structure of the building had to be resistant to water, like a seaworthy vessel. The building had to stand up to the ground water and other natural underground forces. So it's no coincidence that my later underground projects also take the form of ships and submarines."[17] Foster has also said, on different occasions, "The thing about Bucky was that he made you believe anything is possible,"[18] and that "perhaps the themes of shelter, energy and environment—which go to the heart of contemporary architecture—best reflect Bucky's inheritance. . . . For me Bucky was the very essence of a moral conscience, forever warning about the fragility of the planet and man's responsibility to protect it."[19]

At Masdar City, where Foster was realizing one of his most ambitious projects to date, I met Brad, an Irish man in his early forties who had been trained as an architect and who had, since 2009, been mostly managing the relations between Masdar, his employer, and Foster + Partners. Brad had substantial experience working in the Arab world; his previous employer was the Energy City of Qatar, and he had also managed a campus development project in Libya. When I asked Brad if he understood the Masdar City project to represent the Buckminster Fuller legacy, he reminded me, "When Bucky spoke, no one listened to what he had to say." Brad was excited that Fuller's ideas were finally being applied today at Masdar City—at least to a certain extent. Later, in an email exchange, he elaborated on how he related to Buckminster Fuller's work:

> What he did was synergetics, meaning taking a holistic view of things, he was also structure oriented. He looked at nature for instance, at fractals, and then did biomimicry. Bucky, just as we do, understood that the problem was with the system i.e. the industry. Bucky's visions and aspirations all orientated around creating a new system and solution instead of attempting to change the existing establishment. All the resistance he faced was from institutions or unions opposing radical change, hence many of his ideas were never realised, sadly until today, 50–60 years after invented or in some instances—not at all.

But Brad was also aware of the difference between Masdar and the model city Buckminster Fuller had in mind:

> One way that our cities today differ from Bucky's visions, is that a Bucky city would probably have been self-built by communities and perhaps would have been both mobile by nature, and completely off-grid/off-system in all its infrastructure and services. Something that is easier to write or imagine than accomplish in reality, due to various challenges and barriers that are political, social, economical, personal, cultural and regulatory.

The spaceship analogy so often referred to in discussions of Masdar City suggests the possibility of a city that is "mobile by nature, and completely off-grid/off-system in all its infrastructure and services," but Brad did not perceive Masdar to be completely fulfilling these requirements. In addition to underscoring how Masdar is a master-planned city, surely not organic in its development or growth, Brad explained that Masdar was dependent on the grid for its infrastructure and services. According to Brad, Masdar not only relied upon but also celebrated the status quo.

The metaphor of the ship or the submarine continues to inform Norman Foster's design work. For instance, a 2009 article in the *Guardian* suggested that Foster's "reassuringly technical, graceful, silver, white and immaculate" designs would be suitable for architecture on the moon.[20] More recently, in 2015, Foster + Partners publicized renderings for a settlement on Mars, which would be constructed by robots prior to the arrival of humans. "Designing for extra-terrestrial environments provides an exciting platform for experimentation that is at the frontline of innovative technology," one of Foster's partners commented to the *Daily Mail*.[21] In relation to his recent designs for outer space, Foster has noted that he understands practicing architecture in the Arabian Gulf to be similar to lunar exploration,[22] and news commentators have supported this take in their continued fascination with the idea of constructing an eco-friendly city in the desert: "The inhospitable terrain suggests that the only way to survive here is with the maximum of technological support, a bit like living on the moon."[23] In his autobiography, the leading Emirati entrepreneur and businessman Easa Al-Gurg asserts that Emirati rulers understand the desert as a moonscape; he describes how Sheikh Rashid bin Saeed Al Maktoum of Dubai dismissed the moon landing as a hoax, arguing that the landscape looked like the empty terrain in Ras Al-Khaimah, one of the seven emirates that make up the UAE. "Maybe it was filmed there," Sheikh Rashid said.[24]

When the first phase of the Masdar Institute campus (one of the first buildings to be completed within Masdar City) was finally completed in September 2010, it became, one on-site architect told me, the first building to ever be reviewed on the front page of the *New York Times*. In the review, Nicolai Ouroussoff, the newspaper's architecture critic, labeled the city a "futuristic playground for the rich," and stated that its design "reflects the gated-community mentality that has been spreading like a cancer around the globe for decades." Ouroussoff pointed to how "Its utopian purity, and its isolation from the life of the real city next door, are grounded in the belief—accepted by most people today, it seems—that the only way to create a truly harmonious community, green or otherwise, is to cut it off from the world at large."[25] This commentary received attention and provoked debates on the Masdar City site. An on-site Foster + Partners architect noted that as designers they wanted the eco-city to be contained, specifically because they wished to prevent urban sprawl in Abu Dhabi, then added, "But that does not mean the city will not impact the rest of Abu Dhabi positively." Another on-site architect wondered how there could ever be a city that did not allow car entry but still remain connected to the rest of the city grid, echoing Ouroussoff's critique.

Soon after, the architecture critic Rowan Moore published a review of the building in the United Kingdom's *Observer* newspaper, and responded to the *New York Times* article. "The Masdar plan has been accused of being gated and exclusive. It is not, although there is something spooky in the controls it employs in the name of the environment—a touch of eco-Orwell or at least eco-Huxley," Moore wrote. "The purpose of the institute is to study the effectiveness of Masdar's techniques, so that they can be applied elsewhere."[26] Moore seemed to understand spatial isolation to be an essential condition that would produce the environment necessary for experimentation, allowing the city to more effectively influence, or rather create, the future. A new generation of research and business enterprises would emerge from this isolation, shaping the energy infrastructure of a world without fossil fuels. Masdar City had to be an enclosed space—a spaceship where the future would be incubated. The city's totalizing qualities were rather aggressive, but they would serve an abstract higher good, eventually helping humans address climate change and energy scarcity problems.

According to both critics, Masdar was futuristic and enclosed, moving toward a frontier of innovations to enable a new kind of future for the planet. Ouroussoff's critique underlined how this city was being designed and built in a context of extreme levels of inequality both in Abu Dhabi and around the world, while claiming to mitigate problems of planetary scale. The city would be cut off from Abu Dhabi proper, situated near the Formula 1 tracks, the golf course, and the airport, and would not include "the world at large" in its conception of the future. Its design embodied these inequalities, and did not necessarily seek to challenge them. On the other hand, Rowan Moore pointed to the "spooky" controls that the city used in order to monitor and control energy consumption, and added that it was not gated or exclusive. Once it was developed, the city could impact the rest of the world positively. Both critics referenced means of control, and took up the designers' practices of scaling; in so doing, both underlined how the spaceship could serve a higher good in an elusive future.

The Frontier

In December 2010, Fred Moavenzadeh, then president of Masdar Institute, appeared in a CNN documentary by Richard Quest about Masdar City. He explained that when the United States wanted to send a man to the moon, it produced NASA; now, when the United Arab Emirates wants to transform and diversify its economy, it builds Masdar City. How can we understand and conceptualize the impetus to compare Masdar City with the moon landing or with an exploratory trip to outer space? Looking back at the Apollo space program, David Mindell, a historian of science, explains how President John F. Kennedy seized and mobilized the powerful mythology of the frontier in aiming for the moon.[27] The term *frontier*, originally meaning border or borderline, took on new resonance during the settlement of the American West in the eighteenth and nineteenth centuries. In this narrative, heroic pioneers headed to an unknown geography full of unpredictable dangers as well as antagonistic competitors, where they would make use of self-control, self-reliance, and humility to open up a new frontier.

Laura's spaceship analogy also helped the producers of Masdar City in promoting the reconfiguration of the desert as an undiscovered resource frontier from which a novel means of livelihood would emerge. The analogy served as a conceptual extension of the multiple orientalist projects the British or the French undertook in nineteenth century in order to make a certain form of life possible in the arid geographies of Arabia.[28] In the new adventure, the frontier people of Masdar City would be in charge, both abiding by the principles of the Abu Dhabi government and taking the initiative to produce a next generation of innovators. The frontier people would help Abu Dhabi ensure its survival after oil by replacing fossil fuels with renewable energies. According to this destiny, the students would take charge as astronauts, managing the successful institution of a new resource economy within an oil-exporting country.

The frontier narrative not only reconfigured the "passengers" of Masdar City as resource pioneers; it also obfuscated the idea of resource finitude. While the Masdar project seemingly relied on and reproduced the acknowledgment that fossil fuels would eventually disappear, the eco-city promoted an infinity of sunlight and wind in responding to this verdict. Perhaps fossil fuels were going to be less abundant, but this did not mean energy sources were finite and predetermined. Detached from the burdens of "nature," the spaceship in the desert would journey through endless space, confirming the vision of a boundless frontier where new varieties of resources were to be discovered.[29] In fulfilling its duties as an exploratory vehicle in outer space, the Masdar City project would challenge and resolve the problem of finitude.

The frontier narrative led the producers of Masdar City to conceptualize the present as a moment of potential. It also concentrated their efforts on constructing a future that would be incubated inside this enclosed space within the Abu Dhabi desert. Masdar City could give rise to a new generation of resource pioneers, who would hurtle through unbounded renewable energy and clean technology territory.[30] Accordingly, it was not only the space of the Abu Dhabi desert that awaited another discovery, but also its temporality. The spaceship analogy spoke to a future of technical innovations that would potentially emerge from this enclosed space, possibly allowing the eco-city to be replicated in other settings around the world.

This is what Alan Frost, then director of Masdar City, invoked during a presentation at the World Future Energy Summit in Abu Dhabi in January 2011: "When we started Masdar City, we thought it was an island, we thought that basically we were doing all these things people had not done before, we could do it all on our own, and then we come back and tell everyone about it. But you know what, that's not very healthy. . . . So, the lesson is that you cannot be an island."[31] The master-planned city, whose planning had started in 2006, and which would be fully constructed and thereafter sold and perhaps exported, reformulated its business plan after the economic crisis of 2008, and invited renewable energy and clean technology companies to start building their headquarters within its boundaries. This way, the city's growth would not depend completely on the funds made available by Abu Dhabi authorities. "There is no point in doing something, which you can only do at Masdar. It has to be sustainable and it has to work for Abu Dhabi. . . . Everything at Masdar City has to be translatable and repeatable around the world," Frost continued, inviting third parties to participate in this economic diversification project.

In its revised formula, Masdar City would constitute a test-bed for multiple energy technologies that might later be purchased and used around the world. On top of this, Masdar City as a whole would be conceived as an exportable commodity, leading to the production of replicas around the globe. The Masdar City design had to be mobile, traveling throughout the world. The incomplete eco-city served as a technologically advanced spaceship that could survive in a vacuum. Moreover, it had the potential to further spread that technologically advanced environment in an undefined space and time. In other words, Masdar conveyed and emanated the promise to create that space and time for everyone else.

Meanwhile, Masdar Institute students, the frontier people of Abu Dhabi's emergent eco-city experiment, remained unsure about the translatability of Masdar City into other settings. After the summit, on February 1, 2011, they gathered in the Masdar Institute auditorium to debate whether "Masdar City is an elite enclave of sustainability, unsuitable for the rest of the world." The graduate students, who came to Masdar City from countries including the United States, China, India, Egypt, Jordan, Iran, Turkey, and Iceland, were struggling with such questions, and wished to think about them in the context of a debate club performance.

The team that perceived Masdar City as "an elite enclave of sustainability" argued that Masdar was "too unique" to be applied elsewhere. For one, Masdar was very expensive. Which other country, other than the oil-rich UAE, would be able to devote $22 billion for an eco-city?[32] Second, they recalled how this project had been put together to contribute to the economic diversification of Abu Dhabi, and perhaps would not be financially feasible or meaningful for other countries with different economies. Masdar City was expected to help the UAE transform its brand image from oil producer to technology developer, to induce a perception shift, possibly attracting foreign investments or facilitating the creation of local start-ups focusing on renewable energy and clean technology. Third, the political climate of Abu Dhabi was working in favor of Masdar City by providing prolonged commitment and stability—the government often served as a steady source of financing for the project. In this understanding, Masdar

City would remain an island contingent on a specific set of circumstances only available within the United Arab Emirates. Abu Dhabi's oil capital, its future economic vision, and its political environment were thus perceived as preconditions for launching the spaceship.

In response, the team that defended the global applicability of Masdar City proposed that the eco-city should be understood and framed as a prototype: Abu Dhabi would shoulder the burdens of building the eco-city, and others would benefit. "Every new idea is expensive," one of the students underlined. "Think about the car. First rich people had it and now it has spread around the world." Masdar City could become less expensive in an undefined future. It could be exported to other countries as a whole, in the same way that the car and its infrastructure have been exported. In the meantime, the experiments taking place at Masdar would be learning experiences for students, researchers, and faculty, opening up global horizons for research on renewable energy and clean technology for eventual adaptation to other regions in bits and pieces.

At the end of the meeting, one student approached me to express his dissatisfaction at how none of the students on the debate teams had actually defined what Masdar City *was*, or what exactly they expected it to spread around the world. "No one talked about the personal rapid transit units, or the motion sensors," he specified, pointing to the technological artifacts that seemingly defined the eco-city for him. In which of its materializations did Masdar inhere, and what would it pass on to the rest of the world, he wondered, and what exactly was the future that the spaceship promised?

The Fiction of Shibam

On November 10, 2010, some weeks before the official opening of Masdar City, Daniel, a Foster + Partners architect overseeing the master plan, gave a talk about their design process. His slideshow included a lunar image, juxtaposing a space module with the gray, lightweight cladding of the laboratory buildings on the Masdar Institute campus. The laboratory façades were composed of insulating cushions that, the architects explained, shade the interiors of the building and remain cool to the touch under the desert sun. Yet while the technological infrastructure of Masdar City was critical to the project, the architects also emphasized how they learned from old Arab cities in designing the eco-city. Daniel's slideshow in fact began with references to cities that had architectural principles akin to Masdar. Aleppo, in Syria, and Marrakesh, in Morocco, were among the cities that inspired the city's master plan, along with traditional districts within Abu Dhabi, Dubai, and other cities in the UAE and Gulf region. Many of these cities also had narrow streets, shaded windows, courtyards, and wind towers. The audience, mainly Masdar Institute students and researchers, listened carefully and examined the image that Daniel showed, a bird's-eye view of Shibam in Yemen, taken by George Steinmetz, a *National Geographic* photographer.

A student raised his hand to ask a question, interrupting the presentation: "But does Shibam really exist? Have you ever seen it?" Daniel replied that it was too dangerous to travel to Yemen these days, so he had never been to Shibam, adding that he would love to go there someday. But sure, Shibam existed. This city, or this historical artifact, as Daniel framed it, had been one of the primary inspirations for building Masdar City, an eco-city that strove to be located in the future, that had its roots in a uniquely Arab past.[33]

In his book *Dubai, the City as Corporation* (2011), anthropologist Ahmed Kanna attends to the ways in which international architecture offices like Foster + Partners evoke and deploy flattened understandings of culture and history in contextualizing their projects. According to him, architectural forms designed to invoke the Gulf, whether by deriving formal inspiration from the *souq* (bazaar), *dhow* (traditional sailing vessel), or other vernacular elements such as narrow streets and wind towers, eventually serve the state's political goals. Based on this analysis, such alignments between the ruling elite and design professionals produce an "apolitical representation of local culture," reproducing and redeploying the state's expectations of the built environment, and its vision of the country's future.[34]

The Masdar project provided various opportunities to enact Abu Dhabi's political visions as a regional and global center. By using representations of Shibam and other older Arab cities in architectural presentations, the designers of Masdar City looked for a context to which Masdar City could respond. At the same time, however, they helped serve political goals, assisting Abu Dhabi in achieving a centrality in the Arab

FIGURE 1.3 · A bird's-eye view image of Shibam in Yemen, 2005. Photo by George Steinmetz.

world. In their presentation, Daniel and his fellow architects working with Foster + Partners employed references to the past as material evidence and reasoning, to thereby attain solid historical grounding for their project. By depicting their sources of inspiration, the designers of Masdar City formulated a credible trajectory for the emergent eco-city master plan, and positioned it as a natural conclusion to urban developments in different parts of the Arab world. This imagery did not necessarily claim to be apolitical. Instead, by referencing, reproducing, and advancing this trajectory, Abu Dhabi acquired additional critical weight within the Arab world, constituting a new cultural crossroads.

In these presentations, the old city of Shibam lost its social, political, and even material qualities, and became part of the imaginary world of Masdar City. Did Shibam really exist? No one in the audience, including the architects, seemed to have experienced Shibam firsthand. Seen in a bird's-eye view photograph in the Foster + Partners slideshow, Shibam's qualities complemented those of Masdar. Shibam stood in for a mythical

Arab past, relegated to a lost history and unapproachable geography. In this context, Masdar City not only served as the materialization of a displaced longing for this past; it also epitomized the expectations for a mythical Arab future, under construction in Abu Dhabi.

The imaginary world of Masdar had been created step by step in meeting rooms, publicized through marketing and communications campaigns, and finally solidified with the opening of the Masdar Institute campus in November 2010. "When we first started the project," a marketing executive told me, "people thought that these were the quirky ambitions of an oil-led state; people thought that we are not serious." But the opening of Masdar Institute proved that the plans would not swerve and that Abu Dhabi's ambitions were not outlandish. Instead, Masdar Institute would constitute a showcase for the other Masdar projects, attracting more attention to and investments in Masdar Power, Masdar Carbon, and Masdar Capital. Masdar City was thus promoted as the "Global Center of Future Energy" and framed in corporate brochures[35] as "an emerging technology hub that positions companies located here at the heart of the global industry." As the corporate brochures suggested, "A place where businesses can thrive and innovation can flourish, Masdar City is a modern Arabian city that, like its forerunners, is in tune with its surroundings."

Official Opening

The official opening of the Masdar Institute campus, perhaps a metonymical representation of Masdar City, was scheduled for November 23, 2010. The campus—which contained laboratories, residential units, classrooms, a cafeteria, a coffee shop, a small gym, and a "Knowledge Center," as well as open landscaped areas between these facilities—was argued to be the first structure of its kind to be powered entirely by solar energy. The residential units boasted terra-cotta walls of reinforced concrete and relied on contemporary interpretations of *mashrabiyas*, vernacular wooden-latticed screens, to block sunlight and allow for privacy. The laboratory buildings incorporated horizontal and vertical fins and brise soleil to ensure shade inside the buildings. The Masdar Institute's students and faculty, who were already living on campus or commuting there daily, reflected on these material conditions in daily conversations and blog posts, and they

FIGURE 1.4 · Masdar Institute courtyard with a view of the dormitory buildings, 2011. Photo by the author.

FIGURE 1.5 · Masdar Institute courtyard with a view of the laboratory buildings and the Knowledge Center, 2011. Photo by the author.

observed and sometimes guided the various architects, consultants, and visitors who regularly inspected the site.

When the day of the inauguration ceremony came, the students had important roles to play in it. A day before the event, they all received an email attachment with instructions on where they would be stationed throughout the ceremony, and how they would approach the high-profile visitors to the building, such as Sheikh Mohammed bin Zayed Al-Nahyan, crown prince of Abu Dhabi. The document specified: "You need to identify yourselves and greet the guests by saying: Thank you for coming to Masdar Institute Inauguration, we are delighted to have you here, we will show you to the PRT cars." While six students were to welcome visitors at the PRT station, fourteen others were asked to be present at the Knowledge Center, "reading, working on laptops, checking books at 1st floor of the library," so as to allow the visitors to experience the building in operation. The remaining hundred or so students would be stationed at different locations on campus at different times.

The students were provided with a fact sheet with answers to questions such as "What makes Masdar City special?" as well as reference points for their potential conversations with guests. They would redeploy Masdar's marketing and promotional campaigns, this time through informal conversations, while making use of the half-working material artifacts on site as props. What they staged would serve as a natural representation of the future of Masdar Institute, with busy students absorbed in their work, "reading, working on laptops, checking books at the 1st floor of the library." When presenting the Institute, it somehow made more sense to introduce that abstract future, rather than showcasing the current state of indeterminacy the fledgling institution was trying to overcome. In this performance, the students not only pretended to exist in the future, they also demonstrated the perpetual potential of the project.[36]

Norman Foster evoked the permanent potential of the present in his inauguration lecture that day:

> Many have dreamed of a utopian project that would be solar powered. Today's official opening of the initial stage of the Masdar Institute campus at Masdar City is a first realization of that quest. Its student community is already active, living and working in their quarters. This community, independent of any power grid, develops a surplus

FIGURE 1.6
Wind tower in a courtyard at the Masdar Institute, 2010. Photo by the author.

> of 60 percent of its own energy needs, processes its wastewater on-site, which is recycled, and pioneers many energy saving concepts. It is a bold experiment, which will change and evolve over time—already it houses twelve separate research projects with potential worldwide applications.

According to Foster, the opening of Masdar Institute marked a moment in which a science fiction utopia, physically and socially constructed at Masdar, unfolded into material reality. It manifested that the remaining forward-looking statements of Masdar were going to be solidified, in the same way that Masdar Institute was starting its operations. In this sense, the opening of Masdar Institute was more than the sum of its parts, proving how dedicated the professionals at Masdar were to the utopia of Masdar City. As one marketing executive said to me, it demonstrated that Abu Dhabi was "serious" in its endeavors.

Foster spoke of specific examples of the technologies produced and used within Masdar. "There is a breeze that gives one a chill when standing below the wind tower inside the Masdar campus," he noted, referring to a project that had long been under construction. The steel-framed wind tower, which rose above one of the courtyards, attempted to reinterpret an architectural element used for cooling in different parts of the Middle East, most commonly in Iran.

At the top, the 150-foot-tall structure featured louvers and mist jets that aimed to abate high-heat temperatures in the space surrounding its base; it was expected to produce a localized cooling effect. When I discussed Foster's lecture with a postdoctoral researcher from the Institute a few days later, he laughingly asked, "Has Norman Foster even been here and seen that the wind tower does not work, or did they make the wind tower operational just for the moment that he was standing here?" Foster's comments were rooted in a potential and idealized version of the Masdar Institute campus, which would come to exist in an abstract future. He performed that future in his presentation, in the same way that the students performed future versions of themselves at the library.[37]

The science fiction or utopia that Masdar Institute represented was further enacted and confirmed through high-profile visits to the campus. By relying on a predetermined statement about the campus, the marketing department employees introduced the various research projects on site to their guests, which ranged from Hollywood celebrities such as Adrian Brody and James Cameron, to politicians such as U.S. Secretary of State Hilary Clinton and South Korean Prime Minister Kim Hwang-sik, to investors interested in building eco-hotel chains or organic grocery stores. These high-profile visits not only helped showcase the multiple advancements on renewable energy and clean technology, but also supported publicity campaigns in national and international media outlets. When the movie star Clive Owen toured the Masdar Institute, for instance, his comments ran under the headline "Masdar Looks Like a City from the Future: Owen" in the national English-language newspaper *Khaleej Times*.[38] Owen, who had starred in acclaimed science fiction films such as *Children of Men* (2006), suggested that a science fiction film be shot at the Institute.

But some of Masdar's employees voiced concerns about these guided tours. "You can't question the marketing statements," one Masdar executive told me during a conversation in his office. "Then I hear people ridiculing the place on the [private tour] bus, because they're not stupid. So we have to tell them the truth." He continued, "Here, when someone says it works, you have to agree, even though you're wrong." Around the time of our conversation, an article appeared in a German publication titled "The Ruptured Dream of the Desert City Masdar" (Der geplatzte Traum der Wüstenstadt Masdar).[39] The article described Masdar City as "a mirage that falls apart as you get closer to it," and argued that the technologies Masdar promoted did not actually work. Finally, it concluded, Masdar is "a lesson for how delusions of grandeur, technical mistakes, and above all poor planning can rob a fascinating idea of its credibility." Executives at Masdar City, above all Sultan Al-Jaber, the chief executive officer whom the article directly criticized, were enraged. A Masdar employee who was on her way out of the company told me that she very much agreed with the points the article made. While indicating perpetual potential, the repeated performance of a totalizing future could cause the Masdar City project to slowly lose its credibility, rendering it a disappointing mirage.[40]

Abu Dhabi is perceived to be a perfect location for harnessing solar energy. However, according to Mahmood, a thirty-something Egyptian-born engineer at Masdar, this perception was not completely accurate. Upon finishing his PhD at an American university, and wishing to be closer to home, Mahmood had accepted a position at Masdar as his first job. As we chatted outside a solar power station, he stated that high levels of dust and humidity were blocking direct solar rays and causing thick coatings on the solar panels, diminishing their effective functioning. "Although we can't fix the first problem that easily, we have found a solution for the second problem," he continued. "We call it 'man with a brush.'"

There were ongoing experiments at a small solar power station on the Masdar City site as well as many other testing sites around the world,[41] but during the time of our conversation, none of them had been put into large-scale use. In Mahmood's understanding, the man with a brush, a worker dedicated to gently wiping away dust and mud from the solar panels, became part of the picture, only to reveal the infrastructural potential embedded within the solar panels. Man with a brush could perform a feat that extensive technological innovations could not so far handle, and therefore was fundamental to the emergent renewable energy and clean technology sector of Abu Dhabi. The man with a brush was South Asian or perhaps from the Philippines, he shared a room with other workers in a labor camp outside Abu Dhabi, and he walked around the Masdar City site cleaning solar panels on a daily basis. Overall, the immigrant labor force served as a most effective and essential resource for the materialization

FIGURE 1.7 · "Man with a brush" cleaning solar panels at Masdar City, 2011. Photo by the author.

and functioning of renewable energy and clean technology infrastructures in the UAE. Yet these humans, who were making the infrastructure work, were most often perceived as disposable tools. Masdar City attempted to help humanity fight climate change and energy scarcity problems, but its understanding of humanity was particular and selective. It did not include the man with a brush.

When I asked Mohammed, a Bangladeshi man who worked in the kitchen and served the Masdar Institute president's guests, earning six hundred dirham per month (roughly US$160) in exchange for roughly two hundred hours of work,[42] if he knew why so many individuals and groups find the campus worthy of a visit, he shook his head no, then added that a professor at the Institute had told him that solar panels provide energy to the campus. A few days later, Daniel, the on-site architect with Foster + Partners, criticized the conception of renewable energy and clean technology within the compounds of the UAE. "How could sustainability truly be targeted when there is this little attention paid to human capital?" he asked, pointing to the harsh working conditions for the large populations of migrant workers within the United Arab Emirates. Daniel had spent most of his professional career in the United Kingdom prior to moving to Abu Dhabi for the Masdar project, and he had also lived in Germany. He told me that "sustainability is also about claiming some sort of justice, and making sure that what we build leads this very young country toward a better direction. It is also about some kind of equality." Daniel emphasized that the manual labor that was enabling the construction and maintenance of the projects was too often glossed over, at times framed as a disposable tool, and finally excluded from the future of the spaceship in the desert.

At Masdar City, oil would cease to be the main currency, driverless electric pods would replace cars, and, eventually, possible environmental problems would be avoided through meticulous research and technological discovery. In this science fiction–style narrative, the social and political injustices did not seem to matter much.

At the World Future Energy Summit 2011, where Alan Frost gave his talk about Masdar City, many other renewable energy and clean technology companies highlighted their relationship to the future with slogans such as "Tomorrow Is Today," "Enabling the Future," or "For a Better Tomorrow and Greener Earth, ARDECO is at the Forefront of Turning Today's Resources into Tomorrow's Clean Energy." In the words of a writer who blogged about the World Future Energy Summit, "Matter of fact, the most significant word in the name of this global clean energy conference is *future*."[43] Thanks to its current oil exports, the UAE was boasting ski-sloped malls, golf courses, and seven-star hotels, and emitting carbon at a violent pace. Concerned about what this meant for the United Arab Emirates' relationship to clean technology and renewable energy, the blogger came to the conclusion that "The future can't come soon enough."

But perhaps it was not fair to direct such criticism uniquely at the UAE, at its engagement with clean technology and renewable energy infrastructures, especially because global companies, the major players in the industry, seemed to be betting on the future as well.

For instance, when I asked a Siemens representative what they meant by the slogan "Tomorrow Is Today," he argued that Siemens had access to all the technological tools that would be used "tomorrow," but unfortunately people were not ready to embrace what they had to offer. "We test our products at Masdar City," another Siemens representative clarified, "which

FIGURE 1.8 · Siemens Pavilion at World Future Energy Summit, Abu Dhabi, 2011. Photo by the author.

is also in the future." The company was involved in a project called the "Office of the Future," where people worked on optimizing offices. One of these offices would be situated within Masdar City. Elsewhere at the summit, General Electric's marketing slogan announced that the company would be "Enabling the Future" with smart appliances, in addition to other technological gadgets. When I asked him if he could elaborate on these statements, a GE representative stated, "In the future everything will be smart and regulated, just as they are at Masdar City." Less prominent corporate figures, such as Arab Development Establishment (ARDECO), with business operations in a variety of areas including the oil, gas, power, and water sectors, promoted that they would also be part of the "future" energy mix.

Why exactly was the present a rather irrelevant category for the renewable energy and clean technology industry? Asif Ali Zardari, then president of Pakistan, who spoke in 2011 at the World Future Energy Summit, underlined that we must not mourn for the excesses of the last century,

FIGURE 1.9
General Electric Pavilion at World Future Energy Summit, Abu Dhabi, 2011. Photo by the author.

but rather work on developing a vision for the future. While the twentieth century had been a time of decadent pleasures, the future (explored under the wings of governments and the corporate entities present at the summit) would be characterized by responsible consumption of resources. Accordingly, renewable energy and clean technology companies embodied a messianic promise, seeking to liberate humanity from its guilt-ridden consciousness of the twentieth century. In this framework, the present mattered for its perpetual potential, prompting renewable energy and clean technology companies to refer to the abstract planetary-scale transformations they could one day trigger and implement. Perhaps this half-finished and half-working infrastructure would *someday* cultivate a new way of dwelling in the world.

In this context, Masdar remained an exclusive project that aspired to prolong the current social and political conditions by making use of technical adjustments. It supported a conception of utopia or science fiction that did not take into account an improved future for the whole of humanity; the implication was that the status quo was already a best-case scenario. The producers of Masdar already inhabited this utopia, even though this utopia did not necessarily plan for the "man with the brush" or many others who were not included within its confines. In constructing an eco-city, they were building a limited notion of what humanity means, and strengthening existing social boundaries.

The next chapter will study the steps toward building Abu Dhabi's knowledge-based economy. It will show how, through relying on "beautiful buildings" and "research contracts" as networking devices, the pioneers of the Masdar spaceship attempted to generate an economy of technological innovation in the land of fossil fuels.

Beautiful Buildings and Research Contracts 2

Beautiful Buildings

In December 2010, I was approached by Fred, the Iranian-born, U.S.-educated head of the Technology and Development Program (TDP) at MIT and, as of August 2010, the president of Masdar Institute, about whether I would be willing to help organize a student recruitment trip to elite Turkish universities. He had recently met the president of Middle East Technical University (METU), located in Ankara, and found out that a large percentage of their graduates seek out advanced degrees outside of Turkey, mostly in Europe and the United States. He wondered what other universities in Turkey might be similar and asked me to select campuses where Masdar Institute should make presentations in order to attract and recruit highly qualified students. Fred and I had known each other since our initial meeting at MIT in Cambridge in March 2009, and regularly had conversations about my research at Masdar. He thought I would be a good fit for this recruitment trip, as I had moved to the United States to start a PhD at Cornell after finishing undergraduate and master's degrees at Koç University in Istanbul. Fred had also been a graduate student at Cornell. He had met his wife in Ithaca, and often brought up his own experiences there. He also knew that I was an alumnus of Robert College, an American high school in Istanbul that drew his interest due to its success as an institution.[1] Given my background,

FIGURE 2.1 · Slides from Masdar Institute recruitment presentation in Istanbul and Ankara, Living Laboratory, February 2011.

he believed I could talk to Turkish students who would be interested in pursuing graduate degrees abroad.

I assisted with the project as a volunteer, and in mid-February 2011 I traveled to four leading Turkish universities, together with two other Turkish nationals affiliated with the Institute. While Eda and Elif presented the introductory slides that had been provided by the public relations unit at Masdar Institute and shared their respective experiences of working or studying at Masdar Institute, I took notes and photographed their interactions with audience members for a report that we would write upon our return to Abu Dhabi. We stayed in Turkey for about a week, and visited METU and Bilkent University in Ankara, as well as Boğaziçi University and Sabancı University in Istanbul.

During the presentations, our team emphasized Masdar Institute's world-class facilities through a series of photographs and renderings that promoted the experimental infrastructure projects that would give structure to student life there. In line with the marketing and communications material, we framed Masdar Institute not only as a set of "beautiful buildings"—the first set in a series of beautiful buildings that were materializing on the Masdar City site—but also as "a living laboratory," where students could experiment with renewable energy and clean technology in real time. Our presentations happened soon after the first public promotional event took place at Masdar Institute in November 2010, an occasion where students put campus life on view for visitors (see chapter 1). Should students choose to apply to Masdar Institute for graduate degrees, the campus would provide them with a learning opportunity at every point. The students were expected to found renewable energy and clean technology startups in Abu Dhabi after their graduation, translating their experiences on campus to innovative and profitable ventures.

This chapter demonstrates how knowledge, as represented by the establishment of Masdar Institute, became instrumental to practices of economic development in Abu Dhabi in the early 2000s. Knowledge constituted a possible driver of productivity and economic growth that could ensure that Abu Dhabi would remain a significant player in the world economy well after oil stops being a reliable and steady source of wealth. The knowledge-based economy, defined as a greater economic reliance on intellectual capabilities than on physical inputs or natural resources, would need human capital to supplement productivity and increase innovation. In this conception of the future, individuals with the necessary skills would manufacture and export advanced technological products, seemingly replacing Abu Dhabi's oil resources. Research centers such as Masdar Institute were essential because they would function as test beds from which new, exportable ideas would emerge.

Besides the background, expertise, and stamina of specific individuals like Fred, which were central to the establishment and operation of an organization such as Masdar Institute, two factors were significant in creating knowledge as an economic good in Abu Dhabi. As the rest of this chapter will show, "beautiful buildings" and "research contracts" were critical mediators for attracting new investment opportunities in a transforming oil-based economy. Beautiful buildings and research contracts operated as aesthetic and affective networking devices, creating a "buzz" outside the walls of Masdar City and drawing attention to the growing renewable energy and clean technology knowledge in the UAE.[2] The collaborations that stemmed from beautiful buildings and research contracts would ultimately facilitate the production of economic diversification in Abu Dhabi.

To support Abu Dhabi in its attempt to form a knowledge-based economy that would serve as a regional and global hub for renewable energy and clean technology research, the UAE government was willing to provide incentives such as tax breaks for multinational companies to open up their research and development branches within Masdar City. Given the generous stipends, diverse faculty resources, the MIT certificate, and the specific focus on renewable energy and clean technology, Masdar Institute could attract students from around the world, who would engage in entrepreneurial activities in Abu Dhabi.[3] These entrepreneurial activities would make the region economically livelier, contributing to the materialization of the Silicon Valley or Boston 128 (Route 128) ideals. Silicon Valley and Boston 128 were two centers of electronics innovation that came into being in the period following World War II in California and Massachusetts, powered not only by expertise from Stanford and MIT, but also by a culture of trial and error. In this context, Silicon Valley and Boston 128 stood out as symbols of economic and technological success, and they came to stand in for a future that would give rise to new, innovative, globally competitive companies in the UAE. In expanding the non-resource-based economy of Abu Dhabi and achieving these entrepreneurial ideals, the student body's role would be critical. Masdar Institute administrators planned a number of publicity campaigns to recruit this critical mass of faculty and students from around the world. In supplementing these efforts, they also sent teams to select countries with audiences of desirable students who might consider traveling abroad for higher education.

In some ways, Masdar Institute was like computer software: always in beta mode and ready to mutate based on its mistakes. It therefore could never fail. The campus remained half-finished, which allowed students to toy with different versions of its future appearance and gave them the independence to form new conceptual links regarding its ultimate goals and premises. The promotional material we showed during our visits presented the Masdar Institute building as one big experiment that housed many other, perhaps smaller experiments. By living and breathing these new technologies, the students would not only pioneer in renewable energy and clean technology research, but also become test subjects who would have to respond to the technical adjustments of Masdar City.

At our presentations, Eda, Elif, and I observed that interest in Masdar Institute was significantly higher at public universities (METU and Boğaziçi) than at private universities (Bilkent and Sabancı). We wondered if this could be due to chance, but still noted the finding in our final report. Our report also suggested that such presentations could be utilized to establish intellectual links with other universities around the world. For instance, we learned that Sabancı University was in the process of forming an energy institute and that METU was exploring how they might do exchanges with other universities that had built or expected to build techno-parks. On our trip back to Abu Dhabi, we discussed whether the scholarly merits of Masdar Institute, rather than its beautiful buildings, could become vehicles for collaborative research and possible student recruitment, but how that might come to pass remained unclear to us.

While the Institute organized recruitment events around the world,[4] attempting to create a diverse student body in the "living laboratory," the students who attended Masdar consistently compared it to another emergent regional stronghold, King Abdullah University of Science and Technology (KAUST), founded outside Jeddah in Thuwal to generate technological expertise in Saudi Arabia. KAUST had opened on September 23, 2009, roughly a month after the first cohort of students started studying at Masdar Institute.[5] Masdar Institute and KAUST were analogous national development strategies, emerging from two oil-producing countries as attempts at current economic diversification and as preparations for a time when there would be less oil-based resources. The two institutions of higher education not only shared their future goals and potential, but also attracted similar pools of faculty and students.[6]

Masdar Institute students were most interested in the KAUST campus, and consistently talked about its physical capacities. "Did you know that the KAUST campus has three pools?" Bilal, a Pakistani first-year student at the Institute, asked me; he then expounded on gym buildings he had never seen. He had decided to study in the UAE because it was more liberal than Saudi Arabia, but he pointed out, "You know, I've heard that KAUST is like an oasis, it's not like the rest of Saudi Arabia." The campus was an oasis that would allow him to be indifferent to the social life of Saudi Arabia, liberating him in a way from the various restrictions he might suffer if he were a student there. "KAUST has a beautiful campus, beautiful buildings, something like a forest in the middle of the desert," he said. The "beautiful" site, my interlocutor added, attracted students and faculty from around the world.

The literature on the architecture of science mostly underlines how new institutions of higher education strive to create a buzz inside their walls in order to facilitate serendipitous encounters and unplanned collaborations leading, eventually, to scientific discoveries, with the underlying assumption that the social behavior of a building's users is influenced or even determined by the physical environment they occupy. For example, in an article on the Lewis Thomas Laboratory at Princeton University, James Collins Jr. suggests "there is a direct correlation between the work environment and the workers' intellectual and physical activity. Furthermore, a sense of order, continuity, and cohesive structure are all expected to have a positive impact on the way scientists relate to their surroundings."[7] Similarly, Nigel Thrift analyzes how such "performative" buildings are meant to create continuous flows of people and ideas within institutions, possibly engineering contact among scientists from different disciplines in spaces such as cafeterias, hallways, and bathrooms.[8]

In the case of Masdar Institute, however, the architecture did not necessarily emphasize the buzz inside its walls,[9] but rather functioned as networking devices with the world outside. Even though its structures were mostly incomplete, they attracted attention to the Arab Gulf and served as material evidence for a potential interest in knowledge infrastructure. Through their processes of design and construction, and later advertising and promotion, the buildings embodied and performed the knowledge-based economy in a manner that could easily be communicated to spectators. They were half-finished projects, but they generated and performed potential regarding the possibilities of knowledge in the UAE.

Abu Dhabi's beautiful buildings were means of transforming the relationships that the UAE already had through its oil-export economy, giving them new, more sophisticated qualitative dimensions. The buildings had to create and convey certain affective modalities, acting as material purveyors of a "beautiful" potential. The buildings would accumulate positive affective value as they were passed around, with the expectation that they would generate and preserve connections between the aspirations, materials, and potential of a knowledge-based economy. Through their beauty, the buildings would garner new types of relations. In creating an economy of innovations, the relations that the buildings forged through their beauty seemed to matter more than the day-to-day functioning of the buildings themselves.

Knowledge-Based Economy

At the "Future Energy Research and Education" panel, a knowledge-based economy event at the World Future Energy Summit of 2011, where international corporations were convening to exchange ideas about future technologies (see chapter 1), presidents of UAE universities and administrators from the Ministry of Education discussed potential strategies. A spokesperson from the Abu Dhabi Education Council expressed an interest in attracting scholars from around the world by producing a cultural infrastructure (exemplified by Abu Dhabi's efforts to build a Louvre Museum, a Guggenheim Museum, a Sorbonne University, and a New York University campus on Saadiyat Island in addition to its investments in Masdar Institute). They would thereby produce the "right culture" for the emergence of an intellectual community. The Abu Dhabi Education Council wished to train critical thinkers, starting at the high school level, who could wrestle with the difficulties of a competitive labor market. The participants debated tactics for making sure that the education system would cater to the production of a knowledge-based economy and discussed the essential steps for spurring investment in research and development.

"For developing human capital," the chancellor of the American University of Sharjah stressed, "we need to develop open, collegial dialogue among the universities, where the university will be responsive to government and private sector priorities." American University of Sharjah had been founded in Sharjah in 1997 as a U.S.-style higher education institution, envisaged to be the "leading educational institution in the Gulf region and part of a larger process of the revitalization of intellectual life in the Middle East."[10] American University of Sharjah was an emirate-funded private institution like Masdar Institute, and differed in its financing from federal institutions, such as the United Arab Emirates University and Zayed University, and private, foreign campuses operating in collaboration with federal bodies or specific emirates, such as NYU-Abu Dhabi and the Sorbonne. American University of Sharjah also exemplified how the American model of higher education was becoming more pervasive. In the early years of the UAE, the educational system had mainly been based on the British model, with some inspiration from effective institutions in neighboring countries, but administrators slowly began to emulate aspects of American institutions.[11] For example, current federal quality assurance standards are based on a U.S. model.[12] The United Arab Emirates University, whose provost was present at the meeting, is the oldest institution of higher education in the UAE, founded by Sheikh Zayed in Al Ayn in 1976, five years after the dissolution of the Trucial States and the founding of the United Arab Emirates. The new university offered degrees in arts, science, public administration, and political science.[13] This university relied on higher education institutions in Egypt and Kuwait for its main principles, but kept the needs of the Emiratis in mind, resulting in a segregated campus where male and female students studied in separate buildings but shared the faculty.[14] It is ranked the top university in the country.[15] The provost of the United Arab Emirates University argued that the emergence of doctoral programs within the country would contribute to the production of a research community, and suggested that the UAE universities had to act fast to address the needs of commercial and public sectors. The provost of Zayed University, a federal institution with campuses in Dubai and Abu Dhabi that only accepted Emirati women students for the first ten years of its existence (1998 to 2008) but later became coeducational, agreed that universities had to play a larger role in economic and social development, research, and training.

In these forums, knowledge and universities were perceived as objects with practical end goals. Human capital, an aggregate of knowledge, abilities, and skills acquired throughout an individual's lifetime, was a way to augment economic productivity, as well as a source of long-term innovation within the country. In the long run, well-educated individuals would serve to diversify the economy, eventually enabling the country to rely on sectors other than oil and gas.

The investment in human capital also included an attempt to involve more United Arab Emirates nationals within the work force. Political scientist Christopher Davidson has argued that since the foundation of the UAE in 1971, Emirati nationals have been consistently provided with the material benefits of the oil-extraction economy, and thus are lacking motivation to participate in a competitive labor market. While there are no reliable statistics on the issue, Davidson suggests that the nationals make up about 9 percent of the workforce. To resolve this problem, "the only long-term solution is improved education at all levels," through which Emirati citizens will acquire the necessary skills to compete with the large number of expatriates living in the UAE. Studying the history of the education sector, Davidson finds that the one major problem leading to a lack of education among Emiratis has, rather shockingly, been a "lack of funding." Writing in 2009, he argues, "Although the federal budget allocation for education now exceeds $2 billion, this is only a third of the allocation for military expenditure and, in relative terms, is about a quarter of the educational expenditure of some other Arab states." Given how the members of the ruling families send their children abroad to the United States and the United Kingdom for higher education, establishing institutions of higher education has not been a priority.[16] Accordingly, Davidson forecasts that the new emphasis put on education through the founding of NYU-Abu Dhabi, Masdar Institute, and the Sorbonne will have a highly positive effect, because it will train more qualified Emirati youths and strengthen the profile of the education sector within domestic politics.[17]

At the knowledge-based economy event at the World Future Energy Summit of 2011, representatives of Masdar Institute explained that they had started a foundation course exclusively for Emirati students in the fall of 2010, wherein thirty applicants who were not yet qualified to start master's degrees were provided with the opportunity to take preparatory classes and, if successful, to continue into graduate programs at the Institute. Through programs like this, the youth of Abu Dhabi were encouraged to become active participants in the formation of wealth rather than relying solely on the benefits of oil production. (Of the total number of students graduating from Masdar Institute in 2014, fifty-three were Emiratis and seventy-seven were international students from twenty-nine different countries. By 2016, the institute had grown to 186 students from the UAE and 246 students from around the world, totaling 432 students studying toward MSc and PhD programs and indicating an increasing ratio of Emirati students.)[18] As the representatives of higher education institutions insinuated, the Emiratization of the workforce would be a major challenge in the years ahead.

Again and again, when I observed formal discussions of the UAE's plans to develop its educational resources, government officials and educational administrators spoke of the goal of making knowledge a direct agent in the UAE's transformation into a "more elite" country. Knowledge, both in the technical sphere, symbolized by Masdar City and Masdar Institute, and in the cultural sphere, represented by museums, art fairs, and biennales, would generate a momentum, allowing Abu Dhabi to reengineer and refashion its economy for an oil-less future. In this economic vision, categories of the technical and the cultural merge seamlessly, serving as both products and generators of innovation. The two types of knowledge shared an emphasis on products: the technical knowledge infrastructure would incubate technologically advanced artifacts, while the cultural sector would facilitate investments in the art market.[19]

"By 2030, Abu Dhabi's population is expected to more than triple," a government document summarizing the economic vision of Abu Dhabi predicted.[20] The same document outlined how the emirate sought to boost the non-oil share of the economy to more than 60 percent of GDP from just over 40 percent today. Then NYU President John Sexton promoted the notion of "an idea capital," a model whereby Abu Dhabi would not only generate entrepreneurial skills but also develop new concepts that would have corporate use. In other words, the emirates would build their economic and social value based on ideas presented by prospective local and expatriate youths.[21]

In concluding the knowledge-based economy meeting at the Energy Summit, after the administrators of numerous UAE universities presented their visions of the future, Fred explained:

> Education at all levels is necessary for development, not only for the knowledge, but people have to get accustomed to what type of innovation they are looking at. The corroborative nature of this activity is vital, as all the industry, government, and academic need to come together. Then comes the technology rewards system—the IP [intellectual property] rights in terms of the regulatory system that has to contribute to encourage venture capitalists and development of ideas and applications. Lastly, the relevance to need, especially the work we do, has to reflect on the needs of the economy. There must be a balance between the research and applications to reflect the needs of the society.

Between the lines, he seemed to be calling out to the Abu Dhabi government, warning them that the knowledge-based economy would not materialize quickly. Given the slow speed at which knowledge institutions flourished, and based on his experiences elsewhere in the world, he was worried that his local partners would soon lose interest in the project.

Agreement

When I met Fred for the first time in March 2009 at MIT, he had been the head of MIT's Technology and Development Program (TDP) for thirty-seven years. A soft-spoken man in his seventies, he was open and articulate about his experiences with TDP, and sometimes considered writing a book about his time as director. In those thirty-seven years, Fred had seen the TDP transform from an infrastructure-focused development program to an education-focused institution. TDP did not offer courses or grant degrees to students; rather, it specialized in producing research hubs outside the United States in collaboration with affiliated faculty from MIT. After assisting with transportation projects in Latin America and East Africa (1971–75), the TDP had started engaging with educational restructuring in the Middle East, specifically working with Cairo University (1975–86), Kuwait University (1987–90), and the American University of Beirut (1991–95).[22] They had also extended this work to Mendoza, Argentina (1994–98). Next, they had embarked on two university projects with the goal of establishing brand-new science and technology institutes in Thailand (1996 onward) and Malaysia (1997–2005). While the TDP had been considered successful in their earlier transportation and educational restructuring projects, its universities in Southeast Asia had not progressed as predicted. TDP staff did not describe the specific problems with these campus projects to me, but noted that commitments had wavered and relationships had failed between the different parties involved, preventing them from reaching their goals. Yet at the time of our meeting, Fred was enthusiastic about TDP's relatively new initiative, the Masdar Institute, and he explained to me at length the steps they were taking to establish a renewable energy and clean technology research institute in Abu Dhabi.

TDP had signed an agreement with Masdar in December 2006[23] regarding the founding of a new science and technology institute at the center of Masdar City. Mubadala, a state-owned investment company that owns and manages public assets, would provide funding for the project, acting as a subsidiary of the Abu Dhabi government. Foster + Partners were brought on to design the Masdar Institute campus at Masdar City in 2007, following an invited competition. According to this cooperative agreement, TDP would assist "in the establishment of a graduate institute and . . . collaborate on research projects of interest to both parties," in this case, MIT and the burgeoning Masdar Institute. Classes would begin in Abu Dhabi on August 23, 2009: "five master of science curricula . . . developed for offer in Abu Dhabi fall 2009, namely, mechanical engineering, materials science and engineering, engineering systems and management, information technology, and water/environment. By August 2010, two additional master of science programs [will] be put in place."[24] In August 2010, the Institute started admitting PhD students as well. In its first year of operation (2009–10), Masdar Institute had ninety-two students from twenty-two countries, who were provided with full tuition scholarship, a monthly stipend, travel reimbursement, a personal laptop, textbooks, and accommodations. In my conversations with them, many of these students suggested that what drove them to Abu Dhabi was the attractive funding package, MIT's involvement in the project, the laboratory facilities, and the particular emphasis on renewable energy and clean technology. Faculty members were recruited on four-year contracts and were expected to spend the first of these four years at MIT, building research and teaching connections.

The desire of Abu Dhabi's government for an economic shift had been the driving force in signing an agreement with the TDP. According to the document "Abu Dhabi Economic Vision 2030," the government had identified nine pillars that would form the architecture of the emirate's social, political, and economic future as they attempted to restructure their oil-export-based economy into a knowledge-based economy:[25] "A large empowered private sector, a sustainable knowledge-based economy, an optimal, transparent regulatory environment, a continuation of strong and diverse international relationships, the optimisation of the Emirate's resources, premium education, healthcare and infrastructure assets, complete international and domestic security, maintaining Abu Dhabi's values, culture and heritage, and a significant and ongoing contribution to the federation of the UAE." Fred told me of his excitement that Masdar Institute would add to all of these pillars by contributing to the emergent knowledge infrastructure and initiating new connections that would enable Abu Dhabi and the UAE to grow as an economic, cultural, and scientific center.[26]

FIGURE 2.2 · "Beautiful buildings" of Masdar Institute designed by Foster + Partners, March 2014. Photo by the author.

By investing in a research center like Masdar Institute, Abu Dhabi championed an economic vision that relied on knowledge-intensive products, while demonstrating that it embraced new categories in defining its expectations of the future. In some ways, this was a wake-up call to Emirati citizens, forcing them to be more conscious of the possible depletion of abundant oil supplies and encouraging them to participate in economic diversification projects that would make the emirate less dependent on variable oil prices.[27] In Abu Dhabi, knowledge would begin to constitute a resource in its own right,[28] with the underlying assumption that innovative intellectual products and services could be exported for a high value return.

In this framework, the TDP staff understood their project, the Masdar Institute, to be the backbone of Abu Dhabi's economic restructuring and hoped that problems they suffered from in their Southeast Asia projects, such as a lack of commitment on the side of their local partner, would not negatively impact their future prospects. TDP offered Masdar Institute a five-year renewable contract, explaining that they would halt the collaboration when Masdar Institute became a credible and independent institution that no longer needed the MIT stamp.[29] When administrative problems emerged at Masdar Institute in August 2010, mainly because the incumbent president could not forge good relations with Mubadala or with the Abu Dhabi government, and eventually wished to leave, Fred agreed to move to Abu Dhabi and accept a position as the new president of the fledgling research center, making TDP's work truly hands-on. Fred was shortly to retire, however, and he announced his departure at the 2014 Masdar Institute commencement ceremony, yet remained an important figure in the institute afterward.[30] In some ways, the manner in which his position changed demonstrates how uncertain the institution was, requiring his adaptability even after announcing his retirement.

A Catalyst

On their website,[31] the TDP staff explained their work, underscoring that the "process is complex, and dependent on the individual circumstances each country, each initiative has to face." Their statement continues:

> At the invitation of academic institutions, working with local government, TDP supports the establishment of graduate-level research and educational facilities.
>
> From the start, TDP establishes relationships of cooperation with academic institutions, local government, and industry and works to ensure government supported research facilities are privately managed and independent of governmental administration.
>
> We share our knowledge, providing guidance and assistance in the scholarly assessment of curriculum and top tier faculty. TDP sets a level of quality control in the establishment of these intellectual centers that ensures the development stream essential for the critical thinking necessary for these endeavors. Our organization is lean and agile, flexible to the independent situations and university relationships we cultivate.

TDP was "lean and agile," and could transform quickly to address a project, mainly because the organization had only three members. Fred worked together with Pat, an administrative assistant, and Steve, a staff member, and occasionally relied upon other MIT faculty to support specific projects.[32] Steve had been hired in January 2007 as the executive director for the Technology and Development and the MIT/Abu Dhabi Programs, and was based in Cambridge until August 2010, when he accompanied Fred to Abu Dhabi, and became executive director there.[33]

In February 2010, when I asked Steve how the Masdar Institute project operated, he explained that TDP was helping reproduce five master of science programs that were already operational at MIT. At the time of our conversation, the first batch of students were enrolled in these five programs at Masdar Institute and doing coursework. Upon their completion of these degrees, Masdar Institute would provide these students with a certificate showing that they had graduated from a program that was sponsored by MIT. The professors in charge of these MIT programs would help TDP in this endeavor, assisting them in duplicating these degrees at Masdar Institute. If, for instance, five core classes at MIT made up a master's program on engineering systems and management at MIT, the same classes would be offered at Masdar Institute, with the same content. A Masdar Institute faculty member, who had recently finished his PhD and joined Masdar Institute, explained to me that if a Masdar Institute faculty member wanted to change the syllabus, they would have to let the faculty member teaching the course at MIT know about the decision, and at times provide reasons as to why the syllabus had to be modified. At the end of each year, the TDP would assess how the students at the Masdar Institute had done in each course and compare the results with the students at MIT. Fred told me that the results were comparable for 2009–11, and that in many cases, the Masdar Institute students did as well as their MIT counterparts.

MIT derived research benefits from its agreement with Masdar Institute; for instance, research projects that could not be carried out easily in the United States due to strict institutional review board (IRB) protocols, such as smart grid testing, could be done in the UAE.[34] The absence of procedural agreements on biomedical and behavioral research afforded opportunities as well.[35] While the MIT faculty involved with these projects would not receive intellectual property rights for research taking place in Abu Dhabi, they would be learning from their partners' experiences. In this sense, the research agreements between MIT and Masdar Institute were argued to be reciprocal, granting benefits to both parties.[36]

Despite these relations with MIT, for Fred it was important to emphasize that Masdar Institute was not necessarily part of the "global university" model exemplified in Abu Dhabi by NYU or the Sorbonne.[37] For the time being, MIT was being directly reproduced at Masdar Institute through syllabi and curricula, but TDP wished to frame Masdar Institute as an independent institution. In contrast to many other new universities, Masdar Institute would be an autonomous unit, only initiated with the help of TDP, and promoted in its earlier stages by the brand name of MIT alone. Later it would become a brand of its own.

Scholars have noted that there is little agreement on offshore campus typologies, especially in the Middle East.[38] Given this relative intellectual vacuum, Fred created his own framework, attempting to clarify his terms and to achieve specificity in building categories. During a private conversation at his MIT office, Fred suggested that Masdar Institute was seeking to differentiate itself from readily available blueprints of building higher education institutions, giving examples of various transnational models employed in the Middle East since American missionaries started establishing such institutions there in late nineteenth century. For him, the first model was what he called "the transnational American university":

> There is American University of Sharjah, which was established à la American University of Beirut; that is, it is an American institution, but its campus is in Sharjah . . . and it is funded by the Sharjah emirate. . . . They may have relationships with different American universities, but those are ad hoc. So the core structure is U.S.-based. American University of Beirut is the same. Its core structure is in New York. So that's one model that I think is working.

Despite his intention to conceive of and pursue a new model in the Masdar Institute, Fred recognized that the transnational American university model had proved successful regardless of the university's location.

As Fred agreed, American universities in the region have had historic impact on social, political, and economic relations, producing elites in different sectors. In late nineteenth century, the establishment of Robert College in Istanbul, the American University of Beirut in Lebanon, and the American University of Cairo was associated with the good that can emanate from U.S. presence in the region, functioning as a foreign policy strategy. Not only did these institutions strengthen U.S. authority in the region; they also allowed local politicians in support of these institutions to see themselves as part of the Westernization project. Despite various tensions in the making and maintenance of these campuses, the intricate webs of relations between American philanthropists and local educators produced and sustained some of the most prestigious schools in the region.[39]

The second model of building universities was more small-scale and more recent, dating back to the 1990s and early 2000s. Fred explained that these organizations were "not universities but colleges that are being established to provide manpower to a particular sector of economy for which they have a major foreign partner—aluminum company, microelectronics, aviation. . . . That's another model, where your focus is primarily to provide production engineers." The most prominent of these institutions is perhaps the Petroleum Institute, which was started in 2001 with the sponsorship of major oil companies, such as Total and Shell, and which relied on partnerships with various foreign universities in order to run its specific programs. To give an example of these partnerships, Fred talked about the relationship that the Petroleum Institute had with the University of Maryland, which focused on developing collaborative research and education programs on energy at the undergraduate and graduate levels, but suggested that this relationship is very narrowly defined.[40] "They are doing their jobs, both sides," he said. "There is exchange."

For Fred, branch establishments were a third, completely different category, where the newly founded university would be forever dependent on the mother institution. The University of Wollongong, founded in Dubai in 1993, was the first branch establishment in the country. By 2014, the UAE hosted twenty-six branch campuses, most eminently NYU-Abu Dhabi, the Sorbonne in Abu Dhabi, Middlesex University in Dubai, and Heriot-Watt in Dubai.[41] The branch campuses would provide degrees conferring the name of the mother institution, presumed to be equivalent to those conferred at home. To give an example, Fred referred to our shared alma mater, Cornell University, and its medical school branch campus in Qatar's Education City, a hub outside Doha that houses the branch campuses of several U.S.-based institutions of higher education, such as Cornell, Texas A&M, and Georgetown. "Let's assume that Cornell's president in ten years from now says enough is enough," Fred posited. "What will happen to that campus? Cornell hires the people. . . . Students are getting degrees from Cornell. . . . If Cornell doesn't give that degree, where do students get their degrees? So really, except for a physical facility, Qatar really has nothing to show. So that, in my opinion, is not viable for the long run."[42] According to

Fred, the branch establishment model held fledgling institutions of higher education hostage under their respective brand names, faculty and staff recruitment systems, diplomas, and curriculums, mostly stemming from the United States or Western Europe.[43] "Can you imagine if Robert College was established with that premise?" he finally asked, referring once again to my high school in Istanbul.

Steve stressed to me that Masdar Institute would be an independent stronghold of renewable energy and clean technology research in Abu Dhabi. In many ways, he continued, Masdar Institute could be understood as a catalyst that would translate current oil revenues into research and development—this was the ultimate aim of the MIT Technology and Development Program.[44] Masdar Institute would generate new science and engineering knowledge for the region and the globe, eventually triggering the expansion of a high-tech industry, Steve said, similar to Silicon Valley or Boston 128. For Steve, and for many others at Masdar Institute, Silicon Valley and Boston 128 had come to symbolize economic and technological success, demonstrating how a commitment to the knowledge-based economy could result in a powerful, innovative, and profitable sector.

In thinking about different models of building universities, Fred and Steve imagined the present and future impact of these institutions, contemplating their potential. In their interpretations of the three blueprints, they went back and forth between multiple scales, analyzing how institutions functioned within urban centers as nodes within expanding networks, or as hubs of global knowledge production. Fred and Steve held positions of power and decision-making at Masdar Institute; they negotiated its potential by critically examining the history and the future of related organizations; by talking with the authorities in the UAE about perceived possibilities; and by attempting to formulate the social, material, and regulatory environment that would allow the prospering of research at Masdar Institute. Fred and Steve did not know when TDP's collaboration with Masdar Institute would conclude, as their commitment relied on five-year contracts. They did not know if the UAE government would continue to invest in Masdar Institute and could not fully predict the future trajectory of the research center.

Epitomized by Masdar Institute, renewable energy and clean technology knowledge would together transform Abu Dhabi's resource-based economy into a sustainable knowledge-based model. "Oil is exportable, while the sun is not," Steve succinctly stated, spelling out a most significant difference between these two kinds of energy-based business activities. "The two resources are disconnected in the sense that the former is easily capitalized upon while the latter cannot contribute to the production of goods immediately," he continued. The massive infrastructure—oil rigs, refineries, and pipelines—that enabled the production and distribution of oil had to be gutted and replaced by an infrastructure allowing for facilitating the production and distribution of solar energy. "Masdar City will help create indigenous firepower to make these industries grow," Steve concluded. "And so Abu Dhabi will get into places where they become elite." The knowledge produced inside the Masdar Institute laboratories would enable Abu Dhabi to enter into new relationships and position itself as a center of innovation rather than of oil-exporting, and beautiful buildings and research contracts would serve as mediators in manufacturing and solidifying this new image.

A History of Knowledge-Making

During a long interview on the history of TDP at his MIT office, Fred told me about the beautiful buildings they helped set up at Cairo University. He remarked that TDP's attention to the affective and aesthetic modalities of the buildings at Masdar Institute was not entirely new.

TDP's project with Cairo University had been initiated in 1977, at a time when development models were beginning to foreground knowledge and capacity building.[45] Fred stressed that it was the time after *Small Is Beautiful: A Study of Economics as If People Mattered*, an influential collection of essays by economist E. F. Schumacher that was published in 1973 and that challenged the ways in which economic growth was conceived. For Schumacher, the idea of limitless economic growth did not reflect the realities of a world with limited resources. Writing months before the October 1973 energy crisis, when oil prices quadrupled due to an embargo by the members of the Organization of Petroleum Exporting Countries (OPEC), he asked: "What is 'enough'? Who can tell us? Certainly not the economist who pursues 'economic growth' as the highest of all values, and therefore has no concept of 'enough.' There are poor societies, which have too little: but where is the rich society that says: 'Halt! We have enough'? There is none. Perhaps we can forget about 'enough' and content ourselves with exploring the growth of demand upon the world's resources which arises when everybody simply strives hard to have 'more.'"[46] *Small Is Beautiful* proposes that economic growth should be centered on humans rather than on the transfer of technology, and underlines how the discipline of economics focuses on the production of goods, viewing people as an afterthought.[47] It explains how technology transfer and infrastructural solutions cannot resolve deep economic problems in Third World countries, and criticizes the fascination with growth and bigness, advocating instead for "enoughness" and small-scale capacity-building projects that acknowledge the nonrenewable nature of resources. Schumacher lays out his expectations clearly: "What is it that we really require from the scientists and technologists? I should answer: We need methods and equipment which are cheap enough so that they are accessible to virtually everyone, suitable for small-scale application, and compatible with man's need for creativity."[48] In this intellectual context, Fred was attracted to the development of higher education institutions; he was ready to leave behind his work on infrastructure building in Latin American and African countries for a project on higher education in Egypt.

Fred narrated to me the story of TDP's partnership with Cairo University: "So in Egypt—it was just the time that the Camp David Accord was signed between Anwar Sadat and Menachem Begin—and the U.S. president, Jimmy Carter, was very interested in turning that cold peace into a hot peace, so he asked us to see whether we were interested in working with institutions in Egypt, and we agreed." While managing this project, Fred did not leave Cambridge and relocate to Egypt. Instead, he worked at a distance, but paid frequent visits to Cairo to evaluate developments. He continued: "So we worked with Cairo University for about ten years, eleven years." Conceived as a foreign policy project for the U.S. government, this partnership consisted mainly of collaborative research projects between MIT faculty and Cairo University faculty. In order to run the project, TDP received funding from the U.S. Agency for International Development (USAID).

According to Fred, the program had three main benefits for the partnering institutions. First, if a faculty member at MIT had a project proposal that was related to Egypt, they could easily find faculty members to work with at Cairo University, a large public university, and pay them

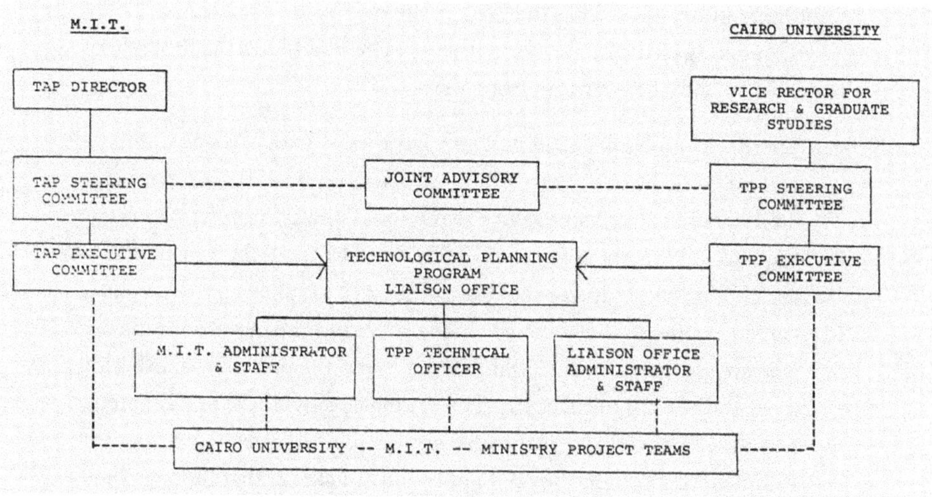

FIGURE 2.3 · Organizational chart of Cairo University and Technology and Development Program (at the time called TPP) Collaboration.

through TDP funds. Second, the kinds of projects a faculty member could research in Egypt were very different from those available in the United States. "For example, the impact of subsidized housing," Fred told me, "the impact of government commitment to provide housing for every family and not being able to deliver, what happened to that market. . . . Or, for example, the Aswan Dam, which at the time was being run by the Ministry of Agriculture."

In addition to its foreseen effects, the agreement would have unexpected structural impacts on the way Cairo University was organized. Through this experience, Fred acknowledged, the TDP learned more about how a university might operate in "socialistic" regimes and the need to contemplate questions such as whether you should educate masses of people with lower standards or educate only a few with very high standards. Along with such large-scale questions, there emerged more practical problems as well. "For example, at MIT, when you have a research contract, you pay MIT an overhead for its infrastructural support," Fred explained. They had decided to apply the same rule at Cairo University, and paid them for costs incurred in the general upkeep of the project. But the Cairo University administration did not operate in this manner. "First of all, the administration did not quite understand what the heck is the overhead," Fred noted. "Why are they giving us the money for nothing?" Then there was the problem of what to do with the overhead from MIT:

> There was no bank account. Cairo University with 120,000 students had no bank account. Everything was coming from the government. So they told us we had to put the money in the government account. We said, "We're not going to do it." We had to go all the way to Sadat, get him to write a decree that Cairo University is allowed to open up a bank account. So they opened a bank account. The question came up, who are going to have the right to sign it. Well, the president didn't want it. He didn't want to get accused of writing checks. So we finally agreed two people have to sign the checks. Quite an interesting scene. . . . And believe it or not, they did not spend a nickel of that money. They didn't want to be accused of anything. They were so afraid of MIT, U.S. government. . . . They had all these elements of explosion. Finally, we convinced them. They had accumulated several million dollars, so we told them that they should build a building for the center, which is a beautiful building. It is still there. It is still operating. And ironically that is the only center in Cairo University that is allowed to enter into contract with an outside board. The last time that I was there, the president of it was telling me that the government charges them overhead!

Through TDP's intervention, a section of Cairo University had transformed from being reliant on government funding to acting as an independent institution that could enter into contracts with outside parties and set up a beautiful building to house such operations.

This would open the way for contract-based research as well, wherein teams of researchers would be able to provide services to private entities. The USAID report published in 1979 states:

> The Center for Development Research and Technological Planning has been established at Cairo University. This center is an autonomous unit, which has its own bylaws and is free from regular governmental financial and administrative regulations. A director and a board of directors have been appointed. An organizational structure, administrative and financial procedures have been developed. The scope of the Center's interest is broader than that covered in the Cairo University/M.I.T.

> Technological Planning Program and has the capability to reach all areas related to development plans for Egypt. Additional time and experience with the Center operation will be necessary in order to fully evaluate its contribution.[49]

The "socialistic" university had started to emulate the U.S. model: contracts with outside parties, managed from the beautiful building, were slowly becoming the modus operandi for conducting research projects.

Next, Fred turned to the beautiful buildings of Kuwait University, TDP's subsequent project in the Middle East, which started in 1987 and lasted until the Gulf War broke out in 1990, and where the primary focus was on developing research projects that would contribute to economic and technological growth. This time they did not rely on USAID funding. "The university was a mess," Fred said. "They had beautiful buildings . . . but it had become Balkanized, in the sense that there was an Egyptian clique, Algerian clique, Palestinian clique—different groups had their own cliques." These cliques were united against Kuwaitis, especially because every young Kuwaiti PhD would immediately be hired with full tenure and they were more likely to be appointed department chairs. They took note of these dynamics, as the academic culture of the university would be important in achieving their research goals. As TDP was doing the groundwork for its collaborations with the faculty at Kuwait University, the Gulf War started, pausing the project. TDP returned to Kuwait after the war was over in 1991 and tried to reinitiate its plans, but eventually pulled out. The university had transformed with the war and was now presided over by people Fred described as Islamists. Fred noted, "ironically Saddam cleaned [the beautiful buildings] out completely, even the air-conditioning plates were gone."

After this short project with Kuwait University, TDP would sign another higher education–related contract in 1990 with American University of Beirut (AUB) in Lebanon. Fred told me that the then president of AUB, Dr. Frederic Herter, had contacted TDP, saying, "I have heard of your work in Egypt, and can you help us, because this is the war time in Lebanon, and our faculty are really trying to leave, and I want to save them, so can you bring them to MIT and put them to work with some of the MIT faculty for any length of time so that their research activities will continue." Fred described the series of events that followed when he asked Dr. Herter where the funding for this project would come from:

> So he brought this guy at the time—his name is Rafiq Hariri—who then became the prime minister. But at that time he was just a rich man. He came and he talked, and I remember Pat [a TDP staff member] talked to him, he said how much does it cost? Pat said, I don't know exactly, but roughly about 10 million dollars. And he said, Who do I write the check to? We said, we have our own bureaucracy, we have to prepare a proposal, submit it, etc. So we did it, and they gave us some money. It went on for about four to five years, going back and forth. We didn't go there, we couldn't go there. It was the war. Many of these people now are in the cabinet. Of course, Hariri himself became the prime minister. His son, who is now the prime minister, was here. So it left a very nice impact.

TDP established the AUB/MIT Collaborative Program in Science, Technology, and Development, a program promoting research and educational activities that would assist the reconstruction and development of Lebanon. As the TDP website notes, "'Reconstruction' extended beyond physical reconstruction to include rebuilding human institutions and the science and technology infrastructure."[50] TDP concentrated on ensuring that research projects would help national economic development, fostering cooperation between various academic, corporate, and governmental bodies. At the same time, knowledge channeled by TDP was utilized to maintain and cultivate foreign relations between the United States and its Middle Eastern counterparts. When the Beirut project was concluded, however, TDP went back to work in South America, in Argentina and Brazil, and then to Malaysia and Thailand, before arriving back in the Middle East with Masdar Institute.

Yet throughout these projects, Fred told me, TDP was transformed, partially because the staff learned how existing bureaucracies in these universities could be major barriers to administering the intended transformations. "So rather than trying to change a system that had tremendous inertia," Fred said, "we thought it's easier to create a new system. Of course, that creates its own problems." That was why they wanted to start new university projects first in Malaysia and Thailand, and now in Abu Dhabi, with Masdar Institute. In concluding our conversation, Fred emphasized how, in all these years, the TDP staff had learned that the institutions they set up had to become "independent, privately controlled, rather than government controlled." Fred finally noted, "And we have to give them, in my opinion, one of the most exciting features of the American university system: the notion of contract research."

Fred had learned how to create higher education centers thanks to his experience as the president of TDP, and he engaged with multiple parties with fluctuating needs during his thirty-seven years there. In each of these projects, beautiful buildings and contractual relations had parts to play, but he knew that the importance of one or the other changed depending on the context. When he took on the responsibility of starting Masdar Institute in 2006, he could draw on his varied experiences with architectures of science and reiterate the significance of contract research there.

Contract Research

Throughout the years in which I knew him, first in the capacity as TDP president and MIT professor, then, starting in August 2010, as the new president of Masdar Institute, Fred reiterated that contract research fostered competition, allowed for multiple channels of funding, and encouraged innovation.

Fred used the example of the United Kingdom's state-sponsored grants to describe how government funding for university research could be disadvantageous. For him, government funding required fulfilling certain predetermined criteria rather than competing against others on the open market, and therefore was not a fruitful way of organizing research. At Masdar, the UAE government was providing research funding, but Fred aspired to change this condition by attracting corporate research sponsors. In criticizing the UK model, he argued: "In Britain, they have [the] university grant commission. And the university grant commission system gives grants—it's not much, but since all the salaries of the faculty and all the fees of the students come from the government, these grants are used for buying equipment, doing some tests. . . . All you have to do is write a short proposal. . . . It does not create a certain competitiveness."

"In the U.S.," he continued, "we by and large do not have a university grant commission, and the money is primarily distributed on a competitive basis. I write a proposal to National Science Foundation, you write a proposal to National Science Foundation. They decide which one of them to fund. I write a proposal to IBM, you write a proposal to IBM. IBM negotiates. This is what I want! If I can do it, I incorporate." In this system, where researchers do not automatically receive funding from the government, Fred argued, "there is a lot of dialog between faculty and the sponsor. At the same time, there is a lot of awareness on the faculty side regarding what's happening to these sponsors. I joke with many MIT presidents that with all the respect to them, they're not all that important to me, because my sponsor is much more important. My sponsor pays for my summer salary, my office, my computers, my telephone, my secretary, and my coffee. All of that comes from contract research! So I have to be worried about my sponsor, to keep him happy! I have to be aware of his needs. I have to identify that. It creates a very different relationship between university and society. That model doesn't exist [in the rest of the world]. To create that takes a lot of effort." The research contract model generated responsibility and liability for the researchers, while requiring them to be in communication with their corporate sponsors, which in his understanding affected the university's relationship to society positively.

In setting up Masdar Institute, the research contract infrastructure was a priority for TDP. While the Abu Dhabi government would pay for the formative stages of the Institute, TDP wanted to have an additional research budget that would be distributed on the basis of proposals. "A proposal not only addresses the need, but it creates obligation," Fred stressed. "I'm going to do it, it takes this much time, it takes this much money, and these are my deliverables, and at the end you have a right to review and tell me whether I did a right job or not. That is a very different mind-set—especially that the students get involved." This was the mentality they sought to create in Abu Dhabi.

Meanwhile, the researchers and faculty at Masdar Institute contemplated the impact of contract research projects on their individual careers. For instance, Michael, a postdoctoral researcher who had been recruited as a faculty member, told me that he was eager to explore opportunities at MIT during the one preparatory year he was expected to spend there before beginning his term as an assistant professor. He thought he should concentrate on microbial communities and explore fundamental research. Yet he did not know how the Masdar community would take it, especially because data mining in regard to microbial communities may not have immediate commercial impact. "Masdar's future prospects involve developing partnerships with companies and receiving finances for research projects—even at MIT they all have their startups on the side," he said. "But for the time being I'm not interested in that, I just want publications." While he did not mind participating in a competitive research infrastructure, where he would submit proposals and expect to receive grants, Michael was worried that conducting fundamental research would be difficult at Masdar Institute.

The Abu Dhabi government encouraged various international corporations such as Siemens, BASF, Bayer, and General Electric to start research and development units within Masdar City, engaging in joint projects with the Masdar Institute faculty and contributing to the flourishing of the eco-city as a clean technology cluster.[51] Eda, one of the postdoctoral researchers at the Institute, explained to me how the Emirate of Dubai had used a similar strategy in setting up themed clusters. "For instance, in Dubai's Media City, they just gave a building to CNN for free, and all the other media companies had to follow and open offices in a zoned area next to that building," she noted. In this sense, contract research would not only advance specific projects; it would also help set up spaces dedicated to such experimentation, thereby creating stronger ties between industry, the academy, and the government. The contracts were then expected to embody relationships, enabling a flow of information between the three parties Fred identified. Consequently, Fred argued, contract research would transform society.[52]

One such research contract, between Masdar Institute and General Electric, materialized in the fall of 2009, and specifically concentrated on the development of "the kitchen of the future" through testing smart grids and smart appliances (see chapter 3).[53] GE had unveiled their plans for the kitchen of the future in July 2009 in their upstate New York research facility. Smart appliances would have the ability to communicate real-time data to a smart meter, and vice versa, so that the appliances could determine when to perform certain functions. For instance, a refrigerator would avoid running its routine defrost cycle during peak energy hours, postponing the operation to off-peak times—say, the middle of the night. Both partners imagined that the Masdar Institute dorms would be ideal for testing the appliances, where they might elicit new research opportunities among the Masdar Institute faculty and students. Laura, the American master's student who wrote about her experiences in the dorms and who had come to Masdar Institute to participate in renewable energy and clean technology experiments, described her studio apartment as a testing ground even before the GE projects took hold: "I keep telling people that it feels like I'm living in a psychology experiment. Every time I flip a light switch in the living room and the faucet in the bathroom starts running, or I desperately push all buttons on the stove to try to turn on a burner, I can't help looking over my shoulder and wondering if there's a scientist observing my behavior and reactions in this strange environment." The students were ready to put the kitchen of the future to a test. A closer look at the project showed, however, that the collaboration between Abu Dhabi and General Electric was not restricted to this research contract. In addition to helping build the kitchen of the future within Masdar Institute, and starting an "Ecomagination Center," a showcase for new water and energy efficiency technologies, inside Masdar City,[54] General Electric benefited from the sovereign wealth funds (SWFs) that the government of Abu Dhabi made available through the Sovereign Wealth Fund Institute.[55] In some ways, Abu Dhabi's investments in General Electric were returning to the emirate through these research projects, but under the GE brand name.

SWFs are state-owned, long-term investments in the global assets of a company, which may be utilized as a tool for fostering national development. In building research alliances for Masdar Institute as well, the SWF had proved to be influential. Mubadala, the larger company that funded Masdar, had recently invested an SWF in General Electric, thereby starting a long-term financial relationship involving the expectation that GE would invest in research projects in Abu Dhabi to help the emirate's technological development. The kitchen of the future, or the Ecomagination Center, then, was only an externality or overflow of a much larger deal that was taking place at another, possibly higher, level. As a short note in one press release suggested, "The Ecomagination Centre is a product of the GE and Mubadala framework agreement, signed in July 2008, on a global partnership encompassing a broad range of initiatives including commercial finance, clean energy research and development, aviation, industry and corporate learning. Building on an already strong relationship and a common view of high growth opportunities in the Middle East and globally, the agreement provides for shared capital commitments to new joint ventures and investment funds."[56] Abu Dhabi's government funds were being directed to Masdar Institute, brand-named as General Electric and as MIT. So, as much as Fred believed contract research would foster ties between industry, government, and the academy, what Masdar's research contracts initially demonstrated was a dependence on the alliances that had already been built through Abu Dhabi's oil wealth, and which were now being utilized for the production of high-tech research facilities.

The research contracts were comparable to the beautiful buildings that were springing up in emergent centers of innovation across the globe. In the same way that the beautiful buildings served as material evidence for how the UAE was investing in a future of science and technology, contract research was understood to create cohesion among the government, the industry, and the academy, demonstrating the steps that the UAE was taking toward the production of knowledge as an economic diversification project. Both research contracts and buildings would reformulate relationships inside and outside the institutions in which they were being produced; in this sense, neither constituted the economic diversification project. The relationships that they triggered seemed to be much more significant.

Exclusions

It is important to remember that building relations, in practice, required exclusions and suspensions: certain individuals or groups were forced, in Abu Dhabi, to relinquish their relationship with the growing knowledge-based economy.[57] In August 2010, while most of the Masdar Institute students were preparing to move into the beautiful buildings on the new campus, six individuals who were about to enter into their second year as master's students received an invitation to a confidential meeting. In this meeting, a high-level Emirati security officer informed them that they had been expelled from the institution and would not be allowed to sign up for classes in the fall of 2010. They had one month before they would be deported from the UAE. No one explained to the students why exactly they were being asked to leave.

Like their classmates, these six students—two Lebanese and four Iranians—had registered their religions and their sects upon applying for visas and enrolling at Masdar Institute.[58] In the process, they had disclosed that they were born Shiʿite, a decision they would later regret. After the meeting, the students quickly started making connections: in the spring of 2010, two Iranian faculty members in Masdar Institute had left with no explanation. This must have been the beginning of a purge, one of the students later told me, where Masdar Institute was being cleansed of Shiʿite Muslims. Slowly, they started learning that other Shiʿites in the UAE were having trouble receiving visas, and realized that this purge was not unique to Masdar Institute. When they tried to find work in the UAE, they could not acquire work permits. Their month was quickly up. After leaving the UAE, they followed diverse routes, going on to pursue graduate degrees in other countries or looking for work back home.

With no time or resources at hand, the students did not take any legal action in response to the discrimination they faced. Later, however, they learned that an Iranian-American Masdar Institute employee who had also been deported during this period was trying her luck in the courts, but was making little headway mainly due to administrative roadblocks. The students heard that no one showed up in the courtrooms and that hearings kept being postponed. It didn't seem worth it, one of the students said; she wanted to go on with her life.

The students lamented the fact that they had spent a year at the Institute without receiving a degree, and saw this as a waste. Given the timing of their deportation, they were unable to join other graduate schools during the fall 2010 semester. "They asked for our religion and the sect of our religion, and I had no idea that I shouldn't mention anything and I wrote that I was born Shiʿa," one student told me. "In spring 2010, they already knew that they wanted to kick us out, but they were gathering evidence to kick us out. If we had known, we could have applied for other schools and not wasted our time, but no one told us anything." Some speculated that the six students could go to MIT as visitors and complete their credits toward a Masdar Institute degree there, but this never happened. "I don't think Masdar could do anything to change this decision," another student assessed, "but they could have helped us and made sure that we didn't suffer during that period. The part that makes me mad about Masdar is how they managed in the months following the decision." One student, who considered herself lucky, joined a program in another country in the spring of 2011 with the help of her Masdar Institute adviser and was able to employ her credits from Masdar Institute toward a degree at her new institution. She noted that her adviser had been one of the few people to understand her situation and to offer sympathy.

At the time of the August 2010 expulsion meeting, Fred was about to start his tenure as president of the Institute. His absence from the meeting where the students were expelled was perhaps indicative of his general detachment from the process. When I asked him what he thought about the students' situation, he emphasized that he did not have a say. When I brought up the MIT partnership, he reiterated that MIT could not challenge a national policy. A student I interviewed in 2016, six years after being expelled from the institute, explained, "I don't think they had any compassion for what we went through or what they put us through. Which is not surprising given all the discriminatory practices prevalent at Masdar and in the UAE."

In regard to the character of the discrimination they faced, the student I interviewed in 2016 underlined how she never felt prejudice during the time she spent at Masdar Institute prior to the meeting. "The people I hung out with didn't mind my being Shiʿite, I didn't feel singled out. But the administration was different," she explained. "It was the UAE security apparatus that enforced these discriminatory practices, not the people around me." For her, this security apparatus operated at a different, more "political" level, exerting pressure on Shiʿites.[59] "If you check the list of students that went to Masdar, it's quite evident that they did not have Shiʿite Lebanese, Shiʿite Syrians, or Iranians. They had problems with Shiʿites, mainly Iran, but also Lebanon, given that Hezbollah was an ally. . . . It's very political. I can't say if it was a policy at the time or if it has changed now, but it was political issues." The student made fun of the marketing material that showcased an international community at Masdar Institute. "All people with red hair, yellow hair, brown hair, black hair," she remembered. While her life as a Masdar Institute student had been comfortable at an everyday level, this global community did not include her.

The purge demonstrated the exclusionary practices that the Masdar project relied upon and reproduced and was one of the rare moments when the UAE's role in international politics became explicit and visible on the eco-city's site. While the Masdar project was often conceptualized as a context-free and floating spaceship in the desert that shut the world out, this event showed this perspective to be an illusion. Masdar was not a building without a neighborhood. In fact, its relations with its neighbors very much determined the lives of its inhabitants.

Harmonious Symphony

Of the possibilities for Abu Dhabi's knowledge-based economy, Sultan Al-Qassemi, a well-known Emirati intellectual, wrote in 2011:

> In order for this vision to be fully realised, it is important to create a network in which the . . . knowledge hubs interact and complement each other rather than exist in isolation. This network should ideally be built in layers, connecting first the hubs in Abu Dhabi with each other, and then branching out across the country and into the wider Arab World. . . . But how would such a network operate? The leaders of these various knowledge hubs must familiarise themselves with each other, along with the heads of universities and even high schools. They could do so by meeting periodically to share expertise and ideas and keep each other updated on future plans. In this way, students in Abu Dhabi will be able to study in world-class universities, undertake internships in world-class institutions and perhaps carry out research in Abu Dhabi's strategic industries. Secondly, these knowledge hubs must launch community outreach programmes to make sure that their benefits reach a wider audience, while also amassing a coalition of stakeholders who are keen on building a knowledge-based future. NYU Abu Dhabi has already launched a successful free public lecture series that feature top professors. By reaching out to others, Abu Dhabi's knowledge hubs can function as musical instruments that, when played together, create the effect of a harmonious symphony.[60]

The new economy of Abu Dhabi would be an outcome of these relationships, here described as a "harmonious symphony" despite its reliance on exclusionary relationships. The purge, while it did have some visibility on the Masdar campus and significantly marked the individuals who were expelled, did not affect the tone of optimism or the voracious appetite for development in the public discussion of Masdar and Abu Dhabi's future.

In further explaining this vision, Anand, an executive at Masdar Carbon, asked me, "Have you heard about Kizad, a 8.5-square-miles industrial area in the outskirts of Abu Dhabi?"—it was going to be the largest industrial zone in the world. "Through Masdar, Abu Dhabi builds relationships," he said, "and through those relationships it will fill these industrial zones. These industrial zones will be the real alternative to oil." According to him,

Abu Dhabi would import raw materials, produce by relying on cheap labor, and then export commodities. In this process, Anand underlined, the Abu Dhabi government would need many partners and collaborators.[61] This was the kind of diversification that would take place in Abu Dhabi's post-oil future. Such developments would change the country's face. Specifically through projects like Masdar Institute, Abu Dhabi would enter these relationships not as an oil-producing economy, but rather as a center of innovation, thereby becoming "more elite." Relations and networks mattered more than anything else. But in order to enter into these relationships, Masdar had to produce some material products.

In the next two chapters, I will examine the making of new experimental infrastructures inside Masdar City, first by exploring the development of an energy currency and next by discussing the implementation of a driverless personal rapid transit (PRT) system.

II TECHNOLOGY

3 Ergos: A New Energy Currency

Table Manners

"If all problems were technical, we would have solved them a long time ago," Nawal, the Emirati sustainability director of Masdar emphasized during a panel on new cities at the Harvard Graduate School of Design in April 2010. Nawal had obtained her BA from UAE University in 1992 and her PhD from Newcastle University in the United Kingdom in 2002, and had written her dissertation on prison buildings in Abu Dhabi. Prior to joining Masdar City, she had served as the first female deputy director of the Abu Dhabi police and published academic articles on prisons and sustainability in hot and humid climates.[1] At Masdar, Nawal managed the START campaign,[2] which aimed to raise awareness regarding the significance of personal habits of consumption, and specifically asked employees to sign a "sustainability pledge" confirming their commitment to a more sustainable lifestyle.[3] Her project aimed at preventing employees from disposing of plastic bottles by providing them with reusable bottles; this involved requesting that all garbage bins be removed from cubicles, thereby forcing employees to walk to shared recycling bins. In private conversations, however, the employees suggested that they were not happy with the new measures implemented within their workspaces; they preferred freedom of choice. Even so, Nawal's team maintained that the employees would get used to the new system and promoted these techniques as means for changing cultural norms. It would only take some time for the employees to adapt to the promoted sustainability mechanisms. "Problems are cultural. Teaching people sustainability is like teaching them table manners," Nawal said. In some sense, teaching sustainability appeared to be her "civilizing mission."

As Nawal concentrated on reeducating Masdar employees, other researchers at Masdar Institute were building infrastructures for an energy currency, reproducing some of the disciplinary and regulatory qualities of her campaigns. Masdar Institute researchers imagined that inhabitants of Abu Dhabi's Masdar City could routinely be issued balance of energy credits called "ergos," which would define their pre-allocated energy budget over the validity period of the credits. A single credit would represent the right to consume a specified quantity of electricity (e.g., 1 kWh) and have a defined expiration period (e.g., 1 month). If the ergos account of any user ran down to zero, electricity would be consumed by buying ergos at spot market prices. If a consumer used exactly the amount of electricity that had been allocated, they would not be subjected to the credit spot price, which was expected to be substantially higher than the subscribed price. Accounts would be filled with energy credits at the beginning of each validity period and diminished or increased commensurate with the user's practices. According to the *Oxford English Dictionary*, *ergos*, etymologically signifying work or action, when in combined form referred to "work, used to form technical terms usually with the sense 'energy,' as ergometer n., ergophobia n." "Everyone has to be part of it," Masdar Institute researchers underlined, "otherwise it does not work."

In a context where researchers and professionals focused on resolving everyday technical problems and helping humanity in the long run, the potential paradoxes of these projects were passingly acknowledged, but not directly confronted. In order to trace energy consumption through ergos, every individual would be assigned a code and would have to use that code in order to access electricity in public spaces—for example, when taking the elevator or charging a laptop at the library. Through ergos, every individual's energy consumption patterns would be followed at every point in time, as long as he or she remained within the boundaries of Masdar City. To some, such an overhaul was justified and even necessary, because it would eventually offer a means to mitigate climate change and overcome energy scarcity, while for many researchers at Masdar the association of these attempts at energy management with the confluence of individual and societal regulation in George Orwell's *Nineteen Eighty-Four* was inevitable. Orwell famously wrote in *Nineteen Eighty-Four*, "If you want a picture of the future, imagine a boot stamping on a human face—forever."[4] This metaphorical boot, taking various forms at Masdar City, most prominently the form of an energy currency, would be protecting humanity from all kinds of existential threats.

This chapter explores the ways in which researchers at Masdar Institute imagined, planned, and implemented the new energy currency ergos, and interrogates how they related to the future consequences of their work. I argue that an investment in half-finished and half-working clean technology infrastructure both triggered and stifled the larger questions regarding the potential social or political meanings of producing an energy currency. While clean technology infrastructures, such as the yet-to-materialize building management system whose construction I will analyze below, remained the focus of everyday conversations and practices, researchers and professionals also consistently argued that their project would serve a higher good, however abstract. The mundane technical challenges prompted researchers to contemplate the planetary-level consequences of their actions and nonactions, allowing them to produce justifications for the risks they unleashed. Ergos were framed as a surgical correction to the monetary system and as a means for helping humanity in confronting energy and climate challenges. The potential of a future where ergos replaced the existing systems of exchange drew attention to Masdar's larger project as an idea city, not only inside Masdar City but also among professionals and researchers around the world.

Presenting

Alexander, a Romanian assistant professor at Masdar Institute, presented his recent research paper to an audience of faculty members, postdoctoral researchers, and graduate students in a spacious classroom on the new campus in October 2010, only a few weeks after the students moved into the new Masdar Institute dorms. Alexander had been working on energy markets and low-carbon technologies since his arrival in Abu Dhabi as a newly minted PhD in late 2007, and was collaborating with more senior colleagues from the Institute. "The way we understand the economy," he began his talk, "is based on a decoupling: a decoupling of the economy and the physical world." Pointing out how "money is a belief about a belief generated by debt in a fractional reserve system," he argued that it was time to make monetary exchange more tangible. Accordingly, his research paper aimed at bringing "the economy and the physical world" together through a new currency based on energy consumption. "In order to link the economy to the physical world, why not have an energy ticket for every service that is provided? Use energy as a currency? Could this be a universal currency?" he inquired, rhetorically, before giving more details about his proposed energy unit, ergos.

In some ways, Alexander's project meant to restore the gap that economic historian Philip Mirowski (1989) laid out in his book *More Heat Than Light: Economics as Social Physics, Physics as Nature's Economics*.[5] Mirowski's book analyzes how the founders of neoclassical economics borrowed the concept of energy from Newtonian physics and used it as a metaphor to formulate the concept of utility. Developed at the end of the nineteenth and the beginning of twentieth centuries in Europe, neoclassical economics was an approach that related supply and demand to an individual's rationality and their ability to maximize utility or profit. Its three main assumptions are: (1) economic agents have preferences, (2) economic agents are maximizers of benefits and minimizers of costs, and (3) decisions are driven by the information available. In this framework, consumers attempt to maximize their gains from purchasing goods or services, and they do this by increasing their purchases until what they gain from an extra unit is balanced by what they give up to obtain it. By behaving in this manner, they maximize utility, defined as the satisfaction derived from the consumption of goods and services.

By using this language and calling each other mathematical theorists, neoclassical economics not only drew inspiration from mechanical physics, but also established that economics was a science that relied on mathematical constructs and that propagated scientific progress. Challenging the neoclassical approach would then be equivalent to challenging scientific progress. Economists such as Thorstein Veblen, in contrast, argued that the perspective of the consumer as a rational agent making calculated decisions was inaccurate and misleading, noting that neoclassical economics assumes the human to be "a lightning calculator of pleasures and pains, who oscillates like a homogeneous globule of desire of happiness under the impulse of stimuli that shift about the area, but leave him intact."[6] Despite the criticism, this transformative perspective led to the development of theories regarding rational behavior, efficiency, and optimality that still inform the discipline of economics today.

Mirowski moves beyond critiquing neoclassical economists' assumptions about the rational consumer, and instead focuses on the conceptual steps that these economists overlook when using energy as a metaphor for utility. According to the neoclassical perspective, the rational economic agents are like atoms and utility like energy pulling them in different directions based on their calculated preferences. In response, Mirowski explains that energy conservation cannot be translated into an economic concept when studied within the framework of utility theory. He argues that conservation—which requires that some quantity, for instance mass or energy, be kept constant in a given system—does not have a counterpart in neoclassical economics; such discrepancies are manifestations of how neoclassical economics fails in its conceptualization of energy as well as utility.

Alexander did not address Mirowski's perspective in laying out his ideas about replacing the dirham with an energy currency. Yet using energy as a currency eliminates this metaphorical understanding and makes energy equivalent to value, without using utility as a mediator for determining the price of a good or service. Instead, an energy currency brings together "the economy and the physical world"—the aspiration of Alexander and his colleagues—especially because it aims at relying on and reproducing the "embodied or sequestered energy" within each action, making humans aware of the energy that is available to them at all times. In this way, "the economy" is no longer a reified object; rather, it is constituted by the material capacities that the energy system allows.

This rectification of the economic system is not the only benefit that ergos presented to the researchers at Masdar, however. According to them, an energy currency could be useful as a method for mitigating the dual problems of climate change and energy scarcity. In the face of uncertainty regarding the future of energy resources, the new energy currency would create an awareness of consumption behavior among Masdar City residents. The number of kilowatt-hours of energy produced within Masdar City boundaries would have to correspond to the amount of ergos reserves that would be available to the eco-city's residents. This setup would give Masdar City a particular independence, since the energy consumed within the city limits would be produced by the renewable energy power stations connected to the facilities on site. Setting the eco-city apart from other renewable energy generation and consumption projects that make use of large networks and super grids, such as Germany's DESERTEC project, which promoted the production of electricity through extensive solar and wind power stations constructed in North Africa and the Middle East, and proposed that this supply could satisfy the energy needs of many regions, including Europe,[7] Masdar City's ergos would contribute to situating the city as a showcase for autonomous independent energy systems that do not partake in or rely on extended networks.

In the question-and-answer portion of his presentation, Alexander clarified that ergos would still function within market dynamics; there would be price volatility, and therefore value to be gained. Initially ergos would operate together with the UAE dirham, especially because the inhabitants of Masdar would be paid in dirhams. Since Masdar City was not yet a completely self-sustaining eco-city, and since the people who lived there would have to purchase goods outside the ergos zone, they could not just abolish dirhams. But it would be best if ergos could become a universal currency, Alexander explained. This is what they aimed at—eventually.

In promoting the use of ergos as a currency uniting initially Masdar City and then the rest of the universe, Alexander dreamed of a semiotic and scalar shift, where national signs of value that had symbolic meaning would slowly be replaced by universal signs of value that have practical use. By replacing dirhams with kilowatts, the Masdar Institute researchers would frame the meaning of a currency as an information-tracking device with possibly global reach. In this sense, Alexander's project would reverse the historic nationalization of money and unite people in harmony with regard to their shared future.[8] The ergos experiment, in other words, would tie consumers together in confronting climate change and energy scarcity by calling for planetary-scale thinking about monetary exchange. The imagined globality of climate change and energy scarcity justified the shift from the national level to the universal, where energy units would be distributed to individuals via a cap-and-trade system and tracked through expansive building management systems and smart grid infrastructures.

Technocratic Dictatorship

Alexander was aware of the potential social implications of the ergos project. Acknowledging that such a commitment to energy constraints could lead to what he called a "technocratic dictatorship," Alexander was compelled to consider whether we could "maintain freedom of action, promote equality, and meet resource constraints" while utilizing technology toward increased energy efficiency.

A postdoctoral researcher who occasionally contributed to the ergos project, and whom I interviewed, pointed out that ergos had a "Big Brother side" to it, suggesting that a utility company could study a consumer's appliance/electricity consumption ratio, develop a better sense of the consumer's habits, and sell this information to vendor companies. This information would easily reflect and include private data about an individual consumer's everyday life and patterns of consumption. As a highly detailed surveillance mechanism, ergos could chart the how and when and how long of any household appliance's use, for example. More broadly, the ergos system could be used to track the inhabitants of Masdar City with the intention of generating novel regulatory mechanisms.

Yet, though the researchers working on the experiment of building an energy currency articulated to me how their proposal could be socially and politically problematic, they were putting their hesitations aside for the time being. The potential implementation of a technocratic dictatorship demonstrated that humans had to choose between maximum flexibility and what the researchers at Masdar called sustainability. In order to conserve energy, certain freedoms had to be surrendered, allowing technocrats to make decisions for global collectives. Promoting a new reading of society and the individual that focused on energy scarcity, ergos would enhance the life of the population at Masdar City, but only insofar as they maintained technocratic social and political relations. The future of humanity was therefore conceptualized as a trade-off between privacy, or the freedom of choice, and the ability to mitigate energy scarcity and climate change. Thus, a specific modality of governance was being generated: the technocratic dictatorship promised that it would protect the collective from experiences of existential threat. As my interlocutors brought forth, this societal fear had already fueled many science fiction narratives, such as George Orwell's dystopian *Nineteen Eighty-Four*, portraying a society embroiled in an omnipresent war, with Big Brother—a powerful, all-seeing leader whose existence is questionable—in charge.

Perhaps the project would someday expand to a planetary level, but, as a start, the Masdar Institute students would act as test subjects for Alexander and his colleagues' forthcoming experiment, making their energy consumption rates available for screening. Articles focusing on the preparatory stages of the ergos project began to appear in UAE newspapers as well as ecology blogs. "When this year's batch of new students at Masdar Institute signed up for their courses, they expected they would be there to learn and conduct research," the English-language United Arab Emirates newspaper the *National* wrote in August 2011, for instance.[9] "They might not, however, have suspected that they would be the subjects of a Big Brother–style social experiment. Other researchers will be watching them closely . . . for their bills. They will be the subjects of a yearlong investigation into which incentives encourage people to use less energy and water."

The ecology blog *Green Prophet*, which began following developments at Masdar City early in 2008 and continued reporting updates, also took up the Big Brother comparison:[10] "Masdar City in Abu Dhabi is aiming for carbon neutrality in an unforgivingly hot and dry environment teeming with young students. Naturally these twenty-somethings—among the world's brightest—will strive to achieve the maximum amount of comfort in their spaceship home away from home even as they are participating in one of the most expensive carbon-less experiments on the planet. But now they are being watched! In an effort to understand what incentives and stimuli drive students to switch their lights and taps on or off, Masdar will track their energy and water consumption over the next year." By pinpointing the kinds of incentives that actually work within the existing student body, researchers and professionals could develop tools for encouraging efficient consumption behavior in the future. The tone of this quotation indicated anxiety at the surveillance society that could be in the works at Masdar.

While the social arrangement required for the information to be gained was drawing some criticism, the end goal of the experiment, many pointed out, seemed to point to a higher good, benefiting humanity as a whole in battling environmental problems. If the experiment was successfully implemented, one commentary on the ergos project noted, the information from the study "could be widely distributed to help other countries develop proven programs that support energy and water conservation." The researchers at Masdar Institute were inventing a rational technique of intervention in order to monitor flows that had not been subject to surveillance before and assisting in the construction of a new smart architecture that would allow and facilitate such surveillance systems—an enhanced Panopticon, to say the least.[11]

In the case of the ergos experiment, energy management manifested itself as one coordinate through which both the small-scale individual risks and infinitely large-scale collective uncertainties that characterize our planet today could be governed.[12] Ultimately, new technologies would manufacture new social relations for the inhabitants of Masdar, altering their habits and conceptions of energy use by introducing nonflexible, technocratic mechanisms.

A Visible Currency

Masdar City, as it developed, was organized by a wide array of technical adjustments that attempted to formulate new ways of imagining the future of energy and climate change. In this context, why did researchers find it necessary to manipulate energy through another system of cultural concern—that is, monetary exchange? What was so particular about it? And what do these emergent and related infrastructures of energy and money tell us about energy and money per se?

"Concerned with the way in which money is symbolically represented in a range of different societies and, more especially, with the moral evaluation of monetary and commercial exchanges as against exchanges of other kinds," economic anthropologists Jonathan Parry and Maurice Bloch emphasize in introducing their edited volume *Money and the Morality of Exchange* (1989) that the worldviews of a particular era give "rise to particular ways of representing money."[13] Parry and Bloch underline how the "meanings with which money is invested are quite as much a product of the cultural matrix into which it is incorporated as of the economic functions it performs as a means of exchange, unit of account, store of value and so on." Similarly, legal and economic anthropologist Bill Maurer, who studies alternative currencies, such as Ithaca, New York's Ithaca HOURS, states that he is "interested in the efforts to remake money in the image of community," and asks: "How did participants in alternative financial systems imagine the boundaries of community? How were these boundaries morally charged? What kinds of exclusions did they create?"[14] Based on these accounts, alternative or complementary currencies may be perceived as symptomatic of the social conditions of a particular time and space and a particular collective.

Taking Bloch and Parry's framework into account, it is crucial to examine the "cultural matrix" into which the ergos project was born. At a time of uncertainty regarding energy resources and economic systems, the ergos experiment embodied a commitment to a set of technical adjustments that would resolve both problems with a single systemic transformation.[15] Such a commitment was the goal of the energy scholars and practitioners at the International Social Transformation Conference I attended in July 2012, themed "Energy Currency: Energy as the Fundamental Measure of Price, Cost and Value," and held in Split, Croatia. The conference venue was situated far from the historical center of Split, a dense urban space dotted with Roman architecture, inhabited continuously for twelve centuries. The venue boasted a glass façade that was markedly distinct, not only from the historic center of the city, but also from the Soviet-era housing projects that characterized the hills surrounding it. The organizers had adorned the building with a large poster featuring Nikola Tesla. At the meeting's start on July 10, 2012, the opening speaker announced that it was Tesla's 156th birthday, and that one intention of the conference was to rectify "the historical injustice" he suffered as an energy physicist. Nikola Tesla is best known for his contributions to the design of the modern alternating current (AC) electricity supply system, used widely to transmit electricity across long distances. Many argue that Tesla did not receive the credit he deserved for inventing systems such as AC electricity, which have become popular across the world. Unlike his rival Thomas Edison, who accrued praise and wealth as a result of his investments in electricity, Nikola Tesla died alone and penniless in a New York hotel room. The conference organizers wished to honor Tesla and assign new meanings to his energy networks.[16] Promoters of energy currencies, including Alexander from Masdar Institute, had gathered in Split to discuss the past, present, and future of their proposed systems.

What I encountered at the conference was a group of scholars and practitioners, including lawyers, architects, and financial experts, searching for

FIGURE 3.1 · Banner featuring Nikola Tesla's image at "Energy Currency" conference, Split, Croatia, 2012. Photo from conference website.

ways out of the Eurozone crisis, a debt crisis that started in 2009. At the time the conference was taking place, Greece, Portugal, Ireland, Spain, and Cyprus were struggling with government debt they had been unable to pay or refinance, and were looking for assistance from third parties. Conditions seemed to be improving, especially in Ireland and Spain, where interest rates were falling, but a sense of uncertainty prevailed. In response, the participants at the conference framed their conversation around market failure; climate change, or energy scarcity for that matter, was not necessarily the central topic of interest. In the context of the International Social Transformation Conference, "our ecological footprint" constituted just one problem involving the existing monetary system, comparable to unemployment or income inequality. "Joining Adam Smith and Nikola Tesla together, we can achieve a world that's better for human beings," one participant exclaimed. All in all, the conference's participants agreed that the current monetary and financial system could not last, specifically because it relied on an "unsustainable means of exchange"—that is, the currency system.

According to participants, one of the most destructive characteristics of the monetary system is its overreliance on growth and expansion. The fact that money is borrowed and lent with interest increases the volume of currency flowing in the financial system; in order to match interest rates, there needs to be constant economic growth. "The global money system therefore requires the further continual expansion of debt in order to avoid financial collapse, as there is not enough money to service the ever expanding debts," Jem Bendell, a strategist and educator on social and organizational change and an advocate of alternative currencies, wrote two years after his participation to the conference. Because of its constant need for expansion, the monetary system, he argued, is triggering environmental collapse. "New loans require further economic activity which, despite a small amount of decoupling economic growth from resource consumption, means an ever greater consumption of natural resources, and pollution of our biosphere," he posited, citing Bernard Lietaer.[17]

The intellectual backdrop for this conference was strikingly Lietaer's book *The Future of Money* (2001) and Richard Douthwaite's *The Ecology of Money* (2000). In asking, "Is energy the money of the future?" participants often referenced Douthwaite's call for a multiplicity of currencies, each with its own purpose, as elaborated in *The Ecology of Money*.[18] Participants, in their discussions, also referred to a system called "scrip," implemented in the United States during the Great Depression. During the early years of the Depression, especially in the spring of 1933, many business leaders had come to believe that alternative local currencies would contribute to recovery efforts.[19] Writing in 1933, Carl Chatters, an economist, explained: "Many barter and exchange organizations have sprung up in the United States. The members of these will trade one service for another, one commodity for another, or a commodity for a service. Where it is not possible for one member to perform the service directly for another, some medium of exchange must be used. This medium is called 'scrip.'"[20] Looking back at this system of exchange, economist Loren Gatch argues, however, "Scrip experiments in the United States never supported any systematic critique of the monetary system or proposals for monetary reform. Economic stresses of the 1930s called forth scrip almost as a reflex; when these conditions disappeared, so did scrip."[21] Lietaer had written about this local exchange system, suggesting that at some point in history complementary currencies would be used all around the world. "Otherwise, we will experience the collapse of cultures and countries," participants said, once again referring to Lietard's writings on future scenarios. Human evolution is the evolution of power, one person remarked, an idea reminiscent of anthropologist Leslie White's work on energy systems, which followed an evolutionary analysis and suggested "cultural development varies directly as the amount of energy per capita per year harnessed and put to work."[22]

At the conference, energy was considered a resource comparable to gold, and therefore as a reference value in "the real world." According to the gold standard, a system of exchange maintained from the 1870s until World War I by participating countries such as the United States and the United Kingdom, and revived for a short period in late 1920s, a unit of currency was convertible to a fixed quantity of gold, which limited governments' or banks' ability to produce paper currency and created stability in terms of exchange rates.[23] Energy measured in the form of kilowatts, participants argued, is the best model for tracking value that we can think of today, superior to gold. As energy sources became scarcer, it would still remain a master commodity. "Gold," one proponent of energy currencies suggested, "the poor dig it up and the rich bury it under the ground. It does not have any use." But energy, an emergent measure of price, cost, and value was not like that: it could serve as a means of exchange, while maintaining a use value in the real world.[24] Alexander proposed that humans needed to set an objective in terms of economic growth, achievable by employing a predetermined amount of energy. In this way, economic growth would not be infinite. Instead, it would match real-world energy production. By making this link, humans would also place a limit on the banking system and ensure that the debt financial organizations issued would correspond to future energy production. The economy would grow only at the rate energy production grew. "Money should not store value, it should not have interest," others agreed. "Money should be an information system, tracking real-world wealth—planetary resources, and all the energy of the earth."

By asserting that money should be an information system, tracking "real-world wealth," the participants seemingly recalled what economic anthropologist Keith Hart calls "the memory bank," where money is a source of collective social memory and thus will take "as many forms as the plurality of associations we enter."[25] In the form of an energy currency, money would contain detailed information about the amount of energy available to a particular population and depict energy transactions between different individuals. This information would create awareness. It would shift money's definitive characteristics—money would stop carrying a value of its own; it would instead be a marker.

In addition to advocating the use of money as an information-tracking device, the participants urged a shift in the visibility/invisibility of money. Could money be made visible again and serve as a device of measurement, rather than remaining invisible and signifying an abstract and perhaps unlimited resource invested with powers of mediation? In *The Economy of Literature*, literary critic Marc Shell writes, "It is not easy for us, who have used coinage for some twenty-five hundred years, to imagine the impression it made on the minds of those who first used it in their city-states. The introduction of money to Greece has few useful analogies."[26] He continues, "Tales of Gyges [credited with the invention of coinage] associate him with founding a tyranny in Lydia and with a power of being able to transform visibles into invisibles and invisibles into visibles. This power . . . is associated with new economic and political forms that shattered the previous world and its culture." The appearance of money created an abstraction, and facilitated what anthropologist Bill Maurer calls "mediation by a third term."[27] Accordingly, Maurer asks: "How can everything be placed on one scale of value figured in terms of money, and how can this thing called money take on such mediating powers?"[28] Anthropologist David Graeber, known for his work on theories of value, also explains how "whenever one examines the processes by which the value of objects is established (and this is true whether one is dealing with objects of exchange, or wealth more generally), issues of visibility and invisibility always seem to crop up. . . . Money tends to be represented as an invisible potency because of its capacity to turn into any other thing. Money is the potential for future specificity even if it is a potential that can only be realized through a future act of exchange."[29] The act of exchange makes money specific, or in other words, visible.

And yet by making money traceable again (by pegging it to a system of energy production and consumption), the promoters of energy currencies suggested, they could put the monetary system on display: visible. In the case of ergos, visibility might induce a new kind of tyranny, wherein the open tracking of real-world wealth would facilitate the emergence of new rationalities for the operators of the system.

Neo-Energetics

At the Energy Currency conference, I asked Alexander's team and other participants what they thought about the technocracy movement of the early twentieth century in the United States—a historical precedent for an energy-based currency system—but few there were familiar with it. Writing in the 1930s, with the purpose of recommending solutions for the economic depression in the United States, Howard Scott, the founder of the movement, argued, for instance, "To say it in one way, the cause of our troubles lies in the fact that during these years, instead of thinking of our well-being and of the operation of our country in terms of energy, we have thought of it in terms of something purchasable with dollars. If we are to understand the problem at all we have got to grapple with this question of energy; upon it everything else rests."[30] To further his argument, Scott stated,

> It is the fact that all forms of energy, of whatever sort, may be measured in units of ergs, joules or calories that is of the utmost importance. The solution of the social problems of our time depends upon the recognition of this fact. A dollar may be worth—in buying power—so much today and more or less tomorrow, but a unit of work or heat is the same in 1900, 1929, 1933 or the year 2000.

The technocracy movement suggested that, given its stability over time, energy should replace the dollar—in other words, be put into use as a currency. According to this proposal, the net energy budget of the United States would be calculated and divided among the residents of the highly centralized "North American Continental Technate," and residents of the continent provided with energy certificates of "joules" or "ergs." These nontransferable credits would expire after a period of two years. As historian of science William Akin posits, Scott believed that "his system would assure the goals that the technocrats desired: to restore purchasing power, assure maximum distribution of all goods produced, balance production and distribution, and abolish debts and profits."[31] As such, the economic crisis would be managed by what they perceived as apolitical engineering solutions.[32]

Economic historian Philip Mirowski calls movements like Howard Scott's, which argue that energy is identical to economic value, "neo-energetics,"[33] and he differentiates them from others who have been interested in energy as a metaphor for constructing economic principles.[34] "The conviction that there exists a literal identity between the physical concept of energy and the economic concept of value . . . has a long and illustrious history, dating back to the 1860s." According to Mirowski, neo-energetics has been able to survive for so long for two reasons: first, "the energy theory of value was never developed with any seriousness or concerted effort," and second, "it never resided very long within any academic disciplinary boundaries, but rather hopped about peripatetically from one fledgling discipline to another." As such, he argues, a lack of rigor along with multidisciplinary interest in the subject are the main factors contributing to a continued interest in energy theories of value that seek to forge literal connections between money and kilowatt hours.[35] This continued interest is manifest in energy currency projects such as Masdar's ergos, and has led to international meetings, exemplified by "Energy Currency: Energy as the Fundamental Measure of Price, Cost and Value" in Split, where many gathered to consider such possible linkages.

Did Alexander and his team need to consider the precedents of models such as the technocracy movement in proposing ergos at Masdar City? In modern theories of neo-energetics, energy is analyzed as a common denominator for all commodities, just as labor is in Marxist economics. Ernst Berndt, a promoter of modern-day neo-energetics, explains,

> First, much like Marx's labor theory of value in which all commodities represent congealed labor, in the accounting sense commodities can be measured by the direct energy input into their production plus the indirect energy input embodied in capital, material and other inputs. The second sense in which energy tends to be viewed as embodied or sequestered in materials is as thermodynamic potential. From the basic principles of physics and chemistry, it is known that materials have thermodynamic potential which changes as the materials pass through various states in productive processes, encountering heat energy and/or work.[36]

In a similar vein, Robert Costanza, a prominent neo-energeticist, has said, "Can anyone seriously suggest that labor creates sunlight! The reverse is obviously more accurate."[37] In calculating how energy would correspond to value, neo-energeticists also utilize various formalisms and look for ways of sorting out "embodied or sequestered energy" within commodities. In doing so, the movement argues that it is bringing together "biology, physics and economics into a single science." Yet Mirowski states that these theories merely underline the simile between human labor and energy, and do not manage to combine the concerns and priorities of biology, physics, and economics into a single science in the way they postulate. At the same time, all of these perspectives dismiss the various ways in which value becomes generated through the sociality of exchange, as explored through a rich literature in the anthropology of value.[38]

The "Hidden Brain"

When I asked Alexander how he would relate these older energy currency systems to his current experiment, he explained that they are conceptually similar. "But it was not possible to implement them at the time," he continued, "especially because of an absence of information technologies." Now, his team had access to novel technical infrastructure at the Masdar Institute: they could rely on its building management system (BMS), or what Rowan Moore, architecture critic at *The Observer*, referred to as the building's "hidden brain."[39] The BMS was expected to act as a regulatory device for the imagined energy currency system of Masdar City, facilitating the institution of certain disciplinary measures within its buildings.

Building management systems are common technological systems that have been implemented in large buildings since the late 1960s, mostly to control a building's indoor environment. Due to the decreasing price of the hardware required for their manufacture, these systems became widespread during the 1970s. In addition to managing a building's environment by keeping track of heating, lighting, ventilation, air-conditioning systems, and window maintenance, such systems administer security, fire protection, elevator operation, and surveillance mechanisms. Experts on building automation also stress that the historical development of building management systems is interlaced with improvements in technologies of computation, wherein the incorporation of computers, on top of various optimization techniques, provides opportunities to further complicate the machineries of control within large buildings.[40] At Masdar City, the BMS would have an additional function: by tracking the energy use of individual residents, it would provide information in the form of an energy currency, thus acting as a new type of regulatory device. The building's regulatory apparatus was intended to remain outside the conscious awareness of its residents while having a decisive effect on how they live—perhaps the analogy of the "hidden brain" was not so misplaced.

The implementation of the desired BMS machinery would breathe life into the Masdar Institute building, augmenting its capacities of automation and control. It would not only contribute to the centralization of decision-making power and facilitate the dominance of an optimization logic within the building's environment; it would prohibit occupants from interfering with the system as much as they would like to. Thus, once the BMS was fully functional, the raw values that made up the database would be values produced by the "building" and not by its occupants. Unless the occupants matched the profile determined by the BMS control panel, they would have to come to terms with the discomforts of the building's environment. As anthropologist Catherine Fennell, writing on the residents of Chicago's public housing, shows in her ethnography of Project Heat, a term used to denote the very particular kind of heat one had access to while living in a Chicago public housing project, "mandates to control . . . heat also involved compulsions to manage subjective senses of comfort."[41] This aspiration to manage the residents' subjective sense of comfort was also present at Masdar. The BMS control panel on the Masdar Institute campus would engineer new subjective senses of comfort for the building's occupants, stressing that this new sensibility would in turn have planetary effects, helping humanity battle environmental problems. In the case of Masdar, the discomforts of the building's environment would translate to an inflexible sustainability, which would not only decrease the energy demands of the building, but also dictate certain types of behavior for the building's residents.

In responding to these debates, Emma, a British master's student who lived in the Masdar Institute dorms between September 2010 and May 2011, suggested that she felt like a test subject but was rarely credited for it. She argued that this feeling was related to being part of an institution that was just being set up and that did not yet have a strong working infrastructure. The students were encouraged to partake in the making of this new system, in some sense coproducing Abu Dhabi's sustainability measures, but Emma did not know if the administration truly cared about their reactions. Another student from the same class stated that they were simply being experimented on, which is "what happens when technology dictates actions." What kind of a prototype is Masdar City? he asked; that must be what they're trying to test. "Could sustainability be defined through a set of inflexible technologies?" the students wondered as they tried to adapt to their environment.

In practice, the building's temperature had been a topic of heated debate on the Masdar Institute campus. Brad, an executive from Masdar City whom I interviewed on the Institute's campus, offered a lengthy explication, saying at one point, "Temperature and air-conditioning change your mood when you're in a building. But people have different senses of temperature. Would you like to inhabit a room that is 23, 24, or 26 degrees Celsius?" Some on-site architects working with Foster + Partners summed up the discussion on temperature as one occurring between the Emiratis and the non-Emiratis. According to them, the Emirati students had become used to occupying buildings that remained firmly set to 21 degrees Celsius, or even less. "Don't you freeze when you go to shopping malls in this country?" Daniel, the German architect who worked with Foster + Partners, asked me, thereby problematizing temperature as a matter of cultural concern. However, stabilizing the temperature at the desired 21 degrees Celsius level would increase the Masdar Institute building's energy demands significantly. The architects knew the temperature would be somewhere between 21 and 26 degrees; later, after weeks of deliberation, one on-site architect noted to me that they had settled on 24 degrees Celsius. The decision upset some of the occupants, they acknowledged, but it was implemented anyway. One Foster + Partners architect added that the sustainability that was their goal did not allow for flexibility. "It's not possible to have both at the same time," he underlined.

Martyn Potter, as the facilities manager of Masdar Institute, also wanted to make sure that sustainability would not be compromised at Masdar City, even if this would require surrendering flexibility. According to him, this would be the future of energy management in the United States and Europe as well. A 2011 article in *Time* magazine titled "Masdar City: The World's Greenest City?" assessed Potter's position:

> Martyn Potter, Masdar's director of operations and facilities, noted that most Abu Dhabi citizens are used to keeping their air-conditioning as

> low as 60°F (15.5°C)—it helps that electricity is heavily subsidized—but in Masdar, AC needs to be set closer to 77°F (25°C) to keep within its efficiency targets. With the ability to monitor exactly how much electricity every room in the city is using, Potter can keep citizens in line. "It's name and shame," he says. "I'm a green policeman."[42]

Another article, in *The Guardian*, highlighted Potter's regulatory approach:

> Here, residents live with driverless electric cars, shaded streets cooled by a huge wind tower and a Big Brother–style "green policeman" monitoring their energy use. . . . "The city is a laboratory for the future," says Martyn Potter, director of operations at the institute and dubbed the "green policeman." The Big Brother approach to cutting energy is likely to become the norm as computerised smart grids are rolled out in Europe and the U.S., he adds. "I want to know exactly how these buildings work. I can pinpoint who is using the most energy and water, whether in an apartment or the academy. Certain students have been used to having the air conditioning on at 16°C (61°F), here it is 24°C. Yes, they complain. But I have told them that's how it is."[43]

When I asked Brad, the executive from Masdar City, what he thought about these ongoing complaints from the building residents, he responded, "But that's exactly why we have to implement dummy controls." He laid out how dummy controls would work for residents: "You get up and change the environment psychologically. And that saves so much energy." Karim, a young energy efficiency engineer, also argued that occupants would be more satisfied with their living situations if they believed they could change a room's temperature, even if in reality they could not. He lightly referred to a study in China, in which engineers had implemented dummy thermostats in rooms in response to repeated protests by the residents of an office block regarding their lack of control. "The dummy thermostats made everyone much happier," Karim reported. Evidently, in the industry this placebo effect was argued to provide the illusion of control to tenants without compromising on the system's efficiency.[44]

At Masdar Institute, the "hidden brain" of the building would serve as a discrete sense-making apparatus. In her book on the emergence of sick building syndrome, historian of science Michelle Murphy touches upon such sense-making capacities and proposes the concept of "regimes of perceptibility" to describe the ways in which certain phenomenological conditions become blocked while others are accentuated, thus creating a definitive methodology for the building occupant to relate to his or her environment.[45] In the China example offered by Karim, the dummy thermostats had served as material manifestations of the desired "regime of perceptibility" within the building's environment. If they were implemented in the Masdar Institute building, the subjects who privileged sight over thermoception would easily be manipulated into believing that their environment had been improved when, in fact, the thermostat remained fixed at a predetermined temperature. An article on dummy thermostats acknowledged this ambiguity and suggested: "The desired effect is obvious. If someone feels chilly and can feel like they have the control to go over and knock up the thermostat setting a couple of degrees, then perhaps they will 'feel' more comfortable assuming the temperature is changing accordingly. Ideally, I suppose, you could wind up with a room of content people, composed of some folks who are comfortable because it is 71 degrees, and some other folks who are comfortable because they think it is 73 degrees. I'm sure you may be thinking, 'Yes, but other people might walk by, see the thermostat, and start to get "warm" because they think it is actually 73 degrees.' Interesting point. Is this mental trick more effective in making people feel better than worse? We'll leave that for any psychologists among you."[46] The building's machinery would work in what might be called a deceptive manner.

Yet Brad did not think this was troubling. The individuals inhabiting the building would be led to consume less energy and thereby contribute to a higher good. They would be doing so rather unknowingly, but Brad argued that this could well be beside the point. For Brad, dummy thermostats, and the imperceptibility produced through them, seemed like an ideal scenario for the time being, until consumers became more aware of the urgency of energy conservation and efficiency. Brad did not talk about how building occupants would become more aware of their consumption if they were consistently manipulated by a technological infrastructure.

"But tech-cities may begin to use even more resources, and in this way, Masdar could be part of the paradox," Brad then pointed out. "This place looks like *Star Trek*, but maybe ecological places must be low-tech, passive houses. Here, we go high-tech and we pay for efficiency, but that may not work either," he added. The possible realization that Masdar could constitute a paradox, as provocative as it may be, did not necessarily mean the people at Masdar City should reconsider their involvement in the project. Everyday discussions and practices consumed the individuals working within Masdar City and allowed them to live with the paradoxes that they passingly identified.

For now, an energy efficiency engineer confirmed, there were no thermostats in the rooms at Masdar Institute. At one of the regular meetings on BMS implementation, which took place in a meeting room inside the makeshift and provisional offices of Masdar City before the temperature was set at 24 degrees Celsius, it was noted that the absence of thermostats prevented Masdar Institute residents from tinkering with central environmental conditions, dictated by the half-working BMS. Two Masdar Institute students, who attended the meeting as research assistants, shyly provided some feedback to the other nine participants, underlining that their rooms, beautiful and spacious in design, were mostly cold and uncomfortable. The students' complaints were logged. The energy efficiency engineers working with Masdar City promised the building would soon be improved.

The BMS meetings often prompted discussion of how the third-party contractors, such as technology companies LG and Schneider Electric or the initial Masdar City contractor CH2M Hill, all associated with the production of the BMS in some capacity, were not working properly. The workers were underpaid and not well trained; the material used was not chosen correctly or did not reflect the priorities of the project. Yet these inconveniences were instrumental in pushing the researchers and professionals working with Masdar to concentrate on short-term problems and solutions, thereby giving them the capacity to leave aside the larger questions regarding their work. The tensions between different technical layers, which caused delays in implementing the BMS, were critical in pushing the project forward and in increasing the level of anticipation for its imminent launch. The potential paradoxes of the project, passingly acknowledged, then became secondary to minute material victories. The idea of serving a higher good by helping humanity in its quest for energy also enabled the project to continue on a steady course. On the other hand, these preparations produced Masdar Institute students as subjects in an experiment, continuously tested on issues ranging from building design to climatic conditions.

"You guys are learning how to use controls—we need a booklet on how all the systems work; it's weird that you never get a how-to-use book for buildings," Daniel, the Foster + Partners architect, announced during an on-campus presentation to the Masdar students in November 2010. The presentation targeted the students who had moved into the dorms only two months ago and would help them figure things out. "The BMS system is not functioning properly," he said, "and BMS runs this building like a ship, and when you don't maintain the BMS system then you can't run the ship properly. Imagine the BMS as the management unit of the ship," he emphasized. The ship, a life-supporting environment amid an ocean where human life is constantly in danger, was put at risk due to the malfunctioning BMS. But the ship, or what many at Masdar referred to as the spaceship in the desert, would soon be improved with students' cooperation.

Alexander and his colleagues not only proposed a new layer of governance that would rely on this infrastructure—monitoring the energy flow of individuals and the populace as a whole—they also intended to produce what they called a more "real-world" indicator of "visible" economic value. They would later have to assess whether their ergos experiment actually involved instituting what Alexander called "a technocratic dictatorship."

The Zero-Carbon City

The production of ergos as a unit of energy currency, and the building of its associated technical infrastructures, eventually gave rise to questions about the future eco-city that ergos users would inhabit. What kind of a prototype was Masdar City? The marketing department had come up with a promotional statement at the very beginning of the project in 2006, suggesting that Masdar City would be the first "zero-carbon city" in the world. The faculty, students, and professionals at Masdar wondered what "zero-carbon" meant.

In his September 2010 presentation at Masdar Institute, Alexander touched upon this question, reiterating that there were three ways in which an eco-city's carbon emissions could be defined. First there were "strictly zero-carbon" cities, which did not emit any carbon to begin with. Second were "net zero-carbon" cities, where carbon emissions could be eliminated or balanced. Third, a city could be "carbon neutral." In this case, the residents of the city would be required to purchase third-party carbon offsets to balance their carbon emissions. "Of course, we've dropped even these," he said in frustration, pointing out that Masdar City's claims to be a zero-carbon city had slowly faded away. Many in the audience shared Alexander's disappointment with what they conceived to be the foundering ideals of Masdar City and grinned ruefully at each other.

And yet Alexander insisted that ergos would be critical in establishing Masdar as a zero-carbon city. Most importantly, ergos would trigger energy awareness and end-user behavioral changes toward satisfying energy demand within the city's established limits. To produce a zero-carbon city, researchers could not rely only on device-based efficiency. The transformation had to be systemic. It had to have social impact. It had to cause a discursive shift. Ergos, Alexander affirmed, would be able to satisfy these requirements.

In suggesting that ergos would fulfill these expectations, Alexander also insisted that ergos would be key in the transformation of political power within Masdar City. The imagined energy currency would bring in tools that would allow the researchers to discipline and regulate individuals and the population within the eco-city, thereby enabling the city to remain zero-carbon. In other words, the disciplinary measures that would be brought about through the new energy currency were perceived to be essential in preparing for future ecological destruction, energy scarcity, and possible economic failure. Through monitoring individuals as well as populations, Abu Dhabi could safeguard its energy future, along with its economic well-being. At the end of his talk, Alexander once again asked: "Can Masdar City be zero-carbon?" He responded to his own question with a determined yes, and he suggested that it would only come at some cost. "We must keep in mind that our world is running out of fossil fuels—besides, there is climate change," he conclusively stated. The anxiety regarding ecological destruction and energy scarcity resurfaced, serving to justify the decisions taken within the eco-city.

When mapping the future of Masdar City, such formal definitions served as directives and incentives to proceed with the project. The paradoxes of the city were not directly confronted, thereby further facilitating the tendency to remain inattentive to the potential bigger-picture problems. What role would ergos play in creating the zero-carbon city that was once envisioned? The researchers and professionals working on the study were keen to underline how the ergos system was key to creating awareness regarding energy consumption, uniting the populace toward a shared future of automated energy conservation. However, the steps required for creating ergos triggered side effects that could be avoided for the time being, but that in the end would drastically transform social, political, and economic relations within communities.

Yet how exactly did Alexander and his colleagues make the decision to further commit to technological infrastructure in promoting energy efficiency when they feared a possible technocratic dictatorship? The small, rather mundane steps toward the enactment of the project enabled Alexander and his team to leave these bigger ideas aside, while simultaneously making them more and more ingrained in the discourses and practices required for reaching the final goal. At the same time, the researchers remained convinced that the project would serve an abstract higher good, eventually helping humanity in dealing with energy problems. In discussing the future of their proposal, they moved between various scales, both concentrating on the immediate impact that the project would have for the residents of Masdar City and expounding the global future implications of their model. Having fully grasped the potential risks they unleashed, the researchers seemed confident that technology could be used as an educational mechanism whereby inhabitants of Masdar City would learn more about their consumption behavior. They hoped and believed that an energy currency could allow people to make informed yet free choices. Simultaneously, they thought of their project as a somewhat revolutionary proposal that would change the understanding of money and energy completely. In addition to the everyday discussions and practices associated with the realization of the project, this belief allowed the researchers to disregard the fears associated with a somewhat dystopian future.

Years after the earliest discussion of the ergos experiment, its implementation remained stalled, its potential open-ended, due to the everyday problems of the Masdar Institute's BMS. "The showers and the air conditioning, even those problems still haven't been resolved," one of my interlocutors told me. "They cannot seem to find what is wrong with the building or resolve it." Postponed due to the many interlinked inconveniences, ergos thus became an ungraspable yet consistently anticipated object for researchers and professionals at Masdar City.

In the next chapter, I will explore another emergent artifact at Masdar that also suffered from various operations-related problems, but which nevertheless became categorized as a success, at least by some.

An Expensive Toy 4

Potential

In an article published in January 2011, a journalist from *Time* magazine perceptively described the personal rapid transit system at Masdar City and questioned how practical the transport solution offered at Masdar was, given its cost:[1]

> The doors swish shut and with the press of a touchscreen button, the Personal Rapid Transit (PRT) car is off, gliding through the tunnels beneath Abu Dhabi's new Masdar City. The sleek four-passenger vehicle—which looks like something out of the movie *tron: Legacy*[2]—runs on an electric motor, making it clean and carbon-free. There are no tracks—the car is autonomous, driven by a computer that charts direction with the help of tiny magnets embedded in the road. When my PRT car senses another vehicle waiting in our parking space, it stops and waits for the area to clear, avoiding a collision. PRT is meant to be the future of mass transit within cities, with the environmental benefits of buses and trains but the freedom of a private vehicle. But as my car pulls into an open docking bay, I can't help thinking there's something slightly silly about all this. For all the technology—which isn't cheap—the PRT has taken me to its one and only stop, maybe half a mile (800 m) from the starting point. For a lot less—and not

> much more time—I could have used a much older form of transport: my legs.

According to the plans put together by Foster + Partners and their Milan-based transportation consultant Systematica in 2007, the PRT system would provide energy-efficient automated public transit inside Abu Dhabi's eco-city: private, on-demand, nonstop transportation between any two points on a network that arguably combined the advantages of cars (travel at any time) and public transport (no congestion or parking issues).[3] Connecting the entire eco-city through a twenty-three-mile network, the PRT would accommodate 1,800 vehicles at eighty-seven stations,[4] while also stopping at about 120 freight points to allow for the widespread distribution of goods. Foster + Partners architects and Systematica consultants told me that the PRT had been crucial in the early days of the project. This transportation solution had differentiated the Foster + Partners master plan from proposals by other architecture offices. As the early Foster + Partners renderings of Masdar City demonstrated, this transportation network would be located on the basement level of the eco-city, commonly referred to as the "undercroft," in order to prevent the "pod cars" from disrupting everyday life on Masdar City's streets. This meant that the whole city would have to be built about twenty feet above the existing ground, allowing for the undercroft below. While initially a plausible scenario, the project soon proved to be excessively demanding financially, leading Masdar executives to drop the plans for the PRT completely in December 2010. Instead, they would pursue alternative emission-free means of transport, such as electric buses or cars. And yet there remained one destination that passengers at Masdar Institute could travel to: the parking lot outside the building. This journey lasted two and a half minutes, and was offered free of charge.[5]

In the years that followed the PRT system's launch, students, researchers, professionals, and journalists at Masdar City discussed it in terms success and/or failure, thereby rendering the PRT system materially and conceptually open. The Masdar Institute students I met on the Institute campus in 2010 and 2011 suggested that the pod cars offered "fun" rides. The subcontractors who manufactured the vehicles stated their conviction that people "enjoyed" the pod cars—therefore, the project was a victory. Transport planning consultants offered more moderate praise, assessing the PRT system itself to be innovative and effective, but qualifying this assertion by

FIGURE 4.1 AND 4.2 · Computer rendering of the Masdar City undercroft, 2007. Image by Foster + Partners.

noting that it should have been supplemented by other forms of transit in the eco-city, such as light rail systems. Executives at Masdar City underlined that the PRT suffered from capacity problems, paralyzing the site and staging an indisputable failure. These conversations revealed that what was at stake in the PRT project was not its functionality, effectiveness, or use, but rather the ways in which its materially and conceptually indeterminate existence mobilized potential toward a technically adjusted future.

In examining a project like the PRT, perhaps the first mode of analysis that comes to mind is the study of how and why grand projects fail. A most fitting example is Bruno Latour's *Aramis, or the Love of Technology* (1993), in which, from an anthropologically and sociologically informed standpoint, the author studies the implementation of a PRT network in Paris in the 1970s. Latour conducts what he calls an "autopsy of a failure," mainly by analyzing documentary evidence and interviewing the foremost actors involved.[6] Stylistically, *Aramis* is framed as a quasi-mystery or a detective novel, where two sociologists of technology try to understand how Aramis—the personal rapid transit system that was to be implemented in Paris—was killed. Eventually, they propose that the technology failed not because any particular person involved in the project killed it per se, but rather because the engineers could not adapt to changing social contexts.[7]

Given the variety of perspectives on Masdar's PRT system that I encountered, it is difficult to designate the project a failure or a success in recounting it here. Therefore, in contrast to Latour's book, there is no solving the crime in this present narrative. In detailing my interlocutors' various points of view, I focus on what I label "potential" as a rejoinder to analytics of success and failure, analyzing the discursive and practical qualities of clean technology, and demonstrating how decisions are made and justified and whom these decisions seek to benefit.[8] In the case of Masdar, people cannot agree on what success or failure is on the ground. What I show here is that this confusion is productive—in fact, the confusion indicates the potentiality of the project. My interlocutors could not decide whether their project was a success or failure, and at times postponed this analysis to a later time. I argue that potential was located not only in words and images but also in the material assemblages that made up the PRT system in the present, which stopped, broke down, or carried visitors to the futuristic universe of Masdar City; the PRT system appeared on site as effective transport, experiment in mobility, science fiction fantasy, and "expensive toy." It was not its functionality as infrastructure that made the PRT system visible, but the multiple imaginaries of the future its half-finished and half-functional state made possible.

It is important to note that this half-finished infrastructure gave rise to multiple, at times contradictory, versions of a speculative future. The personal rapid transit system could be considered a success or a failure depending on how an engineer, student, or visitor conceptualized the larger project of Masdar City. It was challenging to classify the PRT project as a success or failure because of its physical and conceptual indeterminacy, while the potential of the PRT as a half-finished marker of a not-yet future emerged precisely from divergent interpretations of success and failure.

FIGURE 4.3 · The PRT pod cars at Masdar Institute, September 2010. Photo by the author.

Unlike a detective story, where readers may reach a solid truth at the end, this chapter does not identify a culprit or offer resolution. In the sections below, I will first provide a brief outline of the history of automated transit, exploring the various contexts in which it emerged in the mid-twentieth century and showing how the imaginary of automation, which fueled the PRT project, may materialize in the future in other ways, say in the form of the self-driving car technology that Google has been developing. Later the chapter will revisit how students and professionals at Masdar discussed the success and failure of the PRT project, allowing for multiple interpretations of the same mechanical infrastructure. Finally, I will recount the story of how the PRT was canceled, formulating what this may mean for the future of clean technology.

The Imaginary of Automated Transit

The PRT pods, which would be the primary means of transportation within Masdar City, had first been exhibited on the opening day of the World Future Energy Summit (WFES) in Abu Dhabi in January 2009,

FIGURE 4.4 · PRT exhibit at the World Future Energy Summit, Abu Dhabi, January 2009. Photo by Imre Solt.

giving visitors a sense of the eco-city's futuristic ambitions.[9] The Masdar Institute campus was on track to be opened in late 2010, and would be equipped with this transportation network, which had been conceptualized by the transportation consultancy Systematica in collaboration with Foster + Partners architects. The pod cars that would be employed as part of this infrastructure were designed by Zagato, an Italian engineering company famous for racing cars, and manufactured in the Netherlands by 2getthere. The PRT infrastructure was promoted as the most innovative element of Masdar City, representing "a breakthrough in the transport world."[10] According to commentators, the public transportation model of the eco-city was "the first attempt to move away from a traditional transport system to an on-demand system that allows almost door-to-door service—an innovation in the world of transport. And maybe a first step to a better future."[11] One blogger who reviewed the exhibit suggested, "The comfort and safety of the pods shows us a rather favorable vision of the future. Ride on cushioned seats, holding hands or facing each other. Have a conversation, catch up on the morning news. The car will stop to let you off at your chosen destination. . . . That's our future? Not bad. Not bad at all!"[12] The pod cars confirmed that humanity's future would be one of technological complexity, just as in science fiction movies. In the face of deeply unsettling environmental conditions, they offered a comforting and enjoyable narrative, suggesting imaginaries of the future as untouched by problems of energy scarcity.

Of course, the WFES exhibit was not the first instance of the materialization of the dream of automated transit. The vision of producing personal rapid transit infrastructures emerged in the mid- to late twentieth century through the development of automated transit technology, the transformation of passive networks of roads and vehicles into adaptive systems capable of responding to fluctuations in supply and demand in real time. Automated transit technology in the form of highways, trains, buses, and driverless cars generates links between institutions that might otherwise seem unrelated, allowing for new forms of social organization. While the development of specific projects has depended on their individual historical contexts, automated transport had drawn on and continues to foster certain shared ideals, such as optimization, efficiency, and responsiveness, bringing vehicles together under a centralized supervisory system.

In the United States, the 1939 World's Fair in New York had included a General Motors exhibition, "Highways and Horizons," in which the future highway was perceived as a means of automation, restricting drivers to specified lanes and thereby preventing accidents.[13] The exhibit also included a radio tower, which communicated with drivers in order to manage the flow of traffic. Foreshadowing the Interstate Highway System that later developed in the United States, this exhibition was a noteworthy instance of the concepts of automation and transportation being thought of together—perhaps for the first time. However, the construction of highways, especially in the United States in the 1960s and 1970s, later became one of the significant reasons why urban public transportation systems became underfunded, triggering future gridlock and congestion and moving away from ideas about automation.[14]

Under the Urban Mass Transportation Act of 1964, research benefiting public transportation became prioritized in the United States, and the concepts of automation and public transit were brought together with funding from the U.S. government. Around this time, Donn Fichter, a transportation planner and researcher at the New York State Department of Transportation, started writing about PRT systems, culminating in a self-published book titled *Individualized Automatic Transit and the City*, which includes his description of a small-car automated transit system named

Veyar. In 1966, the U.S. Department of Housing and Urban Development (HUD) was asked to study new modes of urban transport that could carry people and goods without causing air pollution; this resulted in early theoretical and systems analysis regarding PRT infrastructure. In 1968, the HUD researchers produced a report that explored the various forms of public transit that should be pursued in the future,[15] emphasizing the notion of automation, and in particular listing "Personal Rapid Transit," "Automated Dual Mode Buses," and "Dial-A-Bus" systems. In the report, the PRT system's operations were outlined in the following manner:

> Empty passenger vehicles or "capsules" would be available at each station on the network. The riders would enter one, select and register their destination, and then be transported there automatically, with no stopping. The average speed would be essentially equal to the vehicle speed. The station spacing on a guideway network for the system would have no influence on speed of travel. Passenger demand and station costs would dictate proper station spacing.

Following a rigorous analysis of the system, the researchers concluded that "control problems become even more complex in the areas of merging one vehicle stream into another and of routing numerous small vehicles automatically over a network of guideways, with provisions for switching off the line at stations, of maintaining adequate supplies of empty cars at stations, and of distributing vehicles so that congestion does not result on any line." Still, the results were optimistic, suggesting that in ten years and at a cost of $250 million[16] these problems could be resolved.

In a *Scientific American* article published in July 1969, William F. Hamilton II and Dana K. Nance introduced the results of this research to the public:

> Engineers have described a system called "personal transit" that will operate like a railroad but will transport individual passengers or small groups nonstop to stations of their own selection. Its cars will be small, electrically propelled vehicles, with a capacity of two to four passengers, running on an automated network of tracks called "guideways." All stations will be on sidetracks shunted off the through line. A passenger will enter a waiting car at a station, punch his destination on a keyboard and then be carried to the designated station with no further action

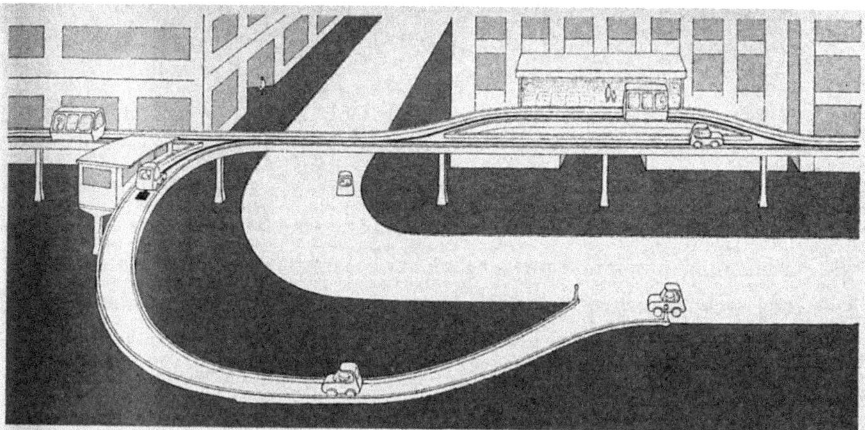

FIGURE 4.5 · Illustration from *Scientific American* article on PRT, July 1969.

> on his part—no transfers, no station stops, no waiting, no driving. It appears that such a system could take the passenger from starting point to destination at an average speed of 60 miles per hour, as against the present average speed of 20 miles per hour counting station stops in U.S. subways.[17]

The article had great impact in shaping later conversation around the PRT, and spurred interest from multiple bodies both inside and outside the United States. In this period, organizations such as Aerospace Corporation, a nonprofit organization that served the U.S. Air Force in the scientific and technical planning and management of missile and space programs, began exploring PRT systems. Thanks to general enthusiasm regarding the new transport system, the Morgantown PRT system was established in West Virginia in 1975, at the time of the oil crisis, when public transit options were more sought out than ever.[18] The PRT mainly served an academic institution, West Virginia University, connecting its three Morgantown campuses to downtown Morgantown. However, the system was not replicated anywhere else in the United States because of its unexpectedly high cost of $120 million.[19] In addition to this, West Virginia

University spends $5 million annually to operate the system six days a week, paying a fifty-five-person crew that repairs the aging cars and the guideway, and that searches for hard-to-find parts for the vehicles.[20]

Automated transport experiments also took hold in Europe and Japan. In 1967, Aramis was the first PRT project to emerge in Europe, sponsored by the aerospace company Matra for deployment in the Paris area.[21] In 1969, German companies Mannesmann Demag and MBB began developing the Cabinentaxi program, concentrating on the construction of a PRT system for Hamburg. Between 1972 and 1978, they tested the Cabinentaxi on an expanding track in Hagen. The Japanese Ministry of International Trade and Industry (MITI) sponsored the development of a PRT system as well, starting in 1968. The Computer-Controlled Vehicle System, known as CVS, was displayed as part of a "traffic game" at the Osaka World Exposition, held from March to September 1970; more than ten specially designed electric vehicles operated individually on a checkerboard-like guideway network, communicating with a central computer by radio through an underground communication channel. Given the excitement at the Expo, Japanese authorities started the Higashimurayama Project in 1971, modeling a track for future pod cars, and began operating it in 1976.

The CVS project was functional for about six months, before it closed due to safety protocols. In 1978, Japan's Ministry of Land, Infrastructure and Transport declined to grant CVS a license under existing safety regulations, citing issues with the short headway distances.[22] While the late 1960s and early 1970s were an exciting time for PRT research, the 1980s saw the enthusiasm die out. The Cabinentaxi project of Hamburg lasted until 1980, yet the application was never realized due to budget cuts. Aramis failed its qualification trials in November 1987, leading executives to drop PRT-related research and concentrate instead on mass-transit systems.

Research on automated transit, and in particular PRT systems, regained momentum in the 1990s, as climate change and energy security issues began receiving more attention, leading to projects such as Masdar City's PRT system or its main competitor, designed by a company called ULTra (short for Urban Light Transit) for terminal 5 at London's Heathrow Airport.[23] Heathrow Airport operator BAA commissioned the British transportation company ULTra in 2005 to design and build the PRT, a twenty-one-vehicle system that covers a total of 2.4 miles along a one-way

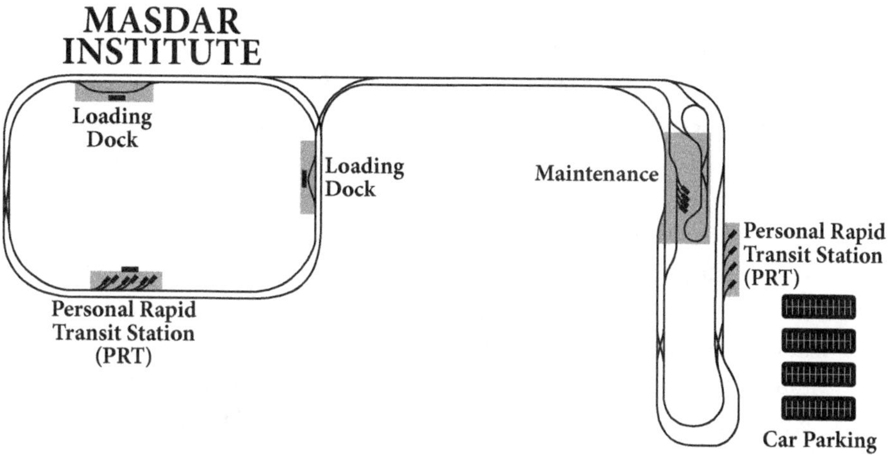

FIGURE 4.6 · Schematic diagram of the PRT track between Masdar Institute and the parking lot.

guideway. ULTra had been founded as a result of a research project at the University of Bristol's Department of Aerospace Engineering, and built the commissioned infrastructure in about six years. The ULTra PRT has been operational since May 2011. While there have been proposals for extending the system beyond the airport, these projects have not materialized.[24] ULTra claims to have reduced design and construction costs in comparison to older systems, making it more competitive. More importantly, the implementation of systems such as ULTra has enabled the technology to be tested again, and within new social, economic, and political contexts. The experiments described above proved significant yardsticks for the development of these more recent PRT systems, but still this transportation system remains a futuristic technology in the imaginary, often labeled "the transport of tomorrow."

Robot Brains

In 2009, soon after Masdar City's PRT pods were unveiled at the World Future Energy Summit, the website Treehugger.com interviewed Luca Guala, a transportation planner and PRT consultant at Systematica, working with Foster + Partners on their Masdar project.[25] Luca was an Italian civil engineer in his early fifties, and held a PhD in transportation technologies and economics. He had been working in Italy, providing transport-planning services to companies and countries around the world. Luca spoke as a richly informed proponent of PRT technology, clarifying his points through multifaceted commentaries whenever he had the chance.

In the interview, Luca gave a detailed explanation of the individual pods, stating that they would speed up to seven meters per second, so that the longest travel time within the city would be between seven and ten minutes, and he provided more information about the possible infrastructure of the PRT. First, passengers would descend a flight of stairs or take an elevator to the station at the undercroft. Next, there would be two options: "You will swipe a smart card through a machine, and a welcome message will appear. One option is that the system will recognize you and greet you personally: 'Good morning, where do you want to go today?' Perhaps the system will remember your usual path, and offer it to you as an option. After you click on your destination, the system will say something like, 'Your car is arriving in two minutes at platform number 3.' You may have to stand in line, and you will be able to identify your car by its number." Then passengers would step into a fully charged pod, and press "go" on the touchscreen control panel. Or, Luca added, "the second option is that you will enter your destination into the system when you are already sitting inside a car."

Luca also highlighted the limits of the PRT system and warned the interviewer that if there happened to be a Rolling Stones show at Masdar, then the PRT would probably fall short of concertgoers' needs because they were not designed for a heavy influx of people. He did not see the PRT system as a stand-alone infrastructure. It could serve Masdar City residents in their day-to-day activities, seating four to six passengers in each pod, but it would need to be complemented with light rail systems with higher carrying capacities. The light rail systems would provide transportation to the residents of the city for longer distances, while the pod cars would be used between locations inaccessible by these trains. Both of these transport networks would be available to the visitors and residents. It was left unclear whether blue-collar workers would be able to benefit from them. Luca emphasized that the Masdar City PRT was a prototype, similar to the Morgantown PRT project, which has been described as the first working PRT system, and which opened in 1975—according to him, prototypes were expensive.

In reflecting on the history of PRT technology, Luca explained to me during an email exchange why he agreed with Bruno Latour's criticism of Aramis,[26] because for Latour the PRT was a "complete object" in the sense that "every element of it is tailored upon the others, and no component can work without the others." According to Luca, *Aramis, or the Love of Technology* demonstrated how the "complete" nature of the project had eventually led to its failure. He explained: "The transport system made of cars, roads, drivers, is very loose: take a car built in Korea, put it on a road in Britain, give it to a Pakistani driver, fill it with UAE fuel, and it will work. All cars are independent one from another: they work together by acknowledging their reciprocal presence and motion by means of 'sensors' (most of which are situated on the driver's head) but there is no central control and supervisory system. The system is 'incomplete' in the sense that you can add or subtract elements and, up to a certain point, it will still work. The PRT system instead is a closed and complete one. You cannot take one of Masdar's PRTs and put it on Heathrow's terminal 5 tracks [replacing an ULTra PRT]: it wouldn't even be able to understand the commands of the central supervisory system, let alone charge its batteries. It would remain still on the tracks, become a dead weight and block the whole system until it is removed."

This criticism is one of the reasons the conversation around automation has switched, as of the late 2000s, to driverless cars, triggering research on their capacities for movement in all weather conditions, the possible partnerships between car companies and technology companies, the ethics of their algorithms, and the institutional infrastructure necessary for their survival. Many technologists and writers have imagined robot cars. For instance, in 1964, when famous science fiction author Isaac Asimov wrote a piece describing the year 2014 for *New York Times*, he argued: "Much effort will be put into the designing of vehicles with 'robot-brains,' vehicles that can be set for particular destinations and that will then proceed there without interference by the slow reflexes of a human driver," and accurately predicted the work that would take hold.[27] Car companies like Ford and Nissan, as well as technology companies like Google, Uber, and Amazon,

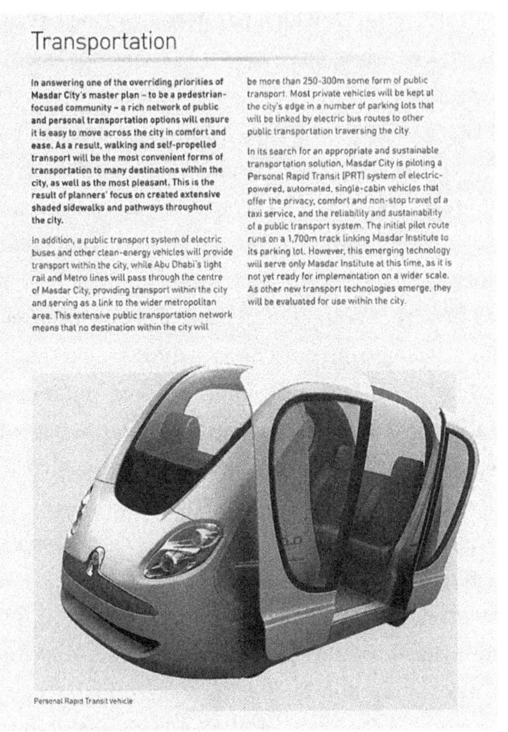

Transportation

In answering one of the overriding priorities of Masdar City's master plan – to be a pedestrian-focused community – a rich network of public and personal transportation options will ensure it is easy to move across the city in comfort and ease. As a result, walking and self-propelled transport will be the most convenient forms of transportation to many destinations within the city, as well as the most pleasant. This is the result of planners' focus on created extensive shaded sidewalks and pathways throughout the city.

In addition, a public transport system of electric buses and other clean-energy vehicles will provide transport within the city, while Abu Dhabi's light rail and Metro lines will pass through the centre of Masdar City, providing transport within the city and serving as a link to the wider metropolitan area. This extensive public transportation network means that no destination within the city will be more than 250-300m some form of public transport. Most private vehicles will be kept at the city's edge in a number of parking lots that will be linked by electric bus routes to other public transportation traversing the city.

In its search for an appropriate and sustainable transportation solution, Masdar City is piloting a Personal Rapid Transit [PRT] system of electric-powered, automated, single-cabin vehicles that offer the privacy, comfort and non-stop travel of a taxi service, and the reliability and sustainability of a public transport system. The initial pilot route runs on a 1,700m track linking Masdar Institute to its parking lot. However, this emerging technology will serve only Masdar Institute at this time, as it is not yet ready for implementation on a wider scale. As other new transport technologies emerge, they will be evaluated for use within the city.

Personal Rapid Transit vehicle

FIGURE 4.7

PRT pods showcased inside a Masdar City catalog, 2011.

have been investing in this form of automation, foregrounding cars as the next turning point in consumer electronics and seeking to reinvent the roads.[28]

An Expensive Toy

In April 2011, toward the end of my fieldwork at Masdar, Elif and Salim, both graduate students at Masdar Institute, gave me a guided tour of the PRT system. Elif had moved to Abu Dhabi in September 2009 to start her master's at Masdar Institute; she held an engineering degree from a well-regarded private university in Istanbul. She often shared her insights about Masdar with me (see introduction and chapter 2). Her family expected her to finish her degree and return to Turkey to join her father's small business—an expectation that she did not yet wish to fulfill. Soon after she arrived in Abu Dhabi, she befriended Salim, a Jordanian engineering student who had been living in the UAE for almost a decade. After his father died, Salim's mother had married an Emirati man and moved from Amman to Abu Dhabi with him. Although he did not hold Emirati citizenship, Salim knew the region well. Elif and Salim were among the first cohort of students to absorb and tackle the strange material conditions of Masdar City. They lived in the Masdar Institute building together with another one hundred students and spent most of their time on campus.

As we rode the pod car from the Masdar Institute building to the parking lot outside, Salim and Elif explained how the PRT system functioned—how the pods were charged by induction during the moments they awaited passengers; how they glided by on magnetic tracks that were regulated by a sensitive supervisory system above; that they relied on energy-efficient lights, featured high-end air-conditioning, offered a panoramic view, and also had cameras inside. While explaining these features, Salim sarcastically quipped that the air-conditioning was "pretty good for a sustainable city" and that the panoramic view was "just like the new Porsche"; he emphasized how the cameras were there "just in case people fooled around." In this way, every material part of the vehicle offered a perspective on the debates regarding Masdar City, addressing its sustainability, wealth, and luxury, as well as its disciplinary qualities. When they were through telling me how the pod cars worked, they began to talk about how and why their future remained uncertain.

In attending to the functions and problems of the PRT network, Salim and Elif found it necessary to break it into parts while also underlining the interactions between these multiple physical elements. For instance, they explained that the uneven concrete surface of the road increased friction, triggering problems for the suspension system. Because of the friction, the brakes and the brake pads wore through easily, making the PRT need more maintenance. The supervisory system was also too sensitive and was unable to interact with the pod cars in the most effective manner. For them, the PRT constituted a conglomerate of various material artifacts, interacting in different ways on every trip and giving rise to at times contradictory interpretations of the same mechanical system. So, in the way that Salim and Elif narrated the new infrastructure, the potential of the project became entrenched and compressed within particular material elements of the PRT—the suspension, the brake pads, the sensors, and so forth—highlighting every fragile part that was essential to the system.

Transport planners like Luca voiced frustration regarding how users and commentators seemed to perceive the PRT system as "the podcars" and not as a "system" made of various components. In Luca's perspective, the PRT consisted of "mobile (the pod cars), fixed (the infrastructure), and ethereal (the control system)" components, working together to advance a new form of transportation. In conceptualizing the PRT, Luca used the analogy of the mushroom: "Try to visualize the PRT system as a mushroom: the pod cars are the part that you see above ground, but as you know, there is a complex network underground that we do not see and cannot appreciate. We think that the mushroom as a creature is just the part that we can see. The PRT is like that." For Luca, it was important to frame the PRT as an open-ended assemblage that triggered the fruition of mushroom-like pod cars, providing productive enjoyment to their users. A materially imperceptible PRT infrastructure allowed the pod cars to communicate and move around.

Salim and Elif, in acknowledging that at times invisible and underappreciated parts ensured that the pod cars moved, saw them as indicative of a future of technical adjustments. Through their repeated motion, they represented the possibility of slightly modified modes of living that would allow humankind to spring over into a new era of prosperity, despite global concerns over climate change and energy scarcity. At the same time, the pod cars were confined, and could never reach their intended twenty-five miles per hour because of the short distance they covered.[29] They experienced unexpected friction due to the material condition of the road. If, in their movement, they allowed the emergence of a future where an exclusive group of technologically advanced humans once again took charge of earth, in their restrictedness they demonstrated the impossibility of this imaginary.

Salim and Elif were among those at Masdar who called the PRT an "expensive toy," rendering its functionality secondary. Especially when the pod cars malfunctioned, leading passengers to be stuck within the vehicles for up to twenty minutes, Masdar Institute students would begin to complain, vowing to take the shuttle bus next time. But the students confirmed that the pod cars were "fun"—an innovative mode of transport that gave the city a futuristic feel, even though it did not have the capacity to transport crowds. In other words, Salim and Elif were at times quick to laud the PRT system, but they also harbored doubts, which extended to the larger project of the eco-city. They suggested that the pod cars served as an appropriate metonym of Masdar City—the whole idea of the eco-city was lavish. The increasing obsession with technological innovation, they stressed, was not unique to Masdar, but rather defined the eco-city concept around the world. Transport planner Luca responded to the "expensive toy" label in an email, explaining to me how he does not see "any contradiction in [the PRT] being a transport system AND 'an expensive fun toy.' Many people drive 'expensive fun toys' to go from home to work, and many more wish they could. Why is that accepted and Masdar's PRT should not be?"

In these discussions, the notion of an expensive toy perhaps sounded dismissive of the pod cars. Yet this description simultaneously permitted the students to frame the project as an exciting occasion. The notion of the expensive toy therefore implied an astonished contemplation that helped the Masdar Institute students surpass the limitations of the present context, and reframed the PRT as something conceptually refreshing, open, and indeterminate.[30] At the same time, such astonishment disclosed the potential embedded in the material infrastructure of the PRT, revealing an impulse calling for ways of experiencing the world that were not quite there. In this case, the pod cars had the capacity to provide technical adjustments, as well as the capacity not to do so. While such emergent infrastructure seemed to define the project of building a renewable energy and clean technology sector in Abu Dhabi, they remained consistently ambivalent and out of reach.

In addition to calling for ways of experiencing the world that were not quite there, the technical adjustments proposed on site seemed to dismiss or exacerbate the race and class divides that characterize the UAE. As such, the so-called spaceship in the desert appeared to be an ark, attempting to mitigate planetary-scale problems by building barriers around an inner core and dressing up its exclusivity as a kind of universalism geared toward resolving climate change and energy scarcity. In the imagined future of adjustments, Abu Dhabi remained a liberal space for Western white businessmen and a space of exclusion for South Asian workers. During an interview, the PRT consultants for Masdar explained to me that the Abu Dhabi authorities enjoyed the pod cars specifically because they took the driver out of the picture. In a sense, they embraced the PRT because it would avoid low-wage immigrants' access to the city, even as workers. The workers who were present on the Masdar City site for various jobs did not take the PRT. Instead, they were shuttled between the Masdar Institute campus and the parking lots outside on buses, or they walked between these locations. Criticism regarding the segregated and walled-in nature of the Masdar project became public to an international readership when the architecture critic of the *New York Times* called the imagined city "a self-sufficient society, lifted on a pedestal and outside the reach of most of the world's citizens."[31]

In response to such comments, Masdar City executives planned the Market @ Masdar, an open house where the residents of Abu Dhabi were invited to experience the eco-city for the first time, advertised online and through newspapers. Framed as a family-focused street fair and organic market, Market @ Masdar took place on April 29, 2011, on the Masdar Institute campus, and promised to "offer Abu Dhabi residents a glimpse at life in one of the world's most sustainable, urban developments." In addition to the organic grocery store, sushi restaurant, coffee shop, and retail spaces located permanently on site, about thirty exhibitors would be displaying or selling their products.[32] Thousands visited that day, leaving their cars in the parking lot and insisting on riding the pod cars rather than the readily available shuttle buses. They lined up for twenty to thirty minutes, as if waiting for a roller coaster ride in an amusement park. Although there was no admission charge, blue-collar workers from Abu Dhabi or the other parts of the UAE were not present on campus due to various structural reasons. Blue-collar workers mostly lived in labor camps far away from the city, and their transportation options were limited. They did not own cars. Especially on weekends, such as the weekend when the Market @ Masdar was held, the labor camps became isolated sites, given the small number of buses serving these spaces. As opposed to the visitors, the blue-collar workers took time-consuming bus rides by necessity rather than choosing to wait a long time for novelty rides.

Sylvia, the operations manager for the PRT subcontractor 2getthere, perceived these long lines as a clear victory. She had previously worked with the London Underground and had experience in real estate development with Dubai World, an investment company that managed businesses for the government of Dubai. She seemed to understand large transport infrastructure and was familiar with professional life in the UAE. She "loved" the pod cars and advocated for their use for Masdar City. "About 4,000 people took the PRT that day," she reported when we chatted about the open

FIGURE 4.8 AND 4.9 · Visitors to Market Day waiting for the PRT, April 29, 2011. Photo by the author.

FIGURE 4.10 · The PRT station at Masdar Institute, 2010. Photo by the author.

house. "There were huge lines, and I was telling people standing in line that there is a bus they can take, but they refused to take the bus—they'd rather stand here and wait, they said they came here to take the PRT." According to her team, the crowds did not indicate a flaw, but rather demonstrated how much everyone appreciated the pod cars and proved how valuable they were for the eco-city. "Some people understand that as a failure, because there were long lines. The system is not designed for such heavy demand; you must understand, our target is the residents at the Institute, which is very small. . . . But others may have misunderstood," she clarified.

Perhaps Sylvia was right—it was an "experience" to ride the PRT and to enter the Masdar Institute building through the beautifully designed undercroft station, where a large screen played an occasional waterfall loop. Later, the loop was replaced with info-screens that provided details of climate change, renewable energy, and clean technology–related developments from around the world. A sculptural staircase greeted the PRT passengers, attempting to entice them not to use the elevator, but rather to walk upstairs to the Masdar Institute reception and laboratories. The aesthetic pleasure of the staircase was expected to be forceful enough to reorganize everyday habits. Some postdoctoral researchers and I often spoke about what a wonderful space this station would be for a party. We "enjoyed" the PRT pods, as well as their undercroft station.

Yet for others the long lines evidenced that the PRT was not an appropriate way of organizing a city's transport system. Among them was Brad, an Irish man in his early forties who had lived in the United Kingdom, worked extensively in the Arab world, and now managed relations between Masdar and Foster + Partners. Brad served as a perceptive and questioning voice throughout my research (see chapters 1 and 3). After the open house, Brad remarked to me over coffee, "On Market @ Masdar City, we witnessed the failure of the PRT. It is just not very practical. It does not work for a city. We saw that you cannot just pay and buy efficiency like that." There were many people attending Market @ Masdar, forming lengthy lines and proving the system was inefficient. Regardless of how much the crowds enjoyed taking the PRT, the system had been incapable of transporting these crowds from one point to another efficiently. Although the system still worked, moving visitors from the parking lot to the Masdar Institute campus, its inefficiency demonstrated to Brad that the system had been unable to perform the most essential function of a transport system—that is, to transport people in an optimal manner.

Brad labeled the PRT "the nervous system of this city," and explained that the whole city failed once it stopped working efficiently. As anthropologist Michael Taussig puts it in his book *The Nervous System* (1992), a nervous system could be characterized by its capacities of "control, hierarchy and intelligence," as well as an ever-present incompleteness and "constant need for a fix."[33] Using the analogy of the nervous system helped Brad explain how the city was paralyzed due to long PRT lines: the experimental transportation network had kept the visitors stuck at the parking lot, preventing them from accessing the building. Brad perceived the nervous system of Masdar to be diseased, so to speak. While for Sylvia the long waiting times showed how desirable, and thus successful, the PRT was as a technology, for Brad they represented the failure of a system that prided itself on user-friendliness and flexibility. Commenting on this disagreement, Luca defended Sylvia's perspective: "Indeed, look at other situations in which crowds gather: is the queue outside Paris' Louvre proof of the failure of the museum? Are queues at Victoria Tube station in London proof of the failure of the London metro? Is a queue outside a theater proof of the failure of the theater?" Such debates, coming to life through experiences such as Market @ Masdar, allowed the producers and users of the PRT to define their expectations of this emergent infrastructure. In this way, the debates were crucial, providing space for the visitors and residents of the city to describe how they understood this new technology.

In this context, the idea of "enjoying" the PRT—perhaps as opposed to "using" it—became significant to the ways in which Sylvia and Brad narrated the project. The observation that the visitors at the Market @ Masdar refused any other means of transport, preferring to line up for the pod cars, implied that they did not understand the PRT as a means of transport per se, but rather as an expensive toy. It was accurate that the system could not cope with such unprecedented demand, but still Sylvia interpreted the PRT to be a successful experiment, because newcomers to the site enjoyed it as a spectacular experience.

Like Elif and Salim, Sylvia also emphasized the multiple material fragments that made up the PRT infrastructure of Masdar City. First, the magnetic track on which the pod cars moved had to be smoother. 2getthere representatives had requested asphalt flooring to ensure this condition, but authorities at Masdar wished to use concrete from the recycled concrete plants on site. The contractor who poured the concrete layer had not fully met the strict specifications, leading to bumpy rides. Second, the supervisory system was very sensitive. "If a bird enters this space," Sylvia explained, "then the PRT stops because it thinks that it's going to hit the bird." In order for the system to function properly, there had to be no birds inside. 2getthere had attempted to preempt this issue and asked for high walls to surround the tracks, containing the vehicle inside a sealed tunnel, but this request was not realized. Third, Sylvia walked me to the PRT doors to show how the runners below were full of sand, arguing that the spaces where two systems contacted each other were the most difficult to manage. Despite the friction, the pod cars were on track—with the goal of transporting or entertaining passengers.[34] The potential of a technically adjusted future was embedded in the frictions of the materials that made up the PRT, producing a sense of flaw as well as a sense of awe at every step.

Yet one incredible story—of a burning pod—showed that the friction between various materials, as well as between aspirations and their practical achievements, was not always endurable in this indeterminate form. A few days before the inauguration ceremony of Masdar City, on November 23,

2010, an overcharged pod car had gone up in flames. "No one was allowed to ride the PRT for a few days," Salim said, "and then they began using only the semi-charged ones." He jokingly pointed at the hatchet that was safely positioned under one of the seats and told me that I should use it in case there was a problem again. The existing frictions between the various material artifacts had transformed into fire, consuming the whole project and triggering a total breakdown. Thus, in order to maintain its potential, the PRT had to be kept a fraction away from total breakdown.[35]

"Anyhow, when they stop building it, and finally give up on the clean technology cluster, Masdar City will probably transform into an amusement park, don't you think?" Salim wondered aloud. He was referring to spaces that were originally conceived of as futuristic communities but later abandoned to constitute objects of amusement, most famously Walt Disney's EPCOT Center (Experimental Prototype Community of Tomorrow), planned for 20,000 residents on a plot of land in Orlando, Florida, which became the site of the theme park Epcot after his death.[36] According to Salim, in a few decades people would come and visit the ruins of an eco-city, or what was meant to be an eco-city, where the ruins would signify not only decay but also traces of an idea once pursued ambitiously. In this imagined future, Masdar would become more of a spectacle, and its ruin would once again offer entertainment to its spectators, in addition to nostalgia for a past where the option of a renewable energy and clean technology future was still available.

Yet such a site provides entertainment markedly different from a ride in a pod car. While the automated transit infrastructure exemplified the work of promoting technical adjustments for a renewable energy economy, the ruins would denote a possible surrendering of that ideal, in a future where this perception functioned as a relic. The specter of ruination denotes how technical solutions are always so close to a complete breakdown, as opposed to indeterminate potential.

Canceling the PRT

Following two years of discussions on the implementation of the PRT at the city scale, the project proved to be more difficult than originally envisioned. In September 2010, rumor had it that the plans for the PRT had been dropped. To some consultants I spoke with, it had become clear in the summer of 2009, when a new executive took over the role of transport planner for Masdar City, that Masdar did not wish to pursue the PRT idea. In June 2011, Masdar presented a new transport plan for Masdar City at the Urban Transport and the Environment conference in Pisa, Italy, and officially eliminated the PRT. The PRT plan was dropped as part of the general financial scaling back of the Masdar project. "O, vehicle of the future, why have you eluded us?" one commentator wondered,[37] inquiring why innovation was so difficult within the transport sector.

The ecology blog *Green Prophet*, an ardent follower of issues related to Masdar City, reported in March 2011:

> Masdar gave us the perfect opportunity to take the next giant leap but we slipped and fell, our Fifth Element [the 1997 feature film] fantasies dashed in the process. Alas, the tiny self-navigating pods were simply too expensive. Or at least, the infrastructure necessary to lift them off the ground would have broken an already strained budget.[38]

The article highlighted that self-navigation had been central to this imaginary of the future, where machines with automation capacities would fully participate in the making of Masdar's urban environments. Due to the cancellation of the project, the possibility of a future informed by science fiction imagery appeared to be in flux. The lively debates around the PRT system did not change the decisions about the cancellation of the project at the city scale. Rather, they brought together different actors into the same conceptual domain, igniting further thoughts on the future of transport systems.

The engineers from Masdar and from its subcontractors, in searching for explanations regarding the cancellation of the project, very often sought to identify an "inherent flaw." They suggested that the main factor in scaling down the project had been the podium-undercroft logic, wherein the city would be raised about twenty feet above the ground to provide a basement space for the PRT tracks. While this plan had become a problem for several reasons, including routing constraints, it was argued that the most important barrier had been the project's costliness. The actual pod car and track technology had to be invented from scratch, and it had been difficult to predict costs and to streamline production.[39] Some wondered if there could have been another way of building the city without raising every new building to create an undercroft. Perhaps developers could have been given stringent guidelines regarding how to situate buildings, allowing space for the PRT tracks between the new facilities. On the other hand, the transportation planners working on the project recalled that this idea was not unique to Masdar City and had proved viable elsewhere. For instance, the La Defence area in Paris was built this way, with a vast pedestrianized platform covering a major highway. The Louvain-la-Neuve in Belgium was another good example—an entire pedestrianized town built on a vast platform of reinforced concrete, with vehicular road systems and parking lots below it.

In responding to the arguments about the project's costliness, Sylvia from 2getthere stated, "You know, the pod cars are all handmade, so they are costly, but if there was more demand, and if we started a factory, costs could have been brought down. Also, we really didn't need such expensive stations with large screens and everything. All we needed was a door, so in fact the costs could have been brought down drastically," thereby pointing to possible miscommunications or decision-making problems. In this way, she suggested that a lack of coordination among various actors involved in the project had caused the city-scale PRT infrastructure to be dropped.

While the various actors discussing the project's demise were unreliable in predicting the destiny of the pod cars, they helped frame a discussion about the topic.[40] Despite the emphasis on budget limitations, many engineers and commentators claimed that the PRT was "a false invention" that was inherently flawed, arguing that this would be a new addition to the history of failed personal transport projects.[41] They provided lists of reasons regarding how and why the PRT had actually been a bad idea from the start. They criticized the Masdar PRT infrastructure specifically for its inefficiency; in particular, the system's energy input was from lithium-powered batteries when it could have been generated through the guideway (comparable to how trams are powered). Their reliance on battery-based energy limited how frequently the pod cars could be used, as each pod car would require extra time to be charged at the docking station.[42] In contrast to Aramis, the PRT of Masdar City enjoyed a much easier technical environment (with abundant space between the pod cars, no need to retrofit existing infrastructures, and very little attention required for transitions between a variety of transport systems), but it suffered from novel impediments. Discussing the Masdar project along with the ULTra PRT system at Heathrow Airport on his PRT-focused blog, Ken Avidor, a Minnesotan with an interest in transportation technologies, came to the conclusion, too, that PRT is a false notion: "[These] are essentially automated, battery-powered golf carts—neither are *personal* (passengers sit awkwardly across from one another, knees almost touching), *rapid* (bikes are faster) or *transit* (totally lacking capacity)."[43]

In responding to these comments, Luca noted that the terms of the discussion demonstrated how producers and users of transport systems prioritize their privileges (space, speed, comfort) over energy conservation, while asking that engineers satisfy such desires in an emission-free manner. In an email, he explained how "the podcars could have been bigger (hence heavier = more energy) and faster (speed = more energy) but not as sustainable as these little, slow, awkward golf carts." He added, "a higher acceleration and speed would be pleasant to have, but it would also have required much more energy: the relationship between energy and speed is a square curve: if you double the speed the energy required becomes quadruple." Essentially, users were calling for technical adjustments that would preserve space, speed, and comfort *and* reduce energy use and carbon emissions. They demanded status quo utopias, which did not interrogate what it meant for humans to demand space, speed, and comfort in the first place.

In the scholarly literature on public transportation systems as well, PRT has often been dismissed.[44] Vukan Vuchic, a professor of systems engineering and a former consultant for the U.S. Department of Transportation who has published widely about urban transit, for instance, argues that "the basic concept of PRT was inherently unsound," and that "the PRT mode is impracticable under all conditions." He explains that the main objective of the PRT concept—bringing together the advantages of private cars and public transportation—would not be achieved without simultaneously experiencing the major disadvantages of the highway system in urban areas, such as "high costs, large space requirements, low capacity, and poor reliability." He suggests that PRT is an unrealistic solution rather than a "future transit mode," reminding his readers that "although it is true that PRT resembles the positive characteristics of the private auto more than any other transit mode, it is also true that due to this similarity PRT has the severe limitations of auto use in urban areas: low capacity, very high cost and energy consumption per space-km, and extremely large

FIGURE 4.11 · Masdar City model, March 2014. Photo by the author.

space requirements for stations, guideway interchanges, and vehicle storage areas." For him, the imaginary of PRT keeps reemerging not because of rational calculations, but rather due to an emotional attachment to an image of cabins gliding through the air over city streets.[45]

Since the 1939 World's Fair, the imaginary of automated transport has continued to evolve, resulting in the PRT experiment at Masdar City, among many other experiments. The scaling back of the Masdar City project did not foreclose discussions regarding automated transit technology; rather, it regenerated a decades-old debate on pod cars and their potential applicability in the transport sector in upcoming years. The cancellation of the project brought various actors into further discussions around the PRT. Masdar would start experimenting with electric cars, I often heard, and in early 2011, I started seeing small test cars by Mitsubishi driving around the building.

"It's difficult to foresee what will happen next with Masdar," Sylvia told me, as we chatted inside the PRT station by the parking lot, months after the cancellation of the project had been made public. She pointed to a large model provided by Foster + Partners to represent the first phase of Masdar City. "As you can see in this model, the PRT moves throughout the buildings, but those plans have been discontinued, though here it is still being advertised as if the city included the PRT." According to Sylvia, this partially proved how the PRT attracted more people to the city, making it a more desirable destination than it was. It also showed how the imaginaries of a future Masdar still had some footing inside the city. Although they had been dropped, the plans for PRT still retained their significance in Masdar City's image as a "futuristic sci-fi eco-city."

The half-finished PRT infrastructure effectively situated automated transit in the interstices between hopefulness and anxiety. On the one hand, the pod cars helped their users escape to a science fiction future, while on the other, they maintained the fantasy as impossible and inaccessible. As they moved back and forth on magnetic tracks, paused to be charged in their docks, and were photographed by the visitors to the site, the pod cars took on various meanings. In the years that followed its launch, students, researchers, and professionals at Masdar City tried to assess the PRT for its success or failure, rendering the pod cars not only materially but also conceptually indeterminate. Gliding back and forth on magnetic tracks, Masdar's pod cars produced, enacted, and simultaneously annulled the possibility of a future with technical adjustments.

The next chapter will go underground, to explore how innovations in policy making related to carbon capture and storage also provided an arena through which the Abu Dhabi government could prove its commitment to the development of renewable energy and clean technology infrastructures.

III GOVERNANCE

Subsurface Workings 5

Preparations

On December 4, 2010, the United Nations Climate Change Conference (COP 16) in Cancún agreed upon the inclusion of carbon dioxide capture and storage in geological formations (CCS) as an eligible option for mitigating greenhouse gas emissions. This meant that the United Nations Framework Convention for Climate Change (UNFCCC) would include CCS in its Clean Development Mechanism (CDM) program[1] and grant carbon credits[2] for the carbon dioxide captured from industrial compounds and stored in underground spaces such as deep saline aquifers, unminable coal seams, or declining oil and gas fields, and specifically in so-called developing countries, officially designated as Non-Annex I, including the United Arab Emirates.[3] CCS is a controversial technology because there is the possibility that concentrated amounts of carbon dioxide will leak or seep from storage sites, and neither short- nor long-term liability protocols related to such incidents are yet in place. At the same time, by injecting carbon dioxide into fields and forcing oil out, oil producers may extend the life span of their oilfields. In further negotiating the means through which CCS would be adopted as a mitigation strategy, interested parties were invited to submit modalities and procedural guidelines to the UNFCCC that would address and resolve issues such as safety and liability protocols.[4]

Upon the declaration of the Cancún CCS decision, some policy consultants at Abu Dhabi's Masdar Carbon admitted that it was a surprise. This could be a turning point for an oil-exporting country like the UAE, they excitedly argued, as it would enable future options for low-carbon oil production and usage, and at the same time it would provide opportunity to earn carbon credits. Besides, it was a perfect occasion for the UAE to demonstrate and publicize its commitment to climate change mitigation goals, improving its image in the international policy sphere; the eventual inclusion of CCS as a climate change mitigation strategy could lead to a major diplomatic success, contributing to the UAE's transformation into a real leader in the international world. Therefore, when it was announced that interested parties could submit modalities and procedural guidelines regarding how carbon capture and storage projects should be initiated, maintained, and monitored, the consultants at Masdar immediately began working on a document, cooperating with other stakeholders: Abu Dhabi National Oil Company (ADNOC), Abu Dhabi Company for Onshore Oil Operations (ADCO), and the Directorate of Energy and Climate Change (DECC) at the Ministry of Foreign Affairs. The document had to be submitted to the UNFCCC by February 21, 2011.[5]

This chapter tracks the production of this CCS policy submission document, drawing on fieldwork with environmental consultants at Masdar as well as with representatives from ADNOC, ADCO, DECC, and the UNFCCC. Similar to many others at Masdar, these environmental consultants had come to the UAE from all over the world for professional purposes and assisted in the production of national and international climate change policy, serving as key players in the climate debate. Beyond the UNFCCC, they pursued opportunities at intergovernmental institutions such as the International Renewable Energy Agency (IRENA) and at consulting companies, namely the "Big Four": Ernst and Young, Deloitte, KPMG, and PwC. They attended climate change summits, followed the debates related to various aspects of climate change governance, drafted reports for internal use and for the development of low-carbon technologies in other countries, and contributed to the policy production and implementation landscape at the intergovernmental level. Internationally experienced, they often changed jobs or moved between organizations, leaving the UAE for positions elsewhere within several years of their arrival. By drawing on how these consultants discussed the CCS document and investigating the language and perspectives they adopted, this chapter examines the methodologies through which the underground became reconstituted as a space to bury carbon dioxide. While the producers of Masdar City reimagined the desert as an undiscovered resource from which novel renewable energy and clean technology projects would emerge (chapter 1), the consultants at Masdar Carbon reconceived the underground as a frontier that would enable them to mitigate climate change, extend the life span of oilfields, and participate in international diplomacy. By tracing the making of CCS policy inside and outside Abu Dhabi, this chapter explores the moral logics of CCS technologies, which obscure how the energy-intensive models of life have triggered climate change in the first place.[6]

By following the production of the UAE's modalities and procedural guidelines submission, I demonstrate that Masdar's investment in new technological developments was ridden with risks and uncertainties. The environmental consultants and engineers in Abu Dhabi created "degrees of acceptable risk" as they attempted to extend the status quo to an uncertain space and time through new technology. In negotiating the different ways of imagining earth—either as a temporary sociopolitical space or as a solid geology—they strove to come up with a shared sensibility regarding potential future risks and uncertainties. Formulated in this chapter as two main discussions, on "particular and global levels" and the "unknowability of the subsurface," the tensions between various actors illustrate the significance of environmental consultants as mediators of risk management and also point to how "degrees of acceptable risk" became crucial in producing climate change mitigation methods that might align with the fossil fuel economy.

Finally, in tracing the production of this document, I examine the indirect ways in which oil companies participated in the making of climate change policy. Referring to specific cases (i.e., the In Salah CCS project), this chapter underlines that each CCS project has its particularities, however sidelined by the desire to create globally applicable policy mechanisms.

Risks and Uncertainties

CCS operates by extracting carbon dioxide from localized sources of pollution, such as power plants; carrying it in solid, liquid, or gas form to storage sites; and injecting it into the subsurface. Issues such as the selection

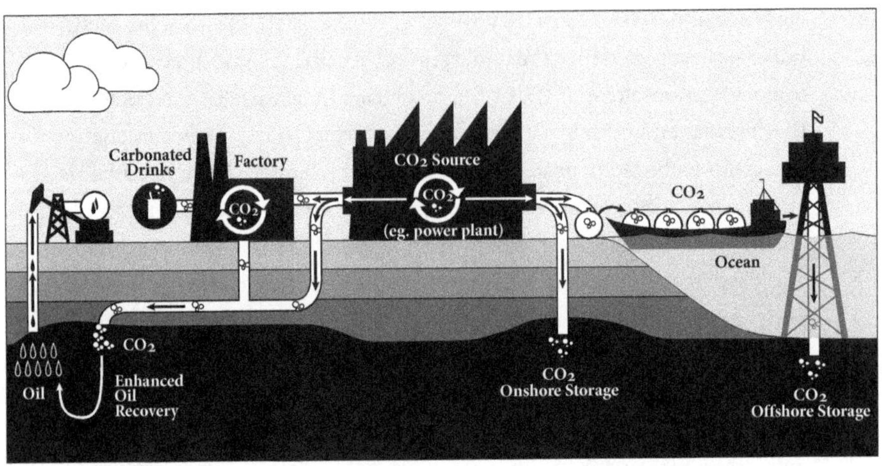

FIGURE 5.1 · An illustration of carbon capture and storage.

of storage sites, monitoring plans for the leakage and seepage of carbon dioxide, and the transboundary effects of gas injection have to be actively addressed in planning for CCS projects.

"We are working at least three kilometers underground!" Marwan, an Algerian consultant at Masdar Carbon, exclaimed, attempting to showcase the various risks and uncertainties of CCS during an interview in early 2011. "If you don't have full understanding of what's underground, you cannot predict all the risks, and these risks will create problems in the future." Marwan and I had met in the fall of 2010 while participating in meetings on the submission document, and we saw each other often in the Masdar Carbon office in the years 2010 and 2011. He had studied chemical engineering as an undergraduate and later received a master's degree in environmental science in France. After working with a large state-owned oil and gas company in North Africa for fifteen years, he had accepted a position as project manager at Masdar and moved to Abu Dhabi. He was focusing on conducting technical assessments and feasibility studies regarding domestic and international climate change policy proposals; in some ways, this was an extension of his previous work in producing environmental regulations for oil fields. He argued that his experiences with the oil industry gave him a rigorous perspective with regard to environmental challenges.

When I asked him how he would define the consultants' role in the implementation of CCS as a climate change mitigation strategy, Marwan continued: "The whole exercise is a risk assessment for future risks. We need to define the mitigation action and to reduce the risk. But the risk can be managed. All we have to do is to define who will be in charge of the risk, and mitigating the risk, and taking care of the accidents." After referring to the Fukushima disaster in Japan, where, following a major earthquake on March 11, 2011, a tsunami disabled the power supply and cooling of three Fukushima Daiichi nuclear reactors, causing a major crisis that at the time of our conversation had shaken the energy industry considerably, he underscored: "There is always error. We just need to be prepared." According to Marwan, the designers and operators of Fukushima nuclear power plant imagined that they knew everything about the plant, but they could not guess that a tsunami would hit and destroy its cooling facilities. What resulted was the second worst nuclear power plant accident in the world, ranked after the 1986 Chernobyl nuclear disaster. "They had models for everything," he reiterated, "but in reality things are different." He framed the production of the modalities and procedures guideline submission as a process of manufacturing a set of directives to be used before and after an inevitable accident or disaster befalls a CCS project. Marwan's position was that through a surgical mapping and management of the risks and uncertainties, interested parties could implement a new mitigation technique at a planetary scale while regulating its possible harmful consequences.

Marwan's words reflected French theorist Paul Virilio's famous argument about accidents from his book *The Original Accident* (2007): "To invent the sailing ship or steamer is to invent the shipwreck. To invent the train is to invent the rail accident of derailment. To invent the family automobile is to produce the pile-up on the highway. To get what is heavier than air to take off in the form of an airplane or dirigible is to invent the crash, the air disaster. As for the space shuttle, Challenger, its blowing up in flight in the same year that the tragedy of Chernobyl occurred is the original accident of a new motor, the equivalent of the first shipwreck of the very first ship." Marwan agreed that accidents were inevitable. Still, he advocated that a strategy of mapping and managing of risks and uncertainties would help expand the underground for reengineering.

The multiple risks and uncertainties regarding CCS technology and policy, often referred to as merely technical problems that awaited resolving, may be considered metonymical expressions of a much larger project that was at play during the preparation of the modalities and procedures submission. In Abu Dhabi, environmental consultants, engineers, and scientists continuously tinkered with a possible redefinition of climate change as a commercially viable business. After all, they were responsible for facilitating business models to compete in the global fossil fuel economy in ways that might contribute to resolving social and environmental challenges. According to many of them, climate change had to be redefined in commercial terms to constitute a plausible topic of interest.

In producing a commercially viable climate change mitigation tool for the fossil fuel economy, the participants also disclosed their personal rifts and tried to make sense of potential contradictions and inconsistencies. "You must know first thing that any project should make money," urged Anand, an Indian environmental consultant at Masdar Carbon who was also involved in drafting the submission document, during an interview in his office. "No one will do something eco-friendly and have loss. Profits may be a little lesser but loss cannot be tolerated." Anand held degrees in mechanical engineering and energy management, and had over twenty years of experience in climate change and sustainability services, having consulted for both private companies and governments. For most of his career, he had worked with one of the Big Four companies in India. During his time at Masdar, he focused on the development of renewable energy and climate change policy for the UAE, representing the country at UNFCCC negotiations, and strategized on the implementation of low-carbon technologies. In remarking that "profits may be a little lesser but loss cannot be tolerated," he insisted on the impossibility of discussing environmental problems independently of commercial valuation.

During a long taxi ride from Abu Dhabi proper to Masdar, I asked Ben, a senior consultant to the DECC at the Ministry of Foreign Affairs, about the possible motivations for working within the emergent green economy. He responded, "The environment is after all a sexy part of the economy." Ben was working on the development and implementation of climate change strategy for the UAE by building policy, training diplomats, and attending negotiations. He was confident that green businesses were going to expand. He had been involved with the renewable energy and clean technology sectors for almost twenty years, but unlike Marwan and Anand, he focused his work on think tanks and nongovernmental organizations (NGOs). Before moving to Abu Dhabi, he had held a prestigious executive position in one of these institutions and regularly traveled to climate change conferences. Reflecting on his experience working in multiple countries, Ben added that "not many of the environmental consultants would self-identify as environmentalists." Still, the development of the modalities and procedures submission served, for many of those involved, as an exercise in bringing together moral domains that may not be immediately compatible with each other—and indeed may be incompatible.

This dilemma was exacerbated because of the UAE's potential as an oil-producing country. When implementing CCS technologies, oil-producing countries are able to use maturing oilfields as storage facilities for the carbon dioxide that they obtain from industrial compounds, as these oilfields may be considered naturally sealed reserves. However, injecting gas into oil reservoirs leads to increased oil production as well, a process commonly known in the industry as enhanced oil recovery (EOR). By injecting carbon dioxide into aging fields and pumping oil out, oil producers may increase the lifetime of the fields by up to 30 percent, while freeing up the natural gas more commonly used in such processes. The inclusion of CCS as an eligible technology for decreasing carbon emissions then becomes a perverse incentive for further oil production; the entities that earn the most carbon credits from CCS activities in turn become oil-producing countries.

For many oil producers, including the UAE, it was important that CCS-EOR become recognized as a climate change mitigation strategy, especially because of its immediate applicability and eventual financial gains.[7] During a meeting with representatives from the DECC, some consultants suggested that the UAE's oilfields are still young and would only require EOR in thirty to forty years' time. Ben, in advance of his participation in the next UN climate summit, asked how far he should push for EOR. "Yes, EOR is significant for us," one consultant responded, "but we would like CCS to be approved as a climate change mitigation technique even if EOR is not approved." Another consultant continued, "We need policy to pay for the environmental premium that we invest in this new technology; we are not looking for a cash cow here." They discussed a potential workshop, wherein experts from the Association of Small Island States (AOSIS)—at the time a major opponent to CCS as a climate change mitigation strategy—would be invited to the UAE, or maybe to Norway, to be shown how CCS functions on the ground. "Bring them, and convince them here," one DECC representative ordered. In the meantime, Masdar Carbon was publicizing plans to capture 800,000 tons of carbon dioxide from Emirates Steel's plant in the Mussafah industrial zone, and to transport it through a 311-mile pipeline to Abu Dhabi's oilfields by the end of 2012. During a lunch break, Ravi, who had been working as a consultant for almost seven years, confessed to me, "Personally, I am against CCS-EOR. But as a consultant, I will do everything to make it approved."

Emergent technological projects open up new moral conundrums for the individuals who research, develop, or implement them.[8] Ravi attempted to resolve his moral dilemma by constructing multiple, at times divergent, perspectives, thereby preventing his personal goals or values from contradicting his professional commitments. An Indian engineer in his early thirties, he had held energy management and consulting positions in India and the UAE, and would soon be moving to Europe for another opportunity. He did not think that EOR projects should receive carbon credits or any further encouragement from policy-making institutions, as they already generated additional amounts of fossil fuels to profit from. But in the end, as he saw it, climate change policy was too extensive an issue for him to effectively influence—his presence or absence in the debates would not change the outcome; they could easily find someone else to do his job. The questions of scale overwhelmed Ravi, making him feel small and unimportant. The scale of the problem also gave him a particular freedom, so that he could act without worrying too much about his own beliefs or actions, submitting to a larger network fully capable of acting in his absence. "Climate change is a business opportunity," he concluded. "We should try to come to terms with that."

Subsurface Is (Not) a Black Box

Increased oil production, and therefore consumption, is not the only reason CCS activities are considered controversial as climate change mitigation strategies. Parties critical of CCS projects point out that besides issues of site feasibility, high operational costs, future safety, and unresolved legal liability that make CCS projects challenging to initiate, implement, and operate, CCS may incur a crowding-out effect, leading investment away from other climate change mitigation strategies, such as renewable energy or energy efficiency projects.

In considering such existing risks and uncertainties, policy consultants at Masdar Carbon would pose a wide range of questions to one another. "What if we pump carbon dioxide into the ground here and it comes out of Iran?" one of them asked during a preparatory in-house meeting, emphasizing the urgency of international legal protocols for resolving liability issues. "What if there is seismic activity due to CCS? Who will be responsible for it in 10,000 years' time? Who will be responsible for it if nation-states disappear?" another consultant brought up, pointing to the deep futurity of current geological engineering projects. They discussed how models for storing nuclear waste could help in planning for carbon dioxide storage. They also spoke about producing new insurance mechanisms to involve new safety funds. Consistently, the indeterminate spatial and temporal boundaries of CCS made it challenging for consultants to conceptualize and attend to the safety and liability issues associated with upcoming projects, prompting them to mobilize multiple temporal and spatial scales at once.

In studying the negotiations for an international legal instrument at a global United Nations conference, legal anthropologist Annelise Riles has concluded, "The 20th-century problem of international institutions has been one of how to grasp [the global, national, and regional] levels, at one and the same time, how to bring them into a single encompassing view."[9] The "levels" problem that Riles identifies did not emerge as a question for the policy consultants at Masdar initially, either during preparatory in-house meetings or in meetings with the Ministry of Foreign Affairs. As time passed, however, the intrinsic characteristics of CCS technologies introduced shifting levels into their debates. The consultants at Masdar addressed questions not only about nation-states, but also about their potential disappearance. They highlighted the arbitrariness of borders, in addition to their transitory nature. They showed that the present, as manageable as it may seem, was not a strong enough temporal unit to work with. In this sense, the document preparation process disclosed and buttressed the precariousness of the categories that international institutions simultaneously relied upon and reproduced, consistently demanding an imagination of alternative futures.

And yet these alternative future scenarios had to be "translated" into the document as it was being composed—formulized according to the thinking that the consultants could currently afford. The consultants had spoken about the possible disappearance of nation-states during their discussions, but when they put down their liability scheme on paper, it did not directly address the possibility of a world without nation-states. Instead, the submission document explained that project proponents would remain liable during the short lifetime of the CCS project, but since the lifetime of underground carbon dioxide was much longer than the lifetime of a CCS project, project proponents would later transfer the liability "to an authorized body designated by the host country after the end of their short term liability period."[10] The financial provision, which the project proponent would provide, had to cover this long-term liability period, and it had to "be based on a long term probabilistic risk assessment, to be approved by the local authorities as per agreed international rules."[11] In short, the submission document pushed the consultants to think about wide temporal and spatial scales and simultaneously locked them within the boundaries of the present.

In another instance, the consultants focused specifically on transboundary projects and engaged in brainstorming about potential liability schemes, mostly by thinking through bilateral agreement methodologies. They wondered how the situation could be managed if several storage projects were conducted in the same reservoir, or if the reservoir stretched beyond more than one area of jurisdiction. "It may make sense to initially limit to single projects," they suggested, meaning that a storage site would have to be entirely located within the territory of a single nation-state. Later, they spelled out the various impossibilities of their protocol. Someone incisively asked, "How do you *know* whether a project will have transboundary impact?" Finally, when putting their thoughts on paper, the consultants simply concluded, "We should have a requirement for upfront liability agreements."

In contrast, the reservoir engineers, geologists, and geophysicists who participated in mid-stage meetings proposed solutions for these problems right away. A particularly telling exchange occurred at a meeting in early February 2011 between Anand, who had been a significant voice at all the early-stage meetings, and Shahab, an Iranian executive at Abu Dhabi Company for Onshore Oil (ADCO), who began to participate in the drafting process only after the initial theoretical parameters had been outlined by the consultants during in-house discussions at Masdar Carbon. "I don't like documents which are only buzzwords, that don't have any meat," declared Shahab upon reading the submission draft. Shahab had earned a PhD in oil recovery and reservoir management from a U.S. university in the mid-1980s, and occasionally taught classes and advised theses on these topics. "We should give more details about the local setting, which we know very well; only then can we produce satisfactory risk matrices," he continued. But Anand, speaking on behalf of Masdar Carbon's team of consultants, quickly rejoined that they were striving for "a floating language" rather than "a fixed one." The floating language that he referred to would be elastic enough to contain global histories and geographies while retaining its meaning at a much smaller scale. Its vagueness would be its strength.

Another policy consultant tried to explain that the document had to be generic, and applicable to all countries that are part of the Kyoto Protocol, an international environmental treaty that set carbon emissions limits for all its signatories and that went into force in 2005. But Shahab protested, "but then how are we going to account for the differences between carbonate oil wells in the UAE and sandstone oil wells in Europe?[12] How will we account for the difference? Where is there anything that shows this will be stringent or robust?" Shahab insisted that the submission include more details. In the meantime, Anand encouraged him to study the issues from a more macro perspective, and grew exhausted. "This is all about negotiation—what is our approach, what are our tactics? We need to state what we want without being apologetic. Descriptive words will make a reasonable submission. Make references to all tools, but make no commitments," he summarized. "Think that you are sitting in the UN and developing guidelines for the globe." While the consultants took the shifts between the local, the global, and the regional for granted, it proved very difficult for them to communicate these necessary "levels" to their ADCO and ADNOC counterparts. "High-level phrases, and not details—that's what you want?" Shahab confirmed in a rather resentful way before he left.

Extending his arguments about the inevitability of errors and accidents, Marwan, who had participated in the preparatory meetings, noted to me in May 2011, "The subsurface is a black box." He then drew a graph in my notebook to communicate the impossibility of representing or knowing

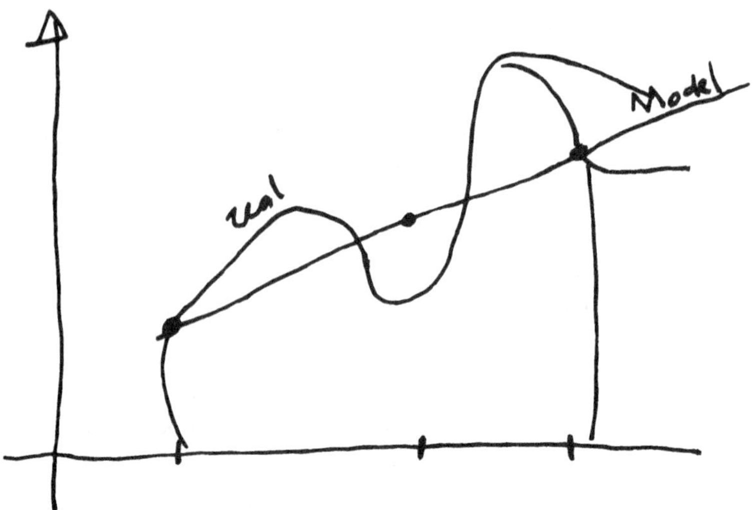

FIGURE 5.2 · Real vs. model graph drawn by Marwan, May 2011.

earth's geology. The graph, with unidentified *x*- and *y*-axes, indicated that in attempting to represent the underground, the steady "model" and the wobbly "real" intersected only briefly, in this case at four specific points. He explained that the representation efforts that took the shape of models were loaded with assumptions, and therefore unable to accurately pinpoint the real.

A belief in this ultimate unrepresentability or unknowability, conveniently contained within this drawing, had made it easier for the consultants to switch levels and contexts between, let's say, carbonate wells in the UAE and sandstone wells in Europe, without fully disputing the physical qualities that they manipulated. As such, for the consultants, uncertainty and risk remained constitutive of policy-making efforts on CCS. They suggested that they needed to act like attorneys and defend the submission as if it were a legal case.

As political scientist Timothy Luke states, moral dilemmas and obligations are ascribed clearly demarcated niches within technical, managerial, and organizational sets of problems and solutions—a mode of management that defines and reflects how environmental challenges should be handled in the present.[13] In his examination of environmental politics in Hong Kong, anthropologist Timothy Choy also reports how "An environmental

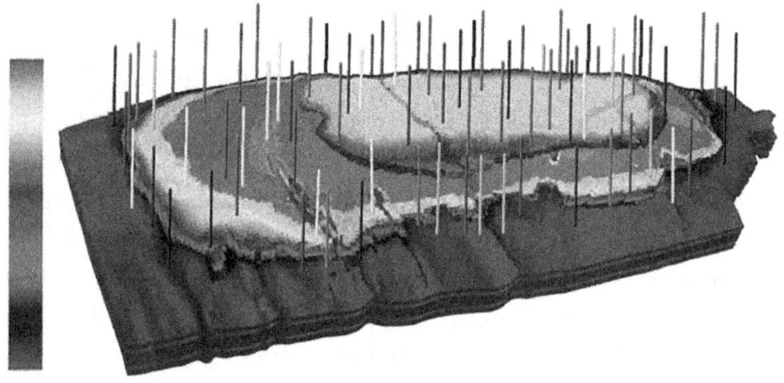

FIGURE 5.3 · Subsurface simulation model, 2011.

consultant based in Hong Kong drew a provocative analogy to describe his role: We're just like lawyers, only with science. A client hires you, and you argue their case. But we use science rather than the law."[14] At Masdar, the legal metaphor that the consultants used allowed them to legitimately distance themselves from this task and enabled them to feel less responsible for any potential implication their claims or decisions might have. The unknowable variables raised in their brainstorming sessions had mostly been left out of the submission document. In defending the document as if it was a legal case, the consultants knew and accepted that it included many unanswerable questions, but still they attempted to produce "degrees of acceptable risk" regarding future CCS projects. The strategies of risk management constituted their main tools for manufacturing such effect.

After the document draft was completed and submitted to the UNFCCC in late February 2011, I visited Shahab and his team at the headquarters of ADCO, hoping to learn more about how they conceptualized the mechanics of the underground. A simulation expert, who worked with Shahab, invited me to his desk to show his work on dynamic models: "It is not only oil that comes out of the reservoirs," he said. "We are also digging for information about the subsurface." He was seated across from a large computer monitor where he manipulated the data that had been collected since 1973, when the first large-scale drilling operations started in Abu Dhabi. He switched from one year to another, changed reservoir pressures, zoomed deeper—seven kilometers below ground. Finally, when he was convinced of the aesthetics of the resulting image—colored in bright pinks and greens—he pressed print and handed me the sheet. Someone else in the office later commented, "The subsurface is *not* a black box."

Embellished with injectors and extractors that resembled spikes, this colorful model was an in-depth representation of pressure levels in the underground at a certain moment. Such a space-and-time-specific model is significant for pursuing geophysical studies, as Geoffrey Bowker notes in elaborating the practices of industrial geophysics during Schlumberger's initial years—before Schlumberger became the world's largest oilfield services company, operating in eighty-five countries. He states, "There was never a perfect fit between figure and ground, and 'general' results were highly particular, rooted to a single site."[15] In this way, he claims that geophysics is similar to medicine: it is a science of the particular, deriving its data and treatment techniques from individual cases. This perception of geophysics may make it somewhat easier to understand the problems that Marwan or Anand suffered from in their relationship with the scientists and engineers at ADNOC and ADCO. While the scientists and engineers believed they would be more successful in attending to individual cases, and pushed the consultants to include case-specific data in the submission document, the consultants refused such contributions, dictating a global thinking. But the geophysical research methodologies did not allow for the floating language that the consultants demanded, thus triggering an inevitable disagreement between the two parties. As such, geophysics unveiled how "the subsurface is *not* a black box" for particular instances, but when it tried to produce more generalizable models, it did fail, reflecting what Marwan called the "real" in only a few instances. The discussion between Anand and Shahab had in fact exposed a pertinent disciplinary characteristic, which possibly made it challenging for the scientists to switch "levels." Accordingly, the discussions regarding the "levels" and "the subsurface as a black box" called attention to the difficulties of the transition from the particular to the general and vice versa, and in different manners. The two knowledges utilized different means of abstraction in linking the particular to global levels.

The reservoir engineers and geologists at ADCO claimed an ever-improving knowledge of the subsurface and evidenced multiple research techniques. Static and dynamic models, in addition to seismic and sonar testing, were crucial in reproducing the underground. They did not have any predictive models at hand, but by relying on a combination of computer modeling and "real-world" monitoring, they would excel at CCS technology. "But it is all about the imagination at the end," Aref, an Emirati reservoir engineer at ADNOC, reflected. He explained that his company organized field trips to Jebel Hafeet, the UAE's most well known mountain—4,098 feet tall at its peak—in order to expose the earth's geology to students and junior engineers. "We explain that there are infinite layers, like the layers you see on the mountain, inside the earth," he continued. The students and junior engineers would observe the mountain and extrapolate.

The imaginative work that the engineers attempted, however, was rather different from the brainstorming sessions at Masdar. Aref stated that such a geological field trip could at times be unnecessary. To understand an oilfield, a student could simply observe a child sipping a drink by using a straw. While every oilfield had particular qualities, what mattered most was to understand simple mechanics that could be applied in multiple contexts. The engineers at ADNOC and ADCO took this infrastructure for granted, in a way that the consultants at Masdar could not. Both parties sought applicability and transferability of conditions. But while the consultants addressed a possible transformation of sociopolitical contexts, albeit temporarily, the engineers and scientists relied on the seeming stability of the earth's crust and its associated mechanics.

Having occupied various positions in the petroleum industry for more than a decade, Aref had worked numerous times with optimum field development plans, which are designed using subsurface static and dynamic models. After receiving his undergraduate degree in mechanical engineering in the UAE, he completed a master's in France, and specialized in well performance, reservoir simulation, and reservoir monitoring at other oil companies. A week after our meeting, in an email exchange, he suggested that these tools were still quite limited, but that they were progressing very fast. "If we focus on the task of collecting all relevant data and building the right tools to model the global climate phenomena, we will be able to play a few global weather forecast scenarios assuming different levels of human activity. Only then, should we be able to seriously think about deliberate manipulation of planetary environment," he concluded. Perhaps the engineers did not believe that the planet was ready for policy making regarding geological engineering projects such as CCS. An executive from ADCO asked, "How could you generate policy without proof of concepts? We may be ignoring the key risks."

The trouble, then, must have been about differing conceptions of risk and uncertainty. Many consultants believed that they had to complete the submission in a way that matched or even exceeded global expectations, regardless of what might lie ahead in terms of CCS or EOR research. On the other hand, the reservoir engineers and geologists attempted to localize the risks and uncertainties, and to produce as much quantitative feedback as they could, which would not be directly useful for other contexts. A week before February 21, 2011, when the consultants were to finally deliver the thirty-six-page proposal to the UAE leadership in order to request final approval, the document had mostly been cleansed of numbers and graphs that described the local context. And yet it included sample uncertainty matrices (see figures 5.4 and 5.5) that had been used for pilot projects in the UAE.

The uncertainty matrices had been provided as clear evidence for the manageability of CCS projects. The introductory text suggested: "Uncertainty can be analyzed and quantified, and if managed properly, reservoir development and risk mitigation can be improved as a result. Consequently, reservoir management, CO_2 injection, process physics, chemistry and ultimately modeling is essential to developing a risk assessment matrix correlated with a mitigation plan." But such manageability would only come at a cost: "Significant capital expenditure and manpower are required to conduct these highly technical and state-of-the-art studies to address uncertainties as described below (conducted by Abu Dhabi National Oil Company)." The adequacy of capital expenditure and manpower would be evaluated based on the particularities of every CCS project, recognizing that these factors could change in relation to every specific application of this technology. The uncertainty matrices served as crisp indicators of a certainty that remained out of reach.

How does one understand the relationship between the different ways of imagining earth—either as a temporary sociopolitical space, or as a solid geology—and the different ways of perceiving risk and uncertainty?

FIGURE 5.4 · (opposite) Uncertainty matrix from the UAE's carbon capture and storage modalities and procedures guidelines submission, February 2011.

Categories	Subcategories	Elements	Rumailta Zone B		Al Dabb'iya Zone B		Al Dabb'iya TZ B		Bab Far North	
			Complexity	Uncertainty	Complexity	Uncertainty	Complexity	Uncertainty	Complexity	Uncertainty
Subsurface	Reservoir Properties	Horizontal Permeability Heterogeneity	4	4	4	4	3	3	4	4
		Vertical Permeability Heterogeneity	4	5	4	4	4	4	3	4
		Stylolite Presence and Development	4	2	3	3	3	3	2	2
		Reservoir Pay Thickness	4	4	4	4	4	4	4	4
		Reservoir Quality (RRT)	4	3	3	4	3	4	2	2
	Reservoir Structure and Geology	Structural Compartmentalization	4	4	4	3	3	3	5	5
		Faulting and Natural Fractures	5	4	4	3	3	3	4	4
		Reservoir Dip	5	5	5	4	4	4	4	4
	Reservoir Rock and Fluid Properties	Oil Properties	3	3	3	4	2	4	5	5
		EOR Injected Gas/Oil PVT	4	3	4	3	4	3	5	4
		EOR Injected Gas/Oil EOS	4	2	3	3	3	3	5	4
		EOR Injected Gas/Oil MMP	5	4	4	4	4	4	5	4
		Waxes/Asphaltene Oil & with Inj Gas	4	4	3	4	3	4	4	3
		Mechanical Property & Mineralogy	4	4	3	3	3	3	2	2
		Routine and Special Core Analysis	4	4	4	4	3	3	4	4
		Gas Misc/Imm Sec. & Ter Corefloods	4	4	4	4	3	3	4	4
Surface	Reservoir Development	Current Development Stage	4	4	3	3	3	3	4	2
		Current Development Mechanism	4	4	3	3	3	3	N/A	N/A
		EOR Gas (e.g., CO_2) Source and Supply	N/A	N/A	3	3	3	3	5	4
		Subsurface Infrastructure	4	4	4	4	3	3	N/A	N/A
	Drilling, Facilities and HSE	HSSE	4	4	3	4	3	3	1	4
		Injection/Production facilities	5	3	3	4	3	4	5	5
		Gas Separation facilities	5	3	3	4	3	4	5	5
		Facilities CO2/H2S Handling Capability	5	3	5	4	4	4	5	5
		Facilities CO2/H2S Injection Capability	5	3	5	3	4	4	5	5
		CO_2/H_2S Breakthrough and Cycling	5	2	5	2	4	4	5	5
		Integrity Management (Corrosion)	5	3	5	3	4	4	4	4
Others	EOR Related Project Objectives Uncertainties	Displacement Efficiency		4		3		3		3
		Vertical Sweep Efficiency		4		3		3		2
		Areal Sweep Efficiency		3		3		3		2
		Recovery Factor		4		3		3		3
		CO_2 Purity		4		4		4		N/A
		MMP Condition/Reservoir Pressure		5		3		3		5
		Reservoir Property Alteration		5		3		3		4
		Asphaltene Precipitation		4		2		2		2
		Injectivity		5		3		3		3
		Well Design		5		3		3		4
		WAG Benefit		4		3		3		2
		Injection/Production Rates Optimization		4		3		3		2
		Monitoring/Surveillance Plan Design		4		3		3		2
			4.125	3.6875	3.6875	3.625	3.25	3.4375	3.875	3.6875

		Activities to Address Uncertainty								Manage Uncertainty	
		Labs		Pilots							
		PVT	SCAL & Corflood	Single Well Pilots (2–3m tl s)	Single Well+ Observations (>1 yr @ 1mm scf/d)	Producer/Injector Pair (+obs.) (>1 yr @ 1mm scf/d)	Single Panel Flood (5/9-spot) (+obs.) >2 yrs @79 mm scf/d	Multiple Pattern Floods	FF Development	Reservoir Modelling	Analogue Review
Uncertainties	Sweep Efficiency (Vertical)										
	Sweep Efficiency (Horizontal)										
	Displacement Efficiency										
	Recovery Factor										
	Mn. Miscibility Conditions (Pressure)										
	CO_2 Purity Requirements										
	Reservoir Property Alteration										
	Asphaltene Precipitation										
	Injectivity										
	Well Design (Angle/completion)										
	WAG Benefits (over CGI) & WAG Design										
	Injection/Production Rates (optimisation)										
	Breakthrough & CO_2 Cycling										
	Surveillance Plan Design										
	Facilities CO_2 Handling Capability										
	Facilities CO_2 Injection Capability										
	Field Demonstration										
	Well/Facility Corrosion Impacts										

FIGURE 5.5 · Uncertainty matrix from the UAE's carbon capture and storage modalities and procedures guidelines submission, February 2011.

In trying to create the modalities and procedural guidelines submission, the consultants knew and repeatedly admitted that they were on risky and uncertain ground. Nevertheless, they tried to conjure a possibility of certainty, charted in vague, floating sentences or uncertainty matrices. In a way, they utilized this document as a means of restraining their imaginations, or a mode of creating stability. Yet the engineers and scientists who were present in the debates thought their imaginations already gave way to a level of certainty, especially on a particular, case-by-case basis. As such, the charts were only a means of representing the stability that they had access to by observing the earth's dynamics—during a mountain excursion, or while watching a child sipping drinks.

Soon after his heated discussion with the ADNOC and ADCO engineers and geologists in February 2011, Anand reiterated, "You cannot reach a destination when you have no road." As indeterminate as they were, the policy-making efforts were more than valid because they would eventually enable engineers and scientists to work toward the betterment of climate change mitigation technologies. They would serve as infrastructure more than anything, and pay for the environmental premiums that governments and corporations are expected to invest. Anand could not understand what it was exactly that the scientists and engineers misconceived. "And there are other examples of CCS projects in the world," Anand said. Like many others in the office often did, he would point to Algeria's In Salah[16] project to support his argument.

The Specifics of CCS at In Salah

Located in the heart of the Sahara in central Algeria, In Salah is a small oasis town frequented by oil and gas professionals from around the world. The In Salah carbon capture and storage project, in operation since August 2004 on a site neighboring this oasis town, is a joint venture between British Petroleum (BP), StatoilHydro, and Sonatrach, the Algerian government-owned oil and gas company.[17] Marwan, who had previously worked for an Algerian ministry in a position loosely associated with the project, quickly became a spokesperson at Masdar Carbon meetings in the planning of the submission document on matters related to Algeria's energy and climate change mitigation policy. "This is the biggest onshore CCS project in the world. Its large scale helps people understand that it can be done," he stated during an interview I conducted with him at the Masdar Carbon office. The impressive scale of the project had been possible due to a specific legal regulation in Algeria, which allowed the national oil company to enter joint ventures. Marwan explained further that the site had been selected especially because of its capacity as a gas reservoir. The gas extracted on site contained high quantities of carbon dioxide, which had to be removed before it was piped, as it would otherwise corrode the pipes. Therefore, the project proponents had indicated that it would be most convenient if the retrieved carbon dioxide were to be reinjected into maturing reservoirs. The construction phase for In Salah—wherein Sonatrach, the national oil company, had a 35 percent share while BP and Statoil respectively owned 33 percent and 32 percent—started in 2001, mainly as a learning exercise for storing carbon dioxide.

"It was a good idea for BP and Statoil," Marwan recounted. "They may need to learn to store carbon dioxide because of the Kyoto Protocol. When they have caps on their emissions, they will be obliged to store carbon dioxide in their own countries. So they used In Salah as an experiment with carbon dioxide." But what about Sonatrach? "Sonatrach had no financial incentive or obligation to do this," Marwan said initially. A little later, he reflected on the inherent inequalities within the project: "The minister of energy at the time decided to go ahead with the project, mainly on his own. . . . So he just handed in thirty-five million dollars, without any obligations. . . . If Sonatrach goes to the North Sea to produce oil there, due to emission limitations, it will be helpful for them to have this experience. But this never happens. I'd say that there is less than 1 percent probability that Sonatrach will work in the developed world. And there is so much that needs to be done in Algeria, in terms of environmental protection, before starting to invest in CCS projects. Treat wastewater! Treat hazardous wastes! The company is not even compliant with regulations at a basic level. But they went on to explore."

By referring to a case outside the UAE, Marwan evidenced how the macro-level arguments that they aimed to put down on paper were not always so constructive. While the policy proposal thus produced would comfortably treat the In Salah case as equivalent to a potential CCS project in the UAE, as someone who had experience with both contexts, Marwan knew that they were drastically different, and that they sparked off divergent problems and questions. As he continued to detail the In Salah case, these clear differences mounted.

The three partners that cooperated in the In Salah project had brought in technology developers and created a monitoring fund. Their main objective was to understand whether the reinjected carbon dioxide remained in place, and to thereby study the seepage and leakage behavior of the storage formation. They implemented tracers that tracked the movement of carbon dioxide underground, which generated further value for the experiment. Still, Marwan insisted that if Sonatrach wanted to "save the environment,"[18] this was the last thing to do. According to him, Sonatrach initially had to attend to problems such as toxic waste, the environmental impact of facilities, and leaking oil pipelines. In other words, money spent on the In Salah project would be better spent on other things. He added, "But for Abu Dhabi [which is also considered a developing country according to the UNFCCC standards] it is different—here there is enhanced oil recovery. . . . So all I'm saying is, Algeria is getting no benefit out of this;

why should it pay for the errors of others, like the United States? Developing countries should initially cling on to their own priorities, others should take care of the damage that they have done to the environment for so many years." In the transformation of climate change into a commercially viable frontier, as Marwan saw it, not every party had the same function or responsibility.

A Shadow Presence

While multinational oil companies had pushed for CCS efforts in Algeria, they took a rather different stance toward the utilization of carbon dioxide in the UAE. BP, Shell, and ExxonMobil, which held a 40 percent share in ADCO, had initially been resistant to doing research on CCS or EOR. "We needed 80 percent to make a decision, so we could not proceed before convincing them that it is a good idea," one executive at ADNOC, the national oil company and 60 percent shareholder at ADCO, told me during an interview. Masdar Carbon consultants had been catalysts for pilot projects on CCS and had advocated to the Abu Dhabi government that ADNOC could make use of carbon dioxide in a way that would add value for oil. First, the oil reservoirs had to be designed in a way that would work better with carbon dioxide. Then ADNOC needed to learn how to work with carbon dioxide in the subsurface. "We regularly use an air separation unit and retrieve nitrogen for gas operations, but we do not have the same infrastructure for carbon dioxide," the ADNOC executive continued. Implementing this infrastructure would serve three main goals. "First, it is good for the environment," he plainly stated. "Second, it is good for the image of Abu Dhabi. And third, of course, there is EOR." In twenty to thirty years, when the oil reservoirs became more mature, it would be necessary to use another injectant to retrieve more oil. "That's how we started doing an earlier assessment of carbon dioxide," he added.

Initially ADNOC had problems with BP, Shell, and ExxonMobil. "Since they didn't want to invest money," he explained, "they were using technical reasons to kill the project." ADNOC insisted that they didn't want politics or economics to take over the discussion. "Just give us your expertise," they protested. Still BP, Shell, and ExxonMobil tried to convince the Abu Dhabi authorities that they did not need carbon dioxide here. Their reservoirs were very rich. "In the end, we said carbon dioxide will increase oil production and will release hydrocarbon gas. We started two offshore studies, only conceptually. We finally agreed."

The ADNOC executive's words were surprising, especially given that, as of 2011, oil companies worldwide were promoting CCS practices.[19] At the World Future Energy Summit (WFES) in Abu Dhabi in January 2011, for instance, executives from ExxonMobil organized a meeting in which they informed participants of how they envisioned the future of CCS. They argued that CCS constitutes 20 percent of the solution toward meeting the three-degree abatement target set by the Kyoto Protocol. For them, CCS was not *the* solution, but it was a major part of the solution. "Half of this has nothing to do with the power industry," the ExxonMobil spokesperson suggested. "Sectors like steel, cement, fertilizers, and gas processing also have to invest in CCS projects." They expected that there would be at least a hundred large-scale CCS projects around the world in 2020, and that more than half of those projects would be located in non-OECD (non–Organization for Economic Co-Operation and Development) countries such as China and India. "We're going to look at fairly significant financial flows here," he said. And that's why CCS had to be economically justified. But during the question-and-answer session, he gave the green light for profit making. "Currently, the bulk of [CCS] projects are EOR projects in the United States, and clearly there are no drivers except for profit making. So they are profitable. They are using carbon dioxide for EOR, and at $80 a barrel of oil, there is money to be made." Then again, the executive continued, "The only reason for doing CCS is climate change, there is no other reason than that." The deployment and commercialization of the technology was perceived to be a complex and fundamental challenge for CCS projects.

It is important to examine the ways in which CCS operations are understood and acted out by multinational oil companies, not only because the oil industry has the most experience with CCS projects due to EOR, but also because multinational oil companies are heavily involved in the implementation and operation of carbon capture and storage policy. Despite their absence in negotiations of the modalities and procedures, in the UAE multinational oil companies indirectly govern the discursive field for climate change mitigation strategies. During a telephone interview, a UNFCCC secretariat representative remarked that oil companies do not attend meetings or prepare submissions, and in this sense mostly remain absent from the debates. Instead, they choose to lobby and pressure the governments they work with. The multinational oil companies had a shadow presence.

"Sooner or later, CCS will become an official part of climate change mitigation strategy, and the negotiations will be concluded," the UNFCCC officer continued. There was too much pressure from OPEC, especially because they wanted EOR to be approved. It was feared that oil producers would refuse to cooperate on other climate change mitigation issues in case CCS-EOR was not endorsed as a mitigation strategy. "Methodologically, it will not be too much of a problem to include CCS-EOR as a climate change mitigation strategy," the UNFCCC employee then stated. The issue would basically not be explicitly addressed. As Anand had suggested during the meetings with ADNOC and ADCO engineers, the vagueness of the document would be its strength.

The oil industry not only influences policy making on climate change mitigation by lobbying and pressuring governments; it also provides labor power for the emergent renewable energy and clean technology sector. Many of the policy consultants at Masdar Carbon had been headhunted from major consulting companies, including Deloitte Touche Tohmatsu, PwC, Ernst and Young, or KPMG, where they had dealt extensively with operations related to the energy industry. But other participants in the preparation of the modalities and procedural guideline submission were currently working for ADCO and ADNOC and had advanced their careers in multinational oil companies like ExxonMobil, Total, and Shell. Oil companies also had an undeniable presence at the climate summits, where such policy proposals were debated and finalized. Many countries did not have the technical expertise to participate in the debates on an emergent technology such as carbon capture and storage. Countries that already have full-fledged oil industries, and thereby first-class geologists and reservoir engineers, were able to negotiate better, given their access to a more rigorous understanding of the subsurface. They could rely upon their oil experts in presenting arguments for and against CCS. As such, it was not surprising that Brazil's CCS delegate at the climate summit in Durban, South Africa, in December 2011 was an executive at Petrobras, the state-owned oil company, while the Saudi Arabian delegate worked with Saudi Aramco. In this sense, expertise seemed to be highly valued in itself in the climate change debates, allowing a Petrobras or Aramco representative to temporarily give up his affiliations and to serve as a delegate for his country. While this enabled countries to have stronger and more reliable perspectives on technical issues, it also raised questions as to whose interests were being represented in the debates.[20] What did the heavy presence of the oil industry mean for the emergent green economy?

Acknowledging the deep connections between climate change mitigation technologies and the fossil fuel economy, well-known climate advocate Larry Lohmann from the British nongovernmental organization The Corner House writes, "Most financial, corporate and government leaders will not be able to find their own way . . . to successful climate investment policies. . . . Their place in society has been carved out and sustained by fossil fuels and fossil fuel substitutes and by the economic and political practices that most need questioning."[21] They will not bite the hand that feeds them. He forecasts that climate change policy will have to be led by a popular movement, not by the oil industry. That is why an economic crash offers the best opportunity for the economy to be transformed into "a force for livelihood and survival."[22] For him, such a crash may help create a "political movement for broad-based, democratic, post-fossil, long-range social planning based on co-operative inquiry," which is what the world needs in order to confront climate change.

Depicting Climate Futures

In March 2012, about a year after the submission of the guidelines, a German UNFCCC secretariat representative told me about the potential dangers of concentrated amounts of carbon dioxide as we had lunch in a Bonn restaurant. I was conducting fieldwork in Bonn to learn more about the ways in which UNFCCC secretariat members evaluated the CCS submissions they received from various countries, such as the UAE, and had been invited to an informal gathering with members of the CCS team. The German secretariat representative began by referring to an incident in Central Africa in 1986: Lake Nyos in Cameroon started emitting large amounts of carbon dioxide, leading to the large-scale asphyxiation of humans and animals in the surrounding areas.[23] The carbon dioxide that leaked from the lake had been completely natural, and demonstrated how fatal such outgassing could be. There were recorded instances of outgassing in Canada as well, where CCS experiments had taken place for some years. Canadian officials did not know to what degree the emissions resulted from injected carbon dioxide—their accounting had come to a dead end. The UNFCCC representative then pointed out that some states (*Länder*) in Germany were now banning potential CCS projects. A 2011 International Energy Agency (IEA) report entitled "Carbon Capture and Storage: Legal and Regulatory Review" included the following assessment: "CCS is still highly controversial in Germany. . . . Additional controversy has been generated by the inclusion of an 'opt-out' clause in the draft act at the insistence of certain Länder, whereby states can designate areas as ineligible for CCS deployment, effectively vetoing CCS in those areas."[24] New CCS regulations became effective in August 2012 in Germany, permitting only research, pilot, and demonstration projects, and allowing for the possibility of restricting carbon dioxide storage to certain parts of the country.[25]

"Right now things are dismal," another UNFCCC representative briskly commented on climate change policy during an interview in his Bonn office. According to him, the main risk regarding CCS specifically and climate change generally was about commitment and willpower issues, as decision-makers did not always exert control to reduce emissions or employ adequate mechanisms to mitigate climate change. "The United States has its own issues to deal with, and the Republicans are hard to crack," he said. Otherwise, he believed that the UNFCCC had a clear road map to resolving uncertainty and risk. As we wrapped up our conversation, he told me, "Solutions are available, and willpower will create clarity, and uncertainty will be resolved in that manner." He was not playing environmentalist—he specified that he understood the profit-making needs of industries. "I would not take a rustic action and propose a radical position saying close everything down," he concluded. Here, "rustic action" meant a move that would work against the interests of the industries, perhaps recalling Larry Lohmann's arguments about how corporate and government institutions could not resolve the climate crisis, and that broad-based political movements had to take charge of the serious issues at hand, signaling the possible benefits of an economic crash.

Like many other environmental consultants at Masdar, UNFCCC representatives endorsed an extension of the status quo. In pushing for climate change mitigation technologies like carbon capture and storage, they also acknowledged the uncertain conditions at hand. Once again, "degrees of acceptable risk" emerged as a useful tool—involving the recognition that carbon dioxide was possibly dangerous, but, with effective expertise, its effects could be kept under control.

The concluding epilogue will show how the plans for Masdar City in particular and the green economy in general shifted, becoming more ambiguous in their expectations for the future.

Epilogue: The Potential Futures of Abu Dhabi's Masdar

On February 16, 2016, the United Kingdom's *Guardian* newspaper ran a piece on Abu Dhabi's Masdar City project, titled "Masdar's Zero-Carbon Dream Could Become World's First Green Ghost Town." Launched in 2006 by the Abu Dhabi government, the eco-city project had attracted a great deal of attention from the media between the years 2007 and 2011. Yet, in the aftermath of the 2008 recession, developers abandoned some of the original goals of the project, and the media hype began to fade away. By 2016, the *Guardian* was imagining that "Years from now passing travellers may marvel at the grandeur and the folly of the futuristic landscape on the edges of Abu Dhabi: the barely occupied office blocks, the deserted streets, the vast tracts of undeveloped land and—most of all—the abandoned dream of a zero-carbon city." The newspaper interrogated whether Masdar City was a failure, and tried to assess its potential alongside other zero-emission projects inside and outside the UAE.[1]

Already in September 2014, a video had surfaced that represented the Masdar City site as a "techno-dystopia" abandoned by its inhabitants.[2] Accompanied by a droning soundtrack, the short clip presented a direct contrast to the early promotional material of Masdar City: it drew attention to the empty buildings and walkways instead of pointing to a soothing and optimistic future enabled by design solutions, business models, and technological innovations. Julien Eymeri, who shot the video, wrote an accompanying text in which he argued that the Masdar City model was too difficult to reproduce, and added that it remained symptomatic of the aspirations of a state obsessed with its future. For him, the Masdar City site was about "facing the fear of death by building quickly (an 'instant city'), to help transition to an Emirates that is a techno-ecological leader." The producers of Masdar City expected businesses to populate the premises, and thus they neglected to invest in public institutions.[3] This strategy, Eymeri wrote, further delayed the fulfillment of plans regarding the site. When he asked a representative whether the project would be cancelled, he learned that "it [was]—politically—unthinkable to abandon such a project." Eymeri called the project an "opening soon city."

These observations were valuable and somewhat accurate, and served as a corrective for the overly sanguine representations of Masdar City in earlier years. At the same time, they reproduced some of the debates that had been happening among the Masdar City staff since the beginning of the project. As active participants in the production of the project, they had been asking if the city could be reproduced elsewhere (chapter 1), analyzing how exactly its beautiful buildings impacted the city (chapter 2), and wondering if they were contributing to the creation of a technocratic dictatorship (chapter 3). Given the extensive marketing efforts, they often expressed how it would be impossible for Abu Dhabi to abandon the project (introduction). Masdar was a means of engaging in international climate change diplomacy (chapter 5). They even spoke about Masdar City's future potential as a ghost town (chapter 4).

In producing a narrative of failure, the later critical commentaries contributed to a dichotomous understanding of the future—as utopia or dystopia—and disregarded the complexities of the project in the same way that Masdar's promotional videos had done years earlier. This book has focused on Masdar employees' and students' commitment to the idea of potential as a response to these discussions of success and failure, understanding Masdar City as a materially and conceptually indeterminate project rather than as a bright prospect for humanity's future or as a symptom of its techno-dystopian demise. Abu Dhabi's renewable energy and clean technology projects continued to generate novel imaginaries, which moved forward and became disseminated globally regardless of their inherent tensions, spawning perpetual potential. The future was never a utopia or a dystopia, but a sometimes uncomfortable in-between space.

In navigating this in-between space, the people working in the renewable energy and clean technology industry developed multiple strategies. Moving across various temporal and spatial perspectives, the individuals concentrating on these projects managed to produce justifications for their participation through a range of actions and nonactions. At times they claimed that their work was going to serve an abstract common good, helping humans battle climate change and energy scarcity. They explained the ways in which these projects would contribute to the economic diversification of Abu Dhabi, allowing the emirate to reconstitute and rebrand itself as a knowledge-based economy. At other times they foregrounded the usefulness of these projects for their own trajectories, focusing on everyday challenges, personal routines, and professional prospects. Rather than subscribing to the neat categories of utopia or dystopia, they created new classifications that explained their attachments to or detachments from the transforming projects, consistently reframing their associations, commitments, and interests based on the material and conceptual qualities of their work.

In closing, this book will track the global horizons of some of Masdar's projects and demonstrate how moving between various scales allowed people to feel potential, enabling them to imagine ways in which they might act upon the future.

Footnotes

In June 2012, a year after completing my fieldwork in Abu Dhabi, I traveled to Cambridge, Massachusetts, to meet Michael and Niko, two friends and research collaborators completing their training year at MIT before departing for the UAE to start as faculty at Masdar Institute. They had been postdoctoral fellows at the Institute during the year I spent in Abu Dhabi, and had subsequently been hired as assistant professors. Michael held a degree from a German university, and it was his first time living in the United States, while Niko had spent many years on North American campuses and knew more about everyday practices and expectations. Throughout their one-year training period at MIT, they were expected to form lasting connections with academics from the United States, develop their research portfolios, and possibly locate grant providers for future projects.

At the time of our meeting, Michael and Niko were about to complete their training, and were busy preparing to head back to Masdar City. During their one-year program, they had increasingly come to realize that MIT was in partnership with Masdar Institute for its financial benefits. MIT had helped with many similar initiatives around the world, which provided assistance regarding educational infrastructures in exchange for a fee. While they did not criticize this general policy on the institution's part, they believed that the nature of this relationship had negatively influenced their training year. "We're sort of invisible here," they said. In this large research institution, the visitors from Masdar Institute had felt somewhat lost. But, convinced that they did not really have the capacity to amend this condition, they concentrated on thinking about forthcoming courses and research projects.

As they prepared to start their positions at Masdar Institute, Michael and Niko shared the worry that their courses would not be attractive to incoming students. Michael planned on teaching courses on algorithms and bioinformatics, while Niko wished to investigate soils and microbiology. They told me about the rather unusual problem of the faculty-to-student ratio at the Institute. Faculty had to offer classes to comply with their contracts, but a class could not be offered unless five students registered for it. "As of May 2012," they told me, "there are about seventy faculty and two hundred students, so the competition is quite tough." In order to become a livelier teaching and research environment, the Institute needed more scholarship opportunities that would attract a larger and more diverse body of students. But as time passed and the Institute was not yet producing renewable energy and clean technology startups, the Abu Dhabi government was becoming impatient; indeed, it was contemplating cutting funding for the Institute rather than making more available.

They were uneasy about their course offerings, but Michael and Niko had more or less settled on their forthcoming research into biofuels. Funded by the Abu Dhabi government, Etihad Airways, Honeywell, Safran, and Boeing, their collaborative project would acquire two hundred hectares of land, on which they would attempt to grow salt-tolerant oilseed plants using as little water as possible. Using lands not suitable for agriculture, the duo aspired to produce biofuels for jet engines—a prospect of intellectual and practical use to the project's investors. Michael had a background in data mining and wished to build foundational knowledge regarding biological approaches for biofuel production, biocarbon sequestration, and waste cleanup. Niko planned on establishing a laboratory focusing on sustainable soil microbiology. Together they would scour the UAE's deserts, coasts, marshes, mangroves, and salt flats for plants that contained sugar or oil. These plants, which had the capacity to thrive in what they described as extreme environments, would metamorphose into fuel. In the long run, these efforts would contribute to the development of an aviation biofuel industry in the emirate; help build a knowledge-based economy; and, perhaps, offer new methods for battling climate change and energy scarcity.

Michael and Niko felt fortunate to have the opportunity to participate in the making of biofuels on Abu Dhabi's nonarable lands because they would be able to conduct some basic science research under the auspices of the project while seemingly working toward a practical commercial end goal. Given how difficult it was to conduct basic science research at the emergent Institute, they understood this to be a rare prospect. Since faculty at Masdar Institute (and many other research institutions around the world) were expected to commit to research contracts with private companies, it was becoming more and more difficult for researchers to obtain funding for nonpractical long-term projects with possibly intangible results. In this context, scientists were developing strategies to include basic science research within economically feasible projects, and managing to capture the benefits of both trajectories.

"Boeing is participating in the project because they would like to develop stronger relations with the UAE," Michael and Niko also underlined, reminding me of an argument that had been prevalent during my fieldwork in Abu Dhabi. My interlocutors had often told me that research contracts and beautiful buildings—rather than serving as effective material artifacts in their own right (see chapter 2)—were ways of expanding networks for Abu Dhabi and its collaborators. In Michael and Niko's case, Boeing had perceived the UAE to be a promising emerging market, and began forming partnerships toward the development of biofuels.

Michael and Niko's research expectations were in line with other projects at Masdar Institute in terms of their focus. Their colleagues worked on solar-powered desalination infrastructure, estimated the future temperatures of the Arab Gulf by relying on regional climate change models, tried to build renewable energy storage facilities, explored methodologies for biorefining waste water, and formulated projections on the pros and cons of smart grids. While Abu Dhabi's authorities did not always find the research center satisfying, especially when it did not produce desirable startups to contribute to the building of a knowledge-based economy, in many ways Masdar Institute did prove to be the most substantial and productive organizational unit within the Masdar project. The faculty members at the Institute built laboratories, gave lectures, produced research results and publications, and trained students in a part of the world not known for its higher education facilities. The research projects on campus responded to local environmental questions and resources by proposing novel technological innovations. They facilitated the emergence of research partnerships with multinational companies, contributed to the emergent renewable energy and clean technology sector, and sponsored Abu Dhabi's future economic diversification.

During the few days we spent together in Cambridge, the conversations Niko, Michael, and I had included innumerable footnotes, further explicating how things "actually" worked. In being pushed forward or papered over, all of these projects were being conceptualized as something other than themselves. The practice of reframing appeared to be the most accessible tool for acting upon the potential of these projects—a strategy that would allow MIT's financial expectations, Michael and Niko's research questions, and Boeing's attempts at building relations to converge on a shared platform. Through ambiguity, the producers of Masdar Institute could have their own interpretations of various projects, at times leaving their hesitations aside. In Masdar Institute's associations with the rest of the world, potential seemingly emerged in these moments when projects could only work if they were reframed, reformulated, and eventually rescaled.

Leaving Social Justice Aside

Susan and Jeff had paid their own way to travel from upstate New York to Split, Croatia, to participate in the "Energy Currency: Energy as the Fundamental Measure of Price, Cost and Value" conference in July 2012 (see chapter 3), where they would present their work on the Human Energy Renewable Measure (HERM). They had been hosting a radio show in New York to develop and discuss their ideas with the public, seeking, in their own words, to design "a fair economic system." They did not know many of the other conference participants, who mostly hailed from nongovernmental institutions and universities, but they shared their interest in using energy as a measure to organize the economy. They also diverged from the other participants in their emphasis on justice and equality rather than the optimization and efficiency of the economic system. On the second day of the conference, when it was their turn to present, they explained how their proposed energy currency, HERM, would work.

"The energy for human thought and human efforts derives directly from renewable solar energy," they began. "Just as energy units can be standardized, human energy can be standardized and used as a renewable energy basis for considering values in a human economy. Human renewable energy is the basis for all economies." They believed that the present valuations of physical and intellectual human accomplishment were subjective—humans received whatever their employers were willing to pay. However, HERM would manage this arbitrariness by suggesting that twenty hours of human labor should equal 7.2 megajoules. In exchange for the 7.2 megajoules, humans would be able to receive education, health care, food, and shelter. Based on their system, the twenty-hour workload would provide humans all over the world with a guaranteed minimum income. "Wage enhancements based on agreed-upon subjective multipliers (higher education, pleasant personality, creativity, etc.) can be applied," they proposed, "but a limit must be set in the form of a pay ceiling, so no one makes more than, maybe, fifty times the base income." By measuring human input through energy, Jeff and Susan imagined creating a universal currency that would defeat income inequality between wealthy countries and poor countries, which would trigger a shift toward a fair economic system.[4]

After spending two days at the conference, however, the pair became concerned about how social justice was being glossed over in the energy currency debates they were attending. Complementary currencies could perhaps alleviate social and economic inequalities, but they were not inherently fair or equitable. The conference's participants had framed complementary currencies as possible ways out of the Eurozone crisis without paying much attention to how economic crises, climate change, and social justice relate. In Susan and Jeff's formulation, labor power would be the basis for an emergent energy currency; but for the conference organizer, the Club of Rome, a global think tank famous for its 1972 report *The Limits to Growth* and that currently works on the world economic system, climate change, and environmental degradation, issues of fairness had been secondary. According to Susan and Jeff, the debates continued in a "wishy-washy" manner, without addressing the most important economic and environmental problems of our time.

I asked Alexander, who participated in the conference to present Masdar Institute's ergos, a new currency based on energy unit expenditure, if he agreed with Susan and Jeff. He responded, "You cannot solve all problems in the world with energy currencies—in the end, they're made for societies and communities that have reached a particular level of sophistication; they are not meant to solve Third World problems." Alexander did not think energy currencies had to be exhaustive measures that would be applicable throughout the world, or that would solve issues of social justice, "but if we have an energy currency that deals with resource constraints, then everyone will be better off." According to him, technical solutions such as energy currencies would enable humanity to deal with climate change and energy scarcity problems.

Alexander's approach privileged the survival and sustenance of what he called "societies and communities that have reached a particular level of sophistication," and assumed that there would be a trickle-down effect, whereby these countries' resources would positively impact what he called the "Third World." Energy currencies would help extend the status quo for countries in the developed world, rather than engaging with Third World problems such as income inequality or social injustice. The technical adjustments discussed at the conference seemed rather distant from "empowering all individuals." Still, Alexander imagined that everyone would be better off once they were put into place.

As Susan and Jeff pointed out, the fundamental conceptual issues of governance related to currencies had been understated during the conference in the hope of moving the debates forward and preserving energy currencies as future possibilities. The conference's participants were united in their criticism of the banking sector. But rather than examining larger questions such as social justice or the impact of new forms of governance, the discussions concentrated on practical issues such as whether complementary currencies should be convertible to national currencies; moving away from issues of social justice, they focused on the narrow technical concerns of various applications of innovative currency regimes. At the same time, by shifting between scales and pointing to ambiguous future results, the conference participants ensured that their projects remained alive and well.

Constructive Ambiguity

The long-winded carbon capture and storage (CCS) deliberations, described in the final chapter of this book, had started at the United Nations Climate Change Conference in Montreal (COP 11) in 2005, and reached a breaking point in 2010 at the COP 16 in Cancún, when the decision was made to include carbon capture and storage as a climate change mitigation technology, with the proviso that safety and liability protocols be resolved. In February 2011, Masdar Carbon was among the parties that submitted proposals regarding modalities and procedural guidelines on CCS projects. After collecting the submissions, the UNFCCC secretariat put together a synthesis report. Next, a technical workshop was organized in Abu Dhabi in September 2011, inviting representatives from various countries and organizations to learn more about the current status of CCS technologies. Following the workshop, the secretariat published a workshop report and a modalities and procedures draft, which was opened for negotiation in the COP 17 Durban meeting in November 2011.[5] After two long contact group discussions, open-ended meetings where representatives negotiated and tried to settle disagreements before forwarding a text for formal adoption, modalities and procedural guidelines were finally accepted on December 3, 2011, but the liability protocols remained the only outstanding issue. The parties had not been able to agree upon whether host countries or carbon credit holders should be liable for the stored carbon dioxide, or if the liability should be shared between the two stakeholders.

During the second week of the COP 17, the liability provisions were finally settled. The provisions called for host countries to develop thorough regulations regarding liability protocols. In addition, they stipulated that project developers place 5 percent of the carbon credits earned from CCS projects in a global reserve fund. The carbon credits in this reserve fund would be awarded to the project proponents only after twenty years of monitoring, provided that no carbon dioxide had leaked from the underground storage site. It was also decided that should a project participant be unable to go on with the project, liability would automatically be transferred to the host country. Such provisions were expected to mitigate concerns around the uncertainties of CCS technologies, especially in regard to long-term liability.

Many of my interlocutors from Abu Dhabi attended the Durban meetings. Together with allies such as Norway and Saudi Arabia, the delegation from Abu Dhabi had long been pushing for the inclusion of CCS in the Clean Development Mechanism (CDM) program. As oil-rich countries, they could make use of carbon capture and storage, not only as a means of decreasing emissions by burying excess carbon dioxide underground, but also as a way to extract more oil from depleting reservoirs through a technology commonly known as enhanced oil recovery (EOR). The inclusion of CCS in the CDM would be considered a long-awaited victory for the Abu Dhabi delegation, which included some of the environmental consultants I worked with at Masdar Carbon.

However, there remained certain inconclusive issues about the policy. For instance, what did it mean to defer the liability for CCS projects completely to host countries? This type of provision evidenced an inability to put together an international treaty on the issue, while making it more difficult for future provisions to be produced, as they could potentially contradict host country rulings. Resolutions on the transboundary movement of carbon dioxide—which would involve capturing carbon dioxide in one nation-state, then transporting it and storing it in another—were also postponed until COP 18, which would take place in November–December 2012 in Doha, Qatar. The making of policy on transboundary flows of carbon dioxide was rather complicated, as it would necessitate defining project boundaries for CCS projects, characterizing carbon dioxide as toxic or nontoxic material, negotiating the legitimacy of this status under other international treaties, and administering the participation of multiple project proponents within a single CCS project. However, as significant as this issue might be for the future implementation of CCS technologies, it did not hinder the process for including CCS in the CDM. By the end of the Durban negotiations, many parties recognized carbon capture and storage to have acquired legitimacy—despite much controversy, CCS had become an official climate change mitigation technology.

While waiting for the CCS in CDM decision to be announced, I chatted with some environmental consultants who worked frequently with the UNFCCC secretariat. "How big is the damage done, you think?" one of them, named Tom, asked another. "The monitoring criteria were supposed to be *stringent*," his colleague replied, referring to the initial policy proposal document. When I asked what adjective would be more appropriate, he laughingly proposed that "wishy-washy" would be a good alternative. "What we are trying to achieve in putting together this document is constructive ambiguity," Tom told me as we had dinner at a café near the conference venue. Tom knew about Masdar Carbon's projects, but had not been employed there. Here, "constructive ambiguity" implied a quick resolution of the debates, without producing further controversy among the delegates. The application of such constructive ambiguity could eventually result in wishy-washy protocols as well, wherein the goal-oriented nature of the negotiations could curtail a rigorous analysis of the final policy decisions. Having worked as an environmental consultant for about a decade, Tom understood the production of constructive ambiguity as an aesthetic challenge, worked through step by step, highlighting the document in different colors, bracketing unresolved sentences, eventually cleansing the text of colors and brackets.[6] He argued that the inclusion of CCS in CDM was more symbolic than anything else. "It will be technically complicated to implement CCS projects and acquire carbon credits in the next few years, with the given state of technology. So even when CCS is included in the CDM, it's not like we're going to have an upsurge of CCS projects," he summarized with much relief.

Often associated with Henry Kissinger's strategies in the Israel-Palestine conflict,[7] the term *constructive ambiguity* is famously defined as "the deliberate use of ambiguous language in a sensitive issue in order to advance some political purpose."[8] The *Dictionary of Diplomacy* explains: "In a negotiation, for example, constructive ambiguity might be employed not only to disguise an inability to resolve a question on which the parties remain far apart, but to do so in a manner that enables each to claim that it has actually obtained some concession. . . . It might also be hoped that, having thereby shelved this particular point in a way that causes neither side excessive discomfort, they will be able to make real progress on other matters. In this way the ground might be prepared for a later return to the unresolved question or it might dissolve altogether with the passing of time." Yet the dictionary continues with a warning: "Such hopes often prove ill-founded and ambiguity in agreements can also generate subsequent controversy. Whether on balance, therefore, such fudging proves 'constructive' in relation to further attempts to resolve a disagreement is for historians to determine." The dictionary suggests that other terms for constructive ambiguity would be "fudging" and "glossing," or "papering over" disagreements.[9]

The CCS debates came to be finalized at the Climate Change Summit in Doha, Qatar, following extensive discussions about two contentious issues: (1) transboundary flows of carbon dioxide, and (2) the global reserve fund. Transboundary flows of carbon dioxide have been regulated by the London Convention, an agreement that does not allow waste products to be carried across borders for purposes of underground storage. If carbon dioxide were to be transported for enhanced oil recovery purposes—that is, as a drilling additive for the oil and gas industry—its transboundary flow could be permitted.[10] But it could not be transported across borders merely to be stored underground. The delegates disagreed about the liability protocols required for such transboundary projects. While the issue would be critical for many forthcoming infrastructure projects involving carbon dioxide, it could not be finalized at the Doha debates.

The global reserve fund, which requires CCS operators to invest an extra 5 percent of their certified emission reductions in a hundred-year reserve, and which would be used in case of a major accident across the world, was also a contentious issue at Doha. The European Union, for instance, argued that the global reserve fund would cause CCS operators to disperse responsibility, exacerbating environmental integrity measures. For them, the already existing twenty-year fund, which was intended for use in a case-by-case manner, would serve as a satisfactory means of protection. On the other hand, Jamaica, representing the Association of Small Island States (AOSIS), ardently supported the global reserve fund. AOSIS had been opposing the implementation of CCS as a Clean Development Mechanism since the beginning of the negotiations. In the meantime, the text changed, attracted different-colored type, gained and lost some brackets. The secretariat members agreed to postpone the debates for another four years, until the forty-fifth Subsidiary Body for Scientific and Technological Advice (SBSTA) meeting in November 2016.

Although the Abu Dhabi delegation suggested that the debates had been successful, they did not have any immediate projects at hand for CCS in CDM. These efforts enabled the delegation to emerge as a rather significant actor at the summits, acquiring international prestige. The negotiations had also overlapped with the National Day of the UAE, and allowed the delegation to celebrate both the inclusion of CCS in CDM and the fortieth anniversary of the founding of the state. During the debates, one member of the delegation, a British national, donned a tie with the UAE flag.

Like a Meteor

Karl, a Swiss environmental consultant who provided services to Masdar during various stages of the project, explained to me in late 2012 that he understood the renewable energy and clean technology initiative as a "star rising and falling like a meteor." I had known Karl as a prominent figure in the climate change debates and had seen him give lectures, but it was only after he came across some of my publications that we started corresponding about renewable energy and clean technology innovations in the Arabian Peninsula. In the fall of 2012, we talked on the phone and met in College Station, Texas, where he was presenting his work at a conference at Texas A&M University. We also saw each other at the COP 18 in Doha, Qatar, in December 2012. Having closely observed the launching of the project while helping with the development of departments like Masdar Carbon, Karl told me how the people at Masdar appeared to be interested in short cuts. Rather than training people inside the emirate, the producers of Masdar hired various experts to give talks or to develop methodologies to help support the initiative. The project had lacked national involvement, consistently relying on climate specialists from around the globe. "How do these people think together and collaborate? No one asked this question," Karl said, in summarizing what he believed to be the main problem with the initiative. "As an effort, Masdar was bold, but not really thought out."

Given his experience consulting for various projects in Saudi Arabia, Karl was able to compare the Masdar projects to other large-scale climate change mitigation efforts in the Arabian Peninsula. "Main difference between Saudi Arabia and the UAE," he explained, "is that Saudi Arabia is committed to developing expertise on climate change, unlike the UAE. Saudi Arabia has been training its own people since the climate change negotiations started. The leadership is more committed to these targets." Thus, Karl supported the Emiratization efforts that were increasingly underway in the UAE (see chapter 2). But secondly and perhaps more importantly, "In Saudi Arabia, once the leadership takes a decision, they commit to it, but Masdar City was not like this," Karl reiterated. "When the challenges came up, they shied away from working on them." As a whole, the Masdar project had been too invested in developing visions rather than resolving the difficult problems that those visions triggered. The producers of Masdar continued to rely upon their physically and conceptually incomplete infrastructure without necessarily addressing the inconsistencies that their project unleashed upon the world. The star could rise again, Karl proposed. If the whole region managed to deal with climate change issues in an innovative manner, Masdar could come back into the picture as an interesting model.

At Masdar City, staircases descend from the elevated platform of the spaceship to the dusty desert ground. The staircases signify a departure from the foundational ideas of Masdar City and mark the cancellation of the master plan. Rather than facilitating a carless-city design, the staircases take Masdar's visitors and residents to large parking lots, which allow them to drive to the Masdar Institute without taking personal rapid transit pods or shuttle buses. Masdar City now consists of half-finished buildings in various parts of the previously designated site; they will someday host various residents, including renewable energy and clean technology companies. In 2013, Hilton DoubleTree showed interest in building a hotel on the Masdar City site, given its proximity to the Abu Dhabi International Airport. A real estate developer, the Majid Al Futtaim group, announced in 2017 that it would open its new My City Centre Masdar mall at the end of 2018.[11] Masdar is also building eco-villas, defined on the Masdar website as pilot projects incorporating water- and energy-saving technologies. The website notes that an Emirati family is moving into an eco-villa in April 2017, and uses a quote from Yousef Baselaib, executive director of sustainable real estate at Masdar: "People expect a sustainable design option to be more expensive, but our Eco-Villa concept challenges this misconception.

FIGURE E.1 · Staircases of Masdar City, March 2014. Photo by the author.

FIGURE E.2 · Masdar City: The City of Possibilities, March 2014. Photo by the author.

The Eco-Villa stays true to Masdar City's principles of sustainable urban development in that it is cost-efficient, environmentally sensitive, and culturally appropriate in both its design and function. Because of its energy and water-efficient design, residents of the Eco-Villa will receive significantly reduced power and water bills."[12] In other words, these will serve as Volkswagens, appealing to a larger segment of the population than would the Formula 1 car that the original designs for Masdar City offered.[13]

Slowly, Masdar will become a special economic zone for renewable energy and clean technology companies, rather than fulfilling its destiny as an eco-city. This is what Masdar advertises on its website, defining the city as an "emerging global free zone cluster that offers business opportunities and investments in UAE."[14] On a trip to Abu Dhabi in March 2014, I saw billboards describing Masdar as a "city of possibilities," expecting the arrival of colorful pie charts, green ideas, and men in suits. The elevated platform of the Masdar Institute campus will perhaps remain an island in the middle of this emerging special economic zone, retaining the qualities of a "spaceship in the desert."

Notes

Introduction: The Soul of Carbon Dioxide

1 Foster + Partners was founded in 1967 by Norman Foster. Currently they operate offices in London, New York, Madrid, Hong Kong, Beijing, Shanghai, Abu Dhabi, Buenos Aires, São Paulo, Silicon Valley, Singapore, and Dubai.

2 The Formula 1 tracks had been hosting the Grand Prix since 2009 on Yas Island. The Al Ghazal Golf Course is older, serving golfers since 1997. All of these zones assisted the drive for economic diversification in Abu Dhabi, while at the same time putting the emirate's name on the map, fostering its brand image for diverse target markets. In their segregation from Masdar City, these carbon-intensive sites staged different pathways toward which Abu Dhabi's economy could be steered. They demonstrated that Masdar City was not necessarily symptomatic of a greening effort across the emirate—it was only one of the experiments toward the production of a future that depended less on oil revenues. They could easily be perceived as unrelated spaces with no common social basis, but the Formula 1 track, the golf course, and the eco-city all attempted to address the challenge of generating non-oil-based revenues for the emirate, which united them under the drive for possible future profit. Despite seemingly contradictory agendas (and drastically different relationships to climate change and

energy scarcity), they collectively served the future economic vision of Abu Dhabi.

3 Polich, *Return of the Children of the Light: Incan and Mayan Prophecies for a New World* (Minneapolis: University of Minnesota Press, 2001), 121–22.

4 Castañeda, *The Teachings of Don Juan: A Yaqui Way of Knowledge* (Berkeley: University of California Press, 1968), 61.

5 Latour, *Aramis, or the Love of Technology* (Cambridge, MA: Harvard University Press, 1996), viii.

6 See, for instance, "Dubai's Six-Year Building Boom Grinds to Halt as Financial Crisis Takes Hold," *The Guardian*, February 13, 2009, https://www.theguardian.com/world/2009/feb/13/dubai-boom-halt, accessed April 21, 2017.

7 See "Abu Dhabi Explores Energy Alternatives," *New York Times*, March 18, 2007, http://www.nytimes.com/2007/03/18/world/middleeast/18abudhabi.html?pagewanted=all, accessed March 15, 2016.

8 *Brink Masdar*, Bloomberg documentary, May 2013, http://www.bloomberg.com/video/masdar-a-green-city-bloomberg-brink-05-13-azsX~xTlSsOJ03BGwXoufg.html, accessed February 7, 2017.

9 Many important books study energy infrastructures (particularly oil) from a systemic, macro perspective, an analysis that I will not provide in this book. For some examples, see Timothy Mitchell, *Carbon Democracy* (New York: Verso, 2012); Robert Vitalis, *America's Kingdom: Mythmaking on the Saudi Oil Frontier* (Stanford, CA: Stanford University Press, 2006); and Daniel Yergin, *The Prize: The Epic Quest for Oil, Money, and Power* (New York: Free Press, 1990).

10 The conversation on climate change is at times couched in an ethical, moral, and political language most often associated with environmentalism. For instance, in his book *A Perfect Moral Storm*, philosopher Stephen Gardiner explains how "the global environmental tragedy is most centrally an ethical failure, and one that implicates our institutions, our moral and political theories, and ultimately ourselves, considered as moral agents." He continues by suggesting that "ethical questions are fundamental to the main policy decisions that must be made, such as where to set a global ceiling for greenhouse gas emissions, and how to distribute the emissions permitted by such a ceiling." Similarly, Dale Jamieson claims that humans must move away from perspectives that focus on "calculating probable outcomes" and instead "nurture and give new content to some old virtues such as humility, courage, and moderation and perhaps develop such new virtues as those of simplicity and conservatism." In *This Changes Everything: Capitalism vs. The Climate*, Naomi Klein proposes: "Fundamentally, the task is to articulate not just an alternative set of policy proposals but an alternative

worldview to rival the one at the heart of the ecological crisis—embedded in interdependence rather than hyper-individualism, reciprocity rather than dominance, and cooperation rather than hierarchy," and explains that social transformation takes place through movements that are "unafraid of the language of morality—to give the pragmatic, cost-benefit arguments a rest and speak of right and wrong, of love and indignation." Stephen Gardiner, *A Perfect Moral Storm: The Ethical Tragedy of Climate Change* (Oxford: Oxford University Press, 2011); Dale Jamieson, "Ethics, Public Policy, and Global Warming," *Science, Technology, and Human Values* 17, no. 2 (1992): 139–53; Naomi Klein, *This Changes Everything: Capitalism vs. The Climate* (New York: Verso, 2014).

11 Anthropologists who study environmental issues and institutions explore how such global problems are vernacularized by actors in specific locales according to the exigencies of their worlds and unpack the ways in which climate change and energy problems are understood, articulated, and confronted. Ethical, moral, and political entailments are described as pertinent for some of these actors. For instance, drawing on an ethnography of matsutake mushrooms, Anna Tsing calls for a reevaluation of principles of progress, and an acknowledgment of indeterminacy and instability in the world. "We can't rely on the status quo; everything is in flux, including our ability to survive," she writes. "Thinking through precarity changes social analysis. A precarious world is a world without teleology. Indeterminacy, the unplanned nature of time, is frightening, but thinking through precarity makes it evident that indeterminacy also makes life possible." Similarly, Elizabeth Povinelli invites her readers to think about the "multitude of geological and meteorological modes of existence," which "have prompted people to demand an ethical and political reconsideration of who and what should have a voice in local, national, and planetary governance." Drawing on a variety of contexts across the globe, these ethnographies forge perspectives that foreground the environmental, economic, and political insecurities of the present, and accordingly call for challenging the status quo. Elizabeth Povinelli, *Geontologies: A Requiem to Late Liberalism* (Durham, NC: Duke University Press, 2016); Anna Tsing, *The Mushroom at the End of the World: On the Possibility of Life in Capitalist Ruins* (Princeton, NJ: Princeton University Press, 2015).

12 Marco, whose story I shared in the beginning of this introduction, is perhaps as an exception to this dominant perspective.

13 Elif informed me that one hundred people responded to the survey. Thirty of these people were Emiratis, whereas the others were expatriates. Of the one hundred people, sixty-two were male and thirty-eight were female. The age distribution was as follows: nineteen people aged between eighteen and

twenty-three, thirty-six people between twenty-four and thirty, twenty-one people between thirty-one and forty, eleven people between forty-one and fifty, eight people between fifty-one and sixty, and four people over sixty. One person did not enter their age.

14 For some examples of this scholarship, please see Ahmad (2017); Al-Nakib (2016); Chatty (1996, 2009); Gardner (2010); Hanieh (2011); Inhorn (2015); Kanna (2011); Limbert (2010); Longva (1997); Menoret (2014); Nagy (2000); Ramos (2010); Stanek (2015); and Vora (2013).

15 Timothy Mitchell's *Rule of Experts* (2002) is an exceptional account of environmental expertise in the Middle East. For other examples of work on the environment in the Middle East, please see Jessica Barnes, *Cultivating the Nile* (Durham, NC: Duke University Press, 2014); Laurie Brand, "Development in Wadi Rum? State Bureaucracy, External Funders, and Civil Society," *International Journal of Middle East Studies* 33, no. 4 (2001): 571–90; Gareth Doherty, *Paradoxes of Green: Landscapes of a City-State* (Berkeley: University of California Press, 2017); Gary Fields, "Landscaping Palestine: Reflections of Enclosure in a Historical Mirror," *International Journal of Middle East Studies* 42, no. 1 (2010): 63–82; Bridget Guarasci, "The National Park: Reviving Eden in Iraq's Marshes," *Arab Studies Journal* 23, no. 1 (fall 2015); Gökçe Günel, "The Infinity of Water: Climate Change Adaptation in the Arabian Peninsula," *Public Culture* 28, no. 2 (2016a): 291–315; Toby Craig Jones, *Desert Kingdom: How Oil and Water Forged Modern Saudi Arabia* (Cambridge, MA: Harvard University Press, 2010); Karim Makdisi, "The Rise and Decline of Environmentalism in Lebanon," in *Water on Sand: Environmental Histories of the Middle East and North Africa*, edited by Alan Mikhail (Oxford: Oxford University Press, 2013), 207–29; Alan Mikhail, *The Animal in Ottoman Egypt* (Oxford: Oxford University Press, 2014); Sophia Stamatopoulou-Robbins, "Occupational Hazards," *Comparative Studies of South Asia, Africa and the Middle East* 34, no. 3 (2014): 476–96; Rebecca Stein, "Traveling Zion: Hiking and Settler Nationalism in Pre-1948 Palestine," *Interventions: International Journal of Postcolonial Studies* 11, no. 3 (2009): 334–51.

16 For some examples of this scholarship, please see Hamdy (2012) and Sanal (2011).

17 Lara Deeb and Jessica Winegar, "Anthropologies of Arab-Majority Societies," *Annual Review of Anthropology* 41, no. 41 (2012): 537–58.

18 For some examples of Zayed's environmental projects, please see http://gulfnews.com/news/uae/environment/zayed-vision-transforming-desert-into-green-haven-1.132209 and http://www.thenational.ae/news/uae-news/environment/sheikh-zayed-laid-groundwork-for-environmental-protection, accessed May 30, 2017.

19 Rosemarie Said Zahlan, *The Origins of the United Arab Emirates: A Political and Social History of the Trucial States* (New York: St. Martin's Press, 1978).

20 Christopher M. Davidson, "After Shaikh Zayed: The Politics of Succession in Abu Dhabi and the UAE," *Middle East Policy* 13, no. 1 (2006c): 42–59.

21 Christopher M. Davidson, "Abu Dhabi's New Economy: Oil, Investment and Domestic Development," *Middle East Policy* 16, no. 2) (2009b): 59–79.

22 Davidson, "After Shaikh Zayed," 44.

23 Yasser Elsheshtawy's work provides a historical framework for Abu Dhabi's urban development and understands the death of Sheikh Zayed as a turning point leading to a globalized city. In describing the projects that characterize Abu Dhabi in the period after 2004, he uses the *souq* by Foster + Partners as an example. While the souq is marketed as "an attempt at reinventing the old market place, giving the city a new civic heart," Elsheshtawy shows that it "excludes these elements which were in some way 'spoiling' the modern metropolitan image that officials are trying to portray. There simply is no room for loitering Pakistani shoppers looking for a cheap bargain, or a gathering of Sri Lankan housemaids exchanging news." The patterns of exclusion that he finds are prevalent across new projects, such as Masdar City. Please see Yasser Elsheshtawy, *The Evolving Arab City: Tradition, Modernity and Urban Development* (London: Routledge, 2008).

24 These cultural projects are under construction on Saadiyat Island (meaning "island of happiness" in Arabic), located 0.3 miles off the coast of Abu Dhabi. NYU-Abu Dhabi opened in 2008 at a temporary site in downtown Abu Dhabi before moving to its permanent campus on the island. Guggenheim Abu Dhabi, designed by American architect Frank Gehry, will show contemporary art and will be the largest of the several Guggenheim Foundation museums internationally. Designed by French architect Jean Nouvel, Louvre Abu Dhabi will exhibit loaned works from the Paris-based collection and will be the French institution's first international branch. Construction of Guggenheim Abu Dhabi has been delayed several times—its opening date is unclear. But Jean Nouvel's Louvre Abu Dhabi was opened in November 2017.

25 For an analysis of how these policies impact migrant communities in the UAE, please see Vora, *Impossible Citizens*. For a comparable reflection on temporariness in Kuwait, please see Ahmad, *Everyday Conversions*. For an exposé of the types of exploitation that the kafala system facilitates, please see the Human Rights Watch 2014 report "'I Already Bought You': Abuse and Exploitation of Female Migrant Domestic Workers in the United Arab Emirates," https://www.hrw.org/report/2014/10/22/i-already-bought-you/abuse-and-exploitation-female-migrant-domestic-workers-united, accessed July 21, 2015.

26 This abuse has been the topic of a story in the *New Yorker*, among other general readership publications. Please see Negar Azimi, "The Gulf Art War: New Museums in the Emirates Raise the Issue of Workers' Rights," *New Yorker*, December 19, 2016, http://www.newyorker.com/magazine/2016/12/19/the-gulf-art-war, accessed February 17, 2017. Also see the Human Rights Watch 2015 report entitled "Migrant Workers' Rights on Saadiyat Island in the United Arab Emirates," https://www.hrw.org/report/2015/02/10/migrant-workers-rights-saadiyat-island-united-arab-emirates/2015-progress-report, accessed July 21, 2015. For a work of fiction that describes these conditions well, see Deepak Unnikrishnan, *Temporary People* (New York: Restless Books, 2017).

27 Please see Abu Dhabi Economic Vision 2030, https://www.ecouncil.ae/PublicationsEn/economic-vision-2030-full-versionEn.pdf, 24, accessed April 14, 2017.

28 Jane Guyer's work is illustrative in showing how the price of oil is constituted. For some examples of this discussion, please see Jane Guyer, *Marginal Gains: Monetary Transactions in Atlantic Africa* (Chicago: University of Chicago Press, 2004), 107 et seq.; Jane Guyer, "Composites, Fictions, and Risks: Toward an Ethnography of Price," in *Market and Society: The Great Transformation Today*, edited by C. Hann and K. Hart, 203–20 (Cambridge: Cambridge University Press, 2009); Jane Guyer, "Blueprints, Judgment, and Perseverance in a Corporate Context," *Current Anthropology* 52, no. 3 (2011): S17–S27; Jane Guyer, "Oil Assemblages and the Production of Confusion: Price Fluctuations in Two West African Oil-Producing Economies," in *Subterranean Estates: Life Worlds of Oil and* Gas, edited by Hannah Appel, Arthur Mason, and Michael Watts (Ithaca, NY: Cornell University Press, 2015), 237–52. For the making of oil price in the United States, listen to five *Planet Money* podcast episodes, http://www.npr.org/sections/money/2016/08/26/491342091/planet-money-buys-oil, accessed January 17, 2017.

29 Mitchell, *Carbon Democracy*.

30 N. Choucri, D. Goldsmith, T. Mezher, "Renewable Energy Policy in an Oil-Exporting Country: The Case of the United Arab Emirates," *Renewable Energy Law and Policy Review* 1, no. 1 (2010): 77–86. Please note that this research paper is a product of the MIT-Masdar Institute collaboration, coauthored by researchers from MIT and Masdar Institute.

31 "Abu Dhabi's oil reserves to last another 150 years," http://www.emirates247.com/eb247/economy/uae-economy/abu-dhabi-s-oil-reserves-to-last-another-150-years-2010-03-31-1.100837, accessed July 10, 2015.

32 Colin J. Campbell, *Campbell's Atlas of Oil and Gas Depletion* (New York: Springer, 2013), 322.

33 As Gary Bowden and Michael Aaron Dennis demonstrate, calculations regarding oil reserves are also linked to the corporate strategies and changing interests of the oil industry. For an overview, see Gary Bowden, "The Social Construction of Validity Estimates of US Crude Oil Reserves," *Social Studies of Science* 15, no. 2 (1985): 207–40; and Michael Aaron Dennis, "Drilling for Dollars: The Making of US Petroleum Reserve Estimates, 1921–25," *Social Studies of Science* 15, no. 2 (1985): 241–65.

34 For a more extensive discussion, see Gavin Bridge, "Geographies of Peak Oil: The Other Carbon Problem," *Geoforum* 41, no. 4 (2010): 523–30.

35 Rogers, "Oil and Anthropology."

36 Limbert, *In the Time of Oil*, 170–76. Also see Mandana Limbert, "Reserves, Secrecy and the Science of Oil Prognostication in Southern Arabia," in *Subterranean Estates: Life Worlds of Oil and Gas*, edited by Arthur Mason, Hannah Appel, and Michael Watts (Ithaca, NY: Cornell University Press, 2015).

37 Todd Reisz, "As a Matter of Fact: The Legend of Dubai," *Log* 13–14 (2008): 127–39.

38 For other examples of contexts where renewable energy and clean technology serve as solutions to present problems, see Dominic Boyer and Cymene Howe, "Aeolian Infrastructures, Aeolian Publics," *Limn* 7 (2016), http://limn.it/aeolian-infrastructures-aeolian-publics/, accessed May 31, 2017; Jamie Cross, "The 100th Object: Solar Lighting Technology and Humanitarian Goods," *Journal of Material Culture* 18, no. 4 (2013): 367–87; Rebecca Slayton, "Efficient, Secure Green: Digital Utopianism and the Challenge of a 'Smart' Grid," *Information and Culture* 48, no. 4 (2013): 448–78.

39 Rowan Moore, "Masdar City, Abu Dhabi: The Gulf between Wisdom and Folly," *The Observer*, December 18, 2010, https://www.theguardian.com/artanddesign/2010/dec/19/norman-foster-masdar-city-review, accessed April 23, 2017.

40 Laura Stupin, "I Live in a Spaceship in the Middle of the Desert," 2010, http://squidskin.blogspot.com/2010/09/i-live-in-spaceship-in-middle-of-desert.html, accessed April 7, 2017.

41 Laura Stupin, blogger profile, https://www.blogger.com/profile/05771450900786731642, accessed April 7, 2017.

42 Scott, *Seeing Like a State*.

43 Ferguson, *Anti-Politics Machine*.

44 Scholarship on infrastructure underlines how systems tend to disappear into the background when they function well. When they break down, however, they are easy to notice. At times, the dysfunctionality of infrastructure, particularly energy infrastructure, represents how people's expectations of

modernity dissipate. In studying the emergence of Abu Dhabi's renewable energy and clean technology infrastructure, I illustrate how these projects' potential to mitigate energy and climate change problems globally made the projects visible. Also see Brian Larkin, "The Politics and Poetics of Infrastructure," *Annual Review of Anthropology* 42 (2013): 327–43.

45 Giorgio Agamben, *Potentialities: Collected Essays in Philosophy* (Palo Alto, CA: Stanford University Press, 2000).

46 Paolo Virno, *Déjà Vu and the End of History* (New York: Verso, 2015).

47 Karen Pinkus, *Fuel: A Speculative Dictionary* (Minneapolis: University of Minnesota, 2016).

48 Gisa Weszkalnys, "Geology, Potentiality, Speculation: On the Indeterminacy of First Oil," *Cultural Anthropology* 30, no. 4 (2015): 611–39, 617. Also see Mette N. Svendsen, "Articulating Potentiality: Notes on the Delineation of the Blank Figure in Human Embryonic Stem Cell Research," *Cultural Anthropology* 26, no. 3 (2011): 414–37; and William Mazzarella, "Beautiful Balloon: The Digital Divide and the Charisma of New Media in India," *American Ethnologist* 37, no. 4 (2010): 783–804.

49 Halpern, *Beautiful Data*. For the logic of the test-bed, see Orit Halpern, J. LeCavalier, N. Calvillo, and W. Pietsch, "Test-Bed Urbanism," *Public Culture* 25, no. 2 (2013): 273–305.

50 In an article on offshore oil production, Hannah Appel studies the ways in which such highly mobile experts attempt to make oil production the same across different geographies despite local entanglements and shows how their paths and their work are hardly seamless. The context of Masdar is rather different from these offshore plants or from the oil industry that Appel describes, mainly because Masdar is located in a country that is almost entirely made up of such modular experts. The modularity and high turnover of the professionals in Abu Dhabi in particular and the UAE in general is at times perceived as a problem that should be mitigated through reformed citizenship protocols that encourage permanent residency in the country. The Emiratization movement, which calls for increased participation of UAE citizens in the economy and seeks to train them for positions of expertise, is another dominant reaction that emerges in other parts of the Arab Gulf as well (see chapter 2). Therefore, the modularity of the workforce is not necessarily a condition that the Abu Dhabi government always celebrates. At the same time, this modularity allows white-collar workers to mistakenly imagine Abu Dhabi as a noncontextual space where local politics can be shut out whenever necessary. Unexpected occurrences such as geopolitical tensions between Iran and the UAE, however, have shown these workers that social and political frictions are not always so easy to shut out (see chapter 2). Hannah Appel, "Offshore Work: Oil, Modularity,

and the How of Capitalism in Equatorial Guinea," *American Ethnologist* 39, no. 4 (2012): 692–709.

51 *Rashomon* is a 1950 Japanese film by Akira Kurosawa, based on two short stories by Ryunosuke Akutagawa in which a murder involving four individuals (suspects, witnesses, and surviving victims) is described in four mutually contradictory ways. Each account of the event, delivered by four different characters, is self-serving, intended to legitimize the narrator. As each of the four narrators testifies, the viewer sees that particular version of the events on film, so the visual image supports each testimony in turn. In this way, *Rashomon* seeks to convince the viewers of the truth of each perspective. Unlike detective stories, where viewers may reach a solid truth at the end, the film refuses to clarify the contradictions it creates. To further explore how this structure may color our understanding of anthropology as a discipline, please see Nur Yalman, "The Rashomon Effect: Considerations for Existential Anthropology," in *Rashomon Effects: Kurosawa,* Rashomon *and Their Legacies*, edited by Blair Davis, Robert Anderson, and Jan Walls (New York: Routledge, 2016).

52 Masdar Institute currently offers the following programs: MSc in Chemical Engineering, MSc in Computing and Information Science, MSc in Electrical Power Engineering, MSc in Engineering Systems and Management, MSc in Materials Science and Engineering, MSc in Mechanical Engineering, MSc in Microsystems Engineering, and MSc in Water and Environmental Engineering.

53 See Gökçe Günel, "Masdar City's Hidden Brain," *The arpa Journal*, 2014, http://arpajournal.gsapp.org/masdar-citys-hidden-brain/, accessed September 25, 2014.

Chapter 1: Inhabiting the Spaceship

1 See video, http://www.masdarcity.ae/en/49/resource-centre/video-gallery/?vid=1, accessed December 22, 2011.

2 The literature on the building of cities from scratch has at times touched upon this futurity. "Ciudad Guayana as an entity exists only in the publicity flyers of the development agency," Lisa Peattie writes, in reviewing the emergence of Ciudad Guayana, a new city that was started in the 1960s when the Venezuelan government invited planners from MIT and Harvard to create an emergent area of growth in the south of the country. "The design focus," Peattie continues, "served to convert the city into a kind of monument to the idea of progress, an ideological construction within which private gain could be thought of as social progress and the general good." This emphasis, according to Peattie, was thought to possibly facilitate the emergence of

an undivided community, while at the same time attracting investment and technically capable individuals to the city. In the case of Masdar, the eco-city would bring together a community of researchers, investors, and professionals working on clean technology and renewable energy infrastructures, thereby functioning as a magnet for investments and technically capable individuals. Through this emphasis on innovation, the eco-city set a stark contrast to the resource-led economy of Abu Dhabi. In discussing the construction of Brasília, James Holston also suggests, "This utopian difference between capital [Brasília] and nation meant that the planning of Brasília had to negate Brazil as it existed. Thus the Master Plan presents the founding of the city as if it had no history. . . . On inauguration day, [the government] planned to reveal a miracle: a gleaming city, empty and ready to receive its intended occupants." This strategy worked for the construction phase of Brasília. And yet, despite the attempts of the Abu Dhabi government, the plans for building a new city could not be put to use. The economic downturn of 2008 prohibited Abu Dhabi from completing the construction of the city fully, demanding that Masdar City be built step by step, together with the investors that it sought to attract. Masdar executives put together a sustainability code, expecting the incoming investors to abide by the city's guidelines. Companies such as Siemens, BASF, General Electric, and Bayer at once agreed to build research centers and office spaces within the clean technology cluster. The Siemens office was opened in 2014, while the others remain in planning stage. See Lisa Redfield Peattie, *Planning, Rethinking Ciudad Guayana* (Ann Arbor: University of Michigan Press, 1987); James Holston, *The Modernist City: An Anthropological Critique of Brasília* (Chicago: University of Chicago Press, 1989); and James C. Scott, *Seeing Like a State: How Certain Schemes to Improve the Human Condition Have Failed* (New Haven, CT: Yale University Press, 1998).

3 See "Abu Dhabi's Masdar Initiative Breaks Ground on Carbon-Neutral City of the Future," http://www.prnewswire.com/news-releases/abu-dhabis-masdar-initiative-breaks-ground-on-carbon-neutral-city-of-the-future-56875567.html, accessed March 14, 2016.

4 "Masdar City—Zero Carbon," http://www.asylum.com/2010/04/22/UAE-Dubai-sustainable-carbon-neutral-masdar-city-abu-dhabi/, accessed July 15, 2014.

5 "Past Sci-Fi Flicks Are the Future of Masdar," http://www.gearfuse.com/past-sci-fi-flicks-are-the-future-of-masdar/, accessed March 15, 2016.

6 Scholars of urban planning, literature, and the history of science have reviewed some of these emergent city projects. On Chinese eco-cities, see Shannon May, "Ecological Citizenship and a Plan for Sustainable Development," *City* 12, no. 2 (2008): 237–44, and Julie Sze, *Fantasy Islands: Chinese*

Dreams and Ecological Fears in an Age of Climate Crisis (Palo Alto, CA: University of California Press, 2014). On the Songdo project in South Korea, see Orit Halpern, *Beautiful Data: A History of Vision and Reason since 1945* (Durham, NC: Duke University Press, 2014). For an analysis of eco-friendly architecture, please see Anne Rademacher, *Building Green: Environmental Architects and the Struggle for Sustainability in Mumbai* (Berkeley: University of California Press, 2017).

7 "Masdar City—A Glimpse of the Future in the Desert," http://www.guardian.co.uk/environment/2011/apr/26/masdar-city-desert-future, accessed March 14, 2016.

8 "American 'Eco-Geek's' First Week at the Masdar Institute," http://www.greenprophet.com/2010/10/american-first-week-masdar/, accessed March 14, 2016.

9 Peder Anker, *From Bauhaus to Ecohouse: A History of Ecological Design* (Baton Rouge: Louisiana State University Press, 2010). Also see Sabine Höhler, *Spaceship Earth in the Environmental Age, 1960–1990* (London: Pickering and Chatto, 2015).

10 For more on the Biosphere 2 project, see Sabine Höhler, "The Environment as a Life Support System: The Case of Biosphere 2," *History and Technology* 26, no. 1 (2010): 39–58.

11 Hans Blumenberg, *Shipwreck with Spectator: Paradigm of a Metaphor for Existence* (Cambridge, MA: MIT Press, 1996), 8.

12 Peter Sloterdijk, *Globes: Spheres 2* (South Pasadena, CA: Semiotext(e), 2014).

13 David Valentine, "Atmosphere: Context, Detachment, and the View from above Earth," *American Ethnologist* 43, no. 3 (2016): 511–24, 513.

14 For a biography of Fuller, please see Steven Sieden, *Buckminster Fuller's Universe: His Life and Work* (New York: Basic Books, 2000).

15 Buckminster Fuller, *Operating Manual for Spaceship Earth* (Rotterdam: Lars Müller, [1969] 2008); also see Anker, *From Bauhaus to Eco-House.*

16 Fuller, *Operating Manual for Spaceship Earth*, 52–54.

17 Ernst von Meijenfeldt and Marit Geluk, *Below Ground Level: Creating New Spaces for Contemporary Architecture* (Basel: Birkhäuser, 2003), 130.

18 "The Pritzker Architecture Prize: Norman Foster, 1999 Laureate," https://www.pritzkerprize.com/sites/default/files/file_fields/field_files_inline/1999_bio.pdf.

19 Thomas Tse Kwai Zung, *Buckminster Fuller: Anthology for a New Millennium* (New York: St. Martin's Press, 2002), 2.

20 "Man on the Moon: Norman Foster Prepares for Architecture's Lift-Off," *The Guardian*, September 22, 2009, http://www.guardian.co.uk/artanddesign/2009/sep/22/moon-norman-foster-architecture, accessed January 24, 2014.

21 "Norman Foster Takes on Mars: Architect's Firm Reveals Their Award-Winning Vision for an Astronaut's Life on the Red Planet," *Daily Mail*, http://www.dailymail.co.uk/sciencetech/article-3253478/Norman-Foster-takes-Mars-Architect-s-firm-reveals-award-winning-vision-astronaut-s-life-red-planet.html, accessed September 30, 2015. Also see "Foster + Partners Reveals Concept for 3D-Printed Mars Habitat Built by Robots," http://www.dezeen.com/2015/09/25/foster-partners-concept-3d-printed-mars-habitat-robots-regolith/, accessed September 30, 2015.

22 "Norman Foster: Building an Oasis," http://www.thenational.ae/arts-culture/norman-foster-building-an-oasis, accessed January 24, 2014.

23 "Masdar: Abu Dhabi's Carbon Neutral City," BBC News, http://news.bbc.co.uk/2/hi/middle_east/8586046.stm, accessed January 24, 2014.

24 Easa Saleh Al-Gurg, *The Wells of Memory: An Autobiography* (London: J. Murray, 1998). Easa Al-Gurg started one of the UAE's most prominent family businesses in 1960 after gaining considerable experience in the fields of banking and finance. He was an adviser to Sheikh Rashid, the late ruler of Dubai, and was also one of the people who attended the meetings in which the UAE was formed on December 2, 1971. Easa Al-Gurg also served as UAE ambassador to the United Kingdom and the Republic of Ireland for almost two decades, starting in 1991.

25 Nicolai Ouroussoff, "In Arabian Desert, a Sustainable City Rises," *New York Times*, September 26, 2010, http://www.nytimes.com/2010/09/26/arts/design/26masdar.html?pagewanted=1&_r=1, accessed January 21, 2014.

26 Norman Foster, "Masdar City, Abu Dhabi: The Gulf between Wisdom and Folly," *The Guardian*, December 19, 2010, http://www.guardian.co.uk/artanddesign/2010/dec/19/norman-foster-masdar-city-review, accessed March 28, 2017.

27 David A. Mindell, *Digital Apollo: Human and Machine in Spaceflight* (Cambridge, MA: MIT Press, 2008), 12.

28 Environmental imaginaries of the desert have long been a point of contestation. While colonizers of the desert, say the French in Algeria, perceived the desert as an arid environment from which only death could emerge, their Algerian counterparts explained to them that they are unable to perceive the riches of this landscape. At times the desert suffered from what Diana Davis calls environmental orientalism, and was conceived as a homogeneous geography. In the case of Abu Dhabi, the desert had the double function of both being a place of wealth—as the source of oil—and a place that was a home for previous generations who knew the specific characteristics of their local environment, but for the contemporary generation could only be navigated by relying on a spaceship. See Diana K. Davis, "Imperialism,

Orientalism, and the Environment in the Middle East: History, Policy, Power, and Practice," in *Environmental Imaginaries of the Middle East and North Africa*, edited by Diana K. Davis and Edmund Burke III (Athens: Ohio University Press, 2011), 1–22. Also see George Trumbull's chapter "Body of Work" in the same edited volume, 87–113.

29 For a longer exploration of this theme, see Rosalind Williams, *Notes on the Underground: An Essay on Technology, Society, and the Imagination* (Cambridge, MA: MIT Press, [1990] 2008), 7.

30 As Sabine Höhler reminds her readers, "Appropriating space by compiling, registering, and neatly arranging the elements within it is a strategy not limited to the modern era of scientific collecting, archiving, and interpreting of the world. The procedure recalls the primal ship representing the inventory of the world, the biblical ark." Höhler, "The Environment as a Life Support System." Also see Höhler, *Spaceship Earth in the Environmental Age*.

31 Presentation at World Future Energy Summit, Abu Dhabi, UAE, January 18, 2011.

32 For a review of these figures, please see "Work Starts on Gulf 'Green City,'" BBC News, http://news.bbc.co.uk/2/hi/science/nature/7237672.stm, accessed March 28, 2017.

33 In recent years, scholars in the social sciences and humanities have become interested in the promissory nature of capitalism, wherein forward-looking statements give life to commercial futures without necessitating material counterparts. For instance, Stefan Helmreich, researching how the ocean becomes marketable, suggests, "In promissory capitalism, after all, money need not be made off marine microbes but can sometimes just as well or better be made off promises about the sunken treasure that will be extracted from them in a possible, artificially selected, blue-ocean future." Likewise, in *Promising Genomics*, Michael Fortun outlines "sequences of speculative activity as they operated across a range of global genomic territories," and studies the "forward-looking statements" that are abundant within his field site. Investigating speculations and promises that are associated with genomic research within Indian techno-science, Sunder Rajan states, "to generate value in the present to make a certain kind of future possible, a vision of that future has to be sold, even if it is a vision that will never be realized. The temporal order of production is inverted away from the present building toward the future instead towards the future always being called into account for the present." In this way, the imaginaries of a future potential constitute the reasons why and how any enterprise may be reliable or successful. Accordingly, he adds, "hype constitutes the grounds on which reality unfolds." All in all, Rajan concludes, for the "biotechnology corporation to exist and

survive it is credibility, rather than truth, with which it is essential to start." But how exactly does a techno-scientific venture produce this credibility? Stefan Helmreich, *Alien Ocean: Anthropological Voyages in Microbial Seas* (Berkeley: University of California Press, 2009); Michael Fortun, *Promising Genomics: Iceland and deCODE Genetics in a World of Speculation* (Berkeley: University of California Press, 2008); and Kaushik Sunder Rajan, "Subjects of Speculation: Emergent Life Sciences and Market Logics in the United States and India," *American Anthropologist* 107, no. 1 (2005): 19–30.

34 See Ahmed Kanna, *Dubai, the City as Corporation* (Minneapolis: University of Minnesota Press, 2011), 93–104. In her seminal article on the Islamic city, Janet Abu-Lughod also notes that "in many parts of the Arab world, and especially in Saudi Arabia and the Gulf, urban planners with a newfound respect for the great achievements of the past are searching for ways to reproduce in today's cities some of the patterns of city building that have been identified as Islamic." She reasons that these decision makers "have been influenced, whether wittingly or not, by a body of literature produced by western Orientalists purporting to describe the essence of the Islamic city." See Janet Abu-Lughod, "The Islamic City—Historical Myth, Islamic Essence, and Contemporary Relevance," *International Journal of Middle Eastern Studies* 19 (1987): 155–76, 155.

35 See one example here: http://masdarcity.ae/digitalbrochure/en/TheGlobalCentreofFutureEnergy/, accessed January 9, 2012.

36 Similar types of performances take place in other new research institutions around the world. For instance, one colleague who worked with a comparable institution in Singapore suggested that he had been "instructed on several occasions to come to work at a specific time, and to sit in front of his computer in formal business attire." After a while an ambassador/minister/CEO walked around the office for about 30 seconds. Upon his departure, everyone was allowed to go back home.

37 In his novel *Remainder*, Tom McCarthy portrays a man who loses his grasp on the world after a traumatizing accident. With the funds he receives from his insurance company, the character in the novel generates looping installations peopled by hired actors, hoping to realize a version of what he perceived as lived experience. In some ways, the Potemkin villages of the Masdar library and the wind tower were like these installations, seeking to generate and perform a particular version of reality for a particular audience. In both of these cases, the idealized repetitions were reminiscent of George Bataille's understanding of exuberance, where the value generated through these performances allows for a possible sovereignty for the characters involved. Tom McCarthy, *Remainder* (New York: Vintage, 2007).

38 "Masdar Looks Like a City from the Future: Owen," http://www.khaleejtimes.com/DisplayArticle.asp?xfile=data/theuae/2010/October/theuae_October373.xml§ion=theuae&col=, accessed April 11, 2012.

39 "Der geplatzte Traum der Wüstenstadt Masdar," http://www.wiwo.de/technologie/modellmetropole-der-geplatzte-traum-der-wuestenstadt-masdar/5258478.html (my translation), accessed January 22, 2012.

40 Increasingly, "the mirage" has become a significant discursive tool in thinking about Masdar City. For instance, this news piece describes Masdar City as a disappointing mirage that did not live up to its promises: http://www.worldcrunch.com/smarter-cities/masdar-city-green-desert-paradise-or-disappointing-mirage-/masdar-city-abu-dhabi-smart-future-city/c15s18332/#.Va17jhNViko, accessed July 20, 2015.

41 See, for instance, this proposal for self-cleaning solar panels: "Self-Cleaning Solar Panels," http://www.technologyreview.com/news/420524/self-cleaning-solar-panels/, accessed July 2, 2014.

42 On labor conditions in the UAE, see David Keane and Nicholas McGeehan, "Enforcing Migrant Workers' Rights in the United Arab Emirates," *International Journal on Minority and Group Rights* 15, no. 1 (2008): 81–115, and Sulayman Khalaf and Saad Alkobaisi, "Migrants' Strategies of Coping and Patterns of Accommodation in the Oil-Rich Gulf Societies: Evidence from the UAE," *British Journal of Middle Eastern Studies* 26, no. 2 (1999): 271–98. For a recent account of struggles to protect immigrant rights in the Arab Gulf, especially in Abu Dhabi, see gulflabor.org, accessed July 15, 2014.

43 "Abu Dhabi: Oil Today, Green Tomorrow?" http://www.marcgunther.com/2011/01/17/abu-dhabi-oil-today-green-tomorrow/, accessed January 21, 2012.

Chapter 2: Beautiful Buildings and Research Contracts

1 Robert College, the oldest American school outside the United States, was established in 1863. Its founders were Christopher Rhinelander Robert (1802–78), a wealthy American philanthropist whose father had made a fortune in the West Indies and who himself built on that fortune by multiple ventures in shipping and mining inside and outside the United States, and Cyrus Hamlin, a missionary with a special interest in education. For more information on the biographies of these founders, please see Özlem Altan-Olcay, "Defining 'America' from a Distance: Local Strategies of the Global in the Middle East," *Middle Eastern Studies* 44, no. 1 (2008): 29–52. Also see Ali Erken, "The Making of Politics and Trained Intelligence in the Near East: Robert College of Istanbul," *European Review of History: Revue européenne d'histoire* 23, no. 3 (2016): 554–71.

2 This was not an entirely new strategy: by exploring TDP's history, this chapter shows that such beautiful buildings and research contracts had been relatively significant to the production of research institutions in countries such as Egypt, Lebanon, and Kuwait as well.

3 In his *Cultural Anthropology* article, Tom Looser asks why students would travel to branch campuses for their education. Although Masdar Institute is not a branch campus, some of his suggestions may apply: "Given these conditions, from a student's perspective, why fly off to one of these campuses? Why fly off to Songdo, or Pudong, or Abu Dhabi, if that is not already home . . . why would a student go? For the moment, the answer generally seems to be money (either scholarship inducements as at Abu Dhabi or cheaper tuition relative to the costs of private universities in the United States as at a place like Yonsei's UIC), and the promise of real, if nonetheless generic, excellence. And perhaps still some interest in a local area." While the generous stipends and excellence in education were influential in making students select Masdar Institute, none of the students I spoke with mentioned an interest in Abu Dhabi's local context, other than the fact that it was close to home for many of them. They compared Masdar with KAUST in Saudi Arabia, and said they preferred Abu Dhabi because it was socially more liberal than Saudi Arabia. Tom Looser, "The Global University, Area Studies, and the World Citizen: Neoliberal Geography's Redistribution of the 'World,'" *Cultural Anthropology* 27, no. 1 (2012): 97–117.

4 "Masdar Institute in US Student Recruitment Drive," http://www.thenational.ae/news/uae-news/environment/masdar-institute-in-us-student-recruitment-drive, accessed March 14, 2016.

5 Discussing the inauguration of KAUST, Toby Craig Jones writes: "[King Abdullah's] focus on science and technology, and his use of oil wealth to build up local expertise, which the king hopes will ultimately help the kingdom diversify its economy, establish a foundation for a future after oil, and make Saudi Arabia internationally competitive in science, are signals that these areas should figure prominently in how both Saudis and outsiders think about the kingdom." Toby Craig Jones, *Desert Kingdom: How Oil and Water Forged Modern Saudi Arabia* (Cambridge, MA: Harvard University Press, 2010).

6 In his overview of educational institutions in the Gulf, architect Kevin Mitchell, a faculty member at the American University of Sharjah, reports on Masdar Institute and KAUST, understanding them as part and parcel of a shared development strategy. Kevin Mitchell, "Design for the Future: Educational Institutions in the Gulf," *Architectural Design* 85, no. 1 (2015): 38–45.

7 Please see James Collins Jr., "The Design Process for the Human Workplace," in *Architecture of Science*, edited by Peter Galison and Emily Ann Thompson (Cambridge, MA: MIT Press, 1999), 410.

8 Nigel Thrift, "Re-Inventing Invention: New Tendencies in Capitalist Commodification," *Economy and Society* 35, no. 2 (2006): 279–306; also see Nigel Thrift, *Knowing Capitalism* (London: SAGE, 2005).

9 The Foster + Partners design suggested that the laboratories would have a "plug-and-play" function, where desks and office spaces would be modular, allowing for interdisciplinary work. However, this feature of the building was much less significant and much less visible than the ways in which it affected relationships with the outside world.

10 Ritchie Lorin and Kathlin Ray, "Incorporating Information Literacy into the Building Plan: The American University of Sharjah Experience," *Reference Services Review* 36, no. 2 (2008), 167–79, 168.

11 D. Kirk and D. Napier, "The Transformation of Higher Education in the United Arab Emirates: Issues, Implications, and Intercultural Dimensions," in *Nation-Building, Identity and Citizenship Education: Cross Cultural Perspectives*, edited by J. Zajda, H. Daun, and L. J. Saha (Dordrecht, Netherlands: Springer Science + Business Media B.V., 2009), 131–42.

12 Stephen Wilkins, "Higher Education in the United Arab Emirates: An Analysis of the Outcomes of Significant Increases in Supply and Competition," *Journal of Higher Education Policy and Management* 32, no. 4 (2010): 389–400.

13 In 1977, 502 students were enrolled at the United Arab Emirates University, of whom 313 were male and 187 were female. By 1990, enrollment had grown to 2,464 males and 5,483 females, or a total of 7,947 students; and in 1992 there were 2,525 males and 6,739 females, or a total of 9,264 students at the university. Please see Khalifa A. Alsuwaidi, "The Future of Higher Education in the United Arab Emirates," PhD diss., University of Southern California, http://ezproxy.library.arizona.edu/login?url=http://search.proquest.com.ezproxy4.1ibrary.arizona.edu/docview/1627800065?accountid=8360.

14 Kirk and Napier, "The Transformation of Higher Education in the United Arab Emirates," 137.

15 For a ranking of the universities, see "Top 10 Universities in the UAE: The United Arab Emirates Offers a Range of Educational Opportunities for Both International and Local Students," *Gulf Business*, http://gulfbusiness.com/top-10-universities-uae/, accessed May 8, 2017.

16 Kirk and Napier, "The Transformation of Higher Education in the United Arab Emirates," 136.

17 Christopher M. Davidson, *Abu Dhabi: Oil and Beyond* (New York: Columbia University Press, 2009), 149–52.

18 "Masdar Institute's Founding President Reflects on Career as Class of 2014 Graduates," http://www.thenational.ae/uae/technology/masdar-institutes-founding-president-reflects-on-career-as-class-of-2014-graduates, accessed May 16, 2017. For figures from 2015–16, please see "Masdar Institute Facts 2015–2016," https://www.masdar.ac.ae/images/pdf/LR-2016-March-MI-Facts-AA.pdf, accessed May 18, 2017.

19 The art market in the UAE started booming in 2006, serving as a space where Middle Eastern artists could auction their work and demonstrating how "for the first time, Middle Eastern art appears definitively to be part of a global scene." "Gold Rush: The Emerging Art Market in the UAE," http://bidoun.org/articles/gold-rush, accessed May 19, 2017. Also see two recent theses on the topic: Taymour Grahne, "The Rise of the Middle Eastern Art Market since 2006," master's thesis, Sotheby's Institute of Art, New York, 2013; and Mert Kaymakçı, "Art and Patronage in the Middle East: The United Arab Emirates," master's thesis, Sotheby's Institute of Art, New York, 2016.

20 http://www.forbescustom.com/abudhabi/index.html, accessed April 10, 2012.

21 For a discussion of the "idea capital" concept, please see Looser, "The Global University."

22 Please note that the organization changed its name from Technology Adaptation Program to Technology and Development Program in 1985.

23 The agreement between Masdar Institute and TDP was renewed in December 2011 and lasted until December 2016. At the time of writing, it is unclear whether the agreement will be renewed again.

24 "MIT Reports to the President 2007–2008," http://web.mit.edu/annualreports/pres08/2008.08.20.pdf, accessed April 6, 2012.

25 See "Abu Dhabi Economic Vision 2030," https://www.ecouncil.ae/PublicationsEn/economic-vision-2030-full-versionEn.pdf, 5, accessed July 20, 2015.

26 Similar types of transformation are taking place in other oil- and gas-rich Gulf countries, where governments increasingly grow concerned about their dependence on finite resources. Like the Abu Dhabi government, the Qatari government invests in arts and education with the expectation of establishing a knowledge-based economy that will safeguard the country's future. One of the major investments in Qatar is Education City, which houses the branch campuses of several U.S.-based institutions of higher education, such as Cornell, Texas A&M, and Georgetown. For an analysis of Education City, please see Neha Vora, "Between Global Citizenship and Qatarization: Negotiating Qatar's New Knowledge Economy within American Branch Campuses," *Ethnic and Racial Studies* 37, no. 12 (2014): 2243–60.

Also see Neha Vora, *Teach for Arabia: American Universities, Liberalism, and Transnational Qatar* (Stanford, CA: Stanford University Press, 2018).

27 As Nigel Thrift argues, this move may be perceived as an attempt "to engineer new kinds of . . . subject positions that can cope with the disciplines of permanent emergency." Nigel Thrift, "Performing Cultures in the New Economy," *Annals of the Association of American Geographers* 90, no. 4 (2000): 674–92.

28 Michel Callon, "An Essay on the Growing Contribution of Economic Markets to the Proliferation of the Social," *Theory, Culture and Society* 24, nos. 7–8 (2007): 139–63.

29 During a conversation in November 2016, a Masdar Institute faculty member suggested that the MIT partnership would soon be phased out, mainly because it was too expensive to keep the U.S. institution as a partner. At the same time, rumors in 2016 indicated that Masdar Institute could be merging with one of the undergraduate universities in Abu Dhabi, another reason the MIT partnership was no longer considered feasible.

30 Fred announced his retirement at the 2014 Masdar Institute commencement ceremony, yet remained an important figure in the institute after his retirement. See http://www.thenational.ae/uae/technology/masdar-institutes-founding-president-reflects-on-career-as-class-of-2014-graduates, accessed July 11 2014.

31 http://web.mit.edu/mit-tdp/about/, accessed February 27, 2012.

32 During my fieldwork at MIT in Cambridge between January and June 2010, I observed that the TDP received criticism for being too insular, and for working with the same faculty members on different projects, rather than involving new people.

33 After Steve moved to Abu Dhabi in August 2010 to work at Masdar Institute, MIT Professor Duane Boning took over Steve's role in Cambridge, and was appointed executive director.

34 An institutional review board (IRB) is a type of committee used in research in the United States that has been formally designated to approve, monitor, and review biomedical and behavioral research involving humans. For an analysis of IRB practices in the United States, please see Laura Stark, *Behind Closed Doors: IRBs and the Making of Ethical Research* (Chicago: University of Chicago Press, 2012).

35 While there were no IRB protocols at Masdar Institute during the years I conducted research there, by 2016 these protocols had been established in the UAE.

36 However, not everyone agreed with this argument about reciprocity. One faculty member at Masdar Institute insisted, for instance, that their faculty

partners at MIT were, most of the time, not invested in these collaborative projects. Referring to the sums of money that the MIT faculty received for providing syllabi and other basic forms of guidance, she emphasized how they enjoyed extensive financial privileges through these contracts.

37 In the past decade, scholars in social sciences and humanities have examined the so-called global university, focusing on the emergence of satellite campuses in Asia and the Middle East. These critics underline how the branch campuses are a reflection of the transforming nature of the North American university system, which relatedly propels changes outside the North American setting. By investigating the types of subjects that branch campuses produce, some scholars emphasize the neocolonial nature of such university functions, while others point to the new types of thinking that are born in these venues. For an article that summarizes these discussions, please see Neha Vora, "Is the University Universal? Mobile (Re)Constitutions of American Academia in the Gulf Arab States," *Anthropology and Education Quarterly* 46, no. 1 (2015): 19–36.

38 For instance, one model proposes that there are seven different ways in which such campuses work and categorizes them as replica campuses (NYU-Abu Dhabi), branch campuses (Cornell Medical), old turnkey campuses (AUB and AUC), new turnkey campuses (AUS), transnational programs (DePaul Business School), foreign campuses (American University in Dubai), and virtual branch campuses (University of Phoenix). According to this model, Masdar Institute would perhaps be categorized as a new turnkey campus, based on the foreign model of higher education, affiliated with or founded in collaboration or consultation with foreign institutions, accredited (or in the process) in the foreign affiliate country and granting degrees recognized in that country, though Fred would resist this category. For more information on these categories, please see Cynthia Miller-Idriss and Elizabeth Hanauer, "Transnational Higher Education: Offshore Campuses in the Middle East," *Comparative Education* 47, no. 2 (2011): 181–207.

39 For a thorough analysis of the production of American higher education institutions in the Middle East, especially Robert College, American University of Beirut, and American University of Cairo, please see Altan-Olcay, "Defining 'America' from a Distance." Also see Erken, "The Making of Politics and Trained Intelligence in the Near East."

40 For more details on the nature of the collaboration between the Petroleum Institute and the University of Maryland, please see http://www.eerc.umd.edu/. For a review of the program from 2008, please see http://www.civil.umd.edu/news/news_story.php?id=2909, accessed May 16, 2017.

41 "Global University Branch Campuses in the UAE Need More Regulation," http://www.thenational.ae/uae/global-university-branch-campuses-in-the-uae-need-more-regulation, accessed May 16, 2017.

42 In an article published in 2014, Neha Vora examines branch campuses in Qatar including Cornell, and analyzes how noncitizen students (many of whom were born and raised in Qatar) respond to the production of a knowledge-based economy in the country. The article investigates the seemingly contradictory categories of "global citizenship" and "Qatarization," which are jointly mobilized in constructing knowledge infrastructure, but does not touch upon the imagined longevity of the branch campus as an institutional model. Please see Vora, "Between Global Citizenship and Qatarization."

43 This independence would also leave wiggle room to both mother and branch institutions, allowing each to assert its own understanding of the politics and ethics of pedagogical practice. In the case of NYU-Abu Dhabi, for instance, issues such as the admission of Israeli students or faculty members had become problematic, requiring the two sides to negotiate on whose principles would be enacted within NYU-Abu Dhabi—NYU's or Abu Dhabi's? The Abu Dhabi government had also impeded scholarly research on the emirate's abuse of workers' rights, basically by preventing certain NYU faculty from entering the country. In this latter case, NYU refused to intervene, suggesting that they could not challenge the country's sovereignty. For an informative news piece on this controversy, please see "N.Y.U. Professor Is Barred by United Arab Emirates," *New York Times*, March 17, 2015, http://www.nytimes.com/2015/03/17/nyregion/nyu-professor-is-barred-from-the-united-arab-emirates.html?_r=0, accessed July 21, 2015.

44 Interview with Steve, February 16, 2010.

45 For in-depth studies of development in Egypt, see Julia Elyachar, *Markets of Dispossession: NGOs, Economic Development, and the State in Cairo* (Durham, NC: Duke University Press, 2005), and Timothy Mitchell, *Rule of Experts: Egypt, Techno-Politics, Modernity* (Berkeley: University of California Press, 2002).

46 E. F. Schumacher, *Small Is Beautiful: A Study of Economics as if People Mattered* (New York: Blond and Briggs, 1973), 21.

47 Schumacher, *Small Is Beautiful*, 21.

48 Schumacher, *Small Is Beautiful*, 29–30.

49 See "Evaluation of the Technological Planning Program Cairo University/Massachusetts Institute of Technology Aid Contract NE-C-1291," http://pdf.usaid.gov/pdf_docs/PDAAM411.pdf, accessed May 16, 2017.

50 "Lebanon: American University of Beirut," http://web.mit.edu/mit-tdp/projects/lebanon.html, accessed May 16, 2017.

51 In early 2014, Siemens moved into a Sheppard Robson–designed building in Masdar City. The city plans to host BASF, Bayer, and Schneider Electric, as well as GE. For a review of the Siemens building, please see "Siemens HQ in Masdar City/Sheppard Robson," http://www.archdaily.com/539213/siemens-hq-in-masdar-city-sheppard-robson, accessed July 24, 2015.

52 I asked Fred how the humanities and social sciences would fare under this model. Given his faith in contract research, he suggested that media organizations such as History Channel could support the humanities and social sciences in their academic inquiries. While this approach would transform the workings of social sciences and humanities, he argued that it would integrate them within the corporate funding model.

53 "GE Moves Smart Appliance Testing to Masdar City: Kitchen of the Future Takes a Trip to Abu Dhabi," http://www.greenchipstocks.com/articles/ge-moves-smart-appliance-testing-to-masdar-city/851, accessed July 22, 2015.

54 "Sovereign Wealth: Abu Dhabi Fund Gains General Electric Stake in $40bn Partnership," *The Guardian*, July 23, 2008, http://www.guardian.co.uk/business/2008/jul/23/generalelectric.sovereignwealthfunds, accessed February 22, 2012. Also see "General Electric Opens 'Ecomagination Centre' in Masdar City," http://www.thenational.ae/business/industry-insights/energy/general-electric-opens-ecomagination-centre-in-masdar-city, accessed May 8, 2017.

55 Please see Daniel Haberly, "Strategic Sovereign Wealth Fund Investment and the New Alliance Capitalism: A Network Mapping Investigation," *Environment and Planning A* 43, no. 8 (2011): 1833–52, and Daniel Haberly, "White Knights from the Gulf: Sovereign Wealth Fund Investment and the Evolution of German Industrial Finance," *Economic Geography* 90, no. 3 (2014): 293–320. Also see Rawi Abdelal, "Sovereign Wealth in Abu Dhabi" *Geopolitics* 14, no. 2 (2009): 317–27.

56 "GE and Mubadala to Launch Multi-Billion Dollar Global Business Partnership," http://www.mubadala.com/en/news/ge-and-mubadala-launch-multi-billion-dollar-global-business-partnership, accessed March 14, 2016.

57 Marilyn Strathern proposes a political and methodological corrective to the study of networks, arguing that scholars should pay attention to the moments of blockage rather than seeing relations as limitless extensions. Paying attention to these moments of exclusion is not only politically significant, providing an opportunity to examine where and how these blockages are built, but also methodologically important in showing limits. Marilyn Strathern, "Cutting the Network," *Journal of the Royal Anthropological Institute* 2, no. 3 (1996): 517–35.

58 In the UAE, it is common for immigrants to state their religions both on employment application forms and on visa application forms. Such declarations are not specific to Masdar Institute.

59 For a geopolitical review of Iran's relations with its Arab neighbors, please see: Anoushiravan Ehteshami, Neil Quilliam, and Gawdat Bahgat, *Security and Bilateral Issues between Iran and Its Arab Neighbors* (London: Springer, 2017).

60 "Linking Capital's Knowledge Hubs Can Fulfill Its Vision, *Huffington Post*, http://www.huffingtonpost.com/sultan-sooud-alqassemi/linking-capitals-knowledg_b_757376.html, accessed March 14, 2016.

61 For an exploration of Abu Dhabi's collaborators at Kizad, please see "Big Names Flood into Abu Dhabi's Kizad," http://www.thenational.ae/business/economy/big-names-flood-into-abu-dhabis-kizad, accessed March 14, 2016.

Chapter 3: Ergos: A New Energy Currency

1 See, for instance, Nawal Al-Hosany and Hisham Elkadi, "Sustainability Approaches for Incarceration Architecture," *Renewable and Sustainable Energy Reviews* 6, no. 5 (2002): 457–70.

2 For more information on the START campaign, please see http://www.masdar.ae/en/MediaArticle/NewsDescription.aspx?News_ID=155&News_Type=PR&MenuID=0&CatID=64, accessed December 22, 2011.

3 For more information, please see "Masdar Trains Staff in Sustainable Practices," http://www.tradearabia.com/news/env_191145.html, accessed December 22, 2011.

4 George Orwell, *Nineteen Eighty-Four* (New York: Signet Classic, 1950), 220.

5 Philip Mirowski, *More Heat Than Light: Economics as Social Physics, Physics as Nature's Economics* (Cambridge: Cambridge University Press, 1989).

6 Thorstein Veblen, "Why Is Economics Not an Evolutionary Science?" *Quarterly Journal of Economics* 12, no. 4 (1898): 373–97, 389.

7 One article about DESERTEC summarizes the aspirations of this now-cancelled initiative: "The Desertec concept is relatively simple; generate renewable energy in sparsely populated deserts and export that energy to population centers. Within six hours deserts around the world receive more energy from sunlight than the humans consume in a year, and 90% of the world's population lives within roughly 1,850 miles of a desert. The Maghreb contains some of the best solar and wind resources in the world. Therefore, clean, renewable electricity can be generated by large scale wind and solar plants in EUMENA and either consumed locally or exported to neighboring countries (primarily from North Africa to Europe). The proponents of the Desertec vision even go on to say that meeting 90% of EUMENA's electricity needs with renewables by 2050 is both economically and technically viable with an interconnected EUMENA grid." For more information on the project,

please see Scott Burger, "Desertec: A Fata Morgana?" *Africa Policy Journal* 8 (2012): 52–53. Also see the project's official website, http://www.desertec.org/, accessed May 7, 2017.

8 See Gustav Peebles, "Inverting the Panopticon: Money and the Nationalization of the Future," *Public Culture* 20, no. 2 (2008): 233–65.

9 "Masdar Students' Energy and Water Use Monitored," http://www.thenational.ae/news/uae-news/technology/masdar-students-energy-and-water-use-monitored, accessed March 14, 2016.

10 "Big Brother? Masdar Monitors Student Energy & Water Consumption," http://www.greenprophet.com/2011/08/masdar-students-energy-water/, accessed March 14, 2016.

11 See Peebles, "Inverting the Panopticon."

12 Also see François Ewald, "Two Infinities of Risk," in *The Politics of Everyday Fear*, edited by Brian Massumi (Minneapolis: University of Minnesota Press, 1993), 221–28.

13 Jonathan Parry and Maurice Bloch, *Money and the Morality of Exchange* (Cambridge: Cambridge University Press, 1989), 19–21.

14 Bill Maurer, *Mutual Life, Limited: Islamic Banking, Alternative Currencies, Lateral Reason* (Princeton, NJ: Princeton University Press, 2005), 4.

15 Ergos is not the only energy currency proposal that has been put together in the early twenty-first century. DeKos, for instance, understood as "a method for securing a more stable value currency via the central bank portfolio using electricity delivery assets," is also an attempt at fixing financial problems and energy problems at once. For more information on DeKos, please see http://papers.ssrn.com/s013/papers.cfm?abstract_id=1802166, accessed March 17, 2012. Also, in 1999, Richard Douthwaite, a philosopher and economist, came up with *ebcu*, meaning environment-backed currency unit, which would enable one to buy goods from other countries in addition to the right to produce carbon dioxide. For more information, on ebcu, see R. J. Douthwaite, *The Ecology of Money* (Totnes, UK: Green, 1999). For more information on the conference, see http://teslaconference.com/, accessed April 2, 2012.

16 For a recent biography of Nikola Tesla, see W. Bernard Carlson, *Tesla: Inventor of the Electrical Age* (Princeton, NJ: Princeton University Press, 2013).

17 Jem Bendell and Ian Doyle, *Healing Capitalism: Five Years in the Life of Business, Finance and Corporate Responsibility* (London: Greenleaf, 2014), 14.

18 See Douthwaite, *The Ecology of Money*, and Bernard Lietaer, *The Future of Money: Beyond Greed and Scarcity* (New York: Random House, 2001).

19 Sarah Elvins, "Scrip, Stores, and Cash-Strapped Cities: American Retailers and Alternative Currency during the Great Depression," *Journal of Historical Research in Marketing* 2, no. 1 (2010): 86–107.

20 C. H. Chatters, "Appendix E: Is Municipal Scrip a Panacea?" *Annals of Public and Cooperative Economics* 9, no. 2 (1933): 323–25, 324.

21 Loren Gatch, "Local Money in the United States during the Great Depression," *Essays in Economic and Business History* 26 (2008): 47–61, 57. Also see Loren Gatch, "Tax Anticipation Scrip as a Form of Local Currency in the USA during the 1930s," *International Journal of Community Currency Research* 16 (D) (2012): 22–35.

22 Leslie White, "Energy and the Evolution of Culture," *American Anthropologist* 45, no. 3 (1943): 335–56, 338. For a review of ideas on energy in anthropology, please see Dominic Boyer, "Energopolitics: An Introduction," *Anthropological Quarterly* 87, no. 2 (2014): 309–33.

23 For more information on the gold standard, please see Barry J. Eichengreen, *The Gold Standard in Theory and History* (New York: Methuen, [1985] 1997). Also see the *Planet Money* podcast titled "Gold Standard R.I.P.," http://www.npr.org/sections/money/2011/02/18/133874462/the-friday-podcast-gold-standard-r-i-p, accessed May 22, 2017.

24 There was disagreement among the participants regarding whether an energy currency was a political project attempting to generating a more ethical economic system. One group explicitly stated, "We understand that if there is a more stable currency, then people may plan more in advance. In this way, energy currency will help economic development and may contribute to fixing inequalities, but this is not our direct goal." However, others had started working on energy currencies with the specific goal of creating a fairer economic model. This debate ensued throughout the conference.

25 Keith Hart, "Money in an Unequal World," *The Memory Bank*, 2000, http://thememorybank.co.uk/papers/money-in-an-unequal-world/, accessed December 22, 2014.

26 Marc Shell, *The Economy of Literature* (Baltimore: Johns Hopkins University Press, [1978] 1993).

27 Bill Maurer, "Does Money Matter? Abstraction and Substitution in Alternative Financial Forms," in *Materiality*, edited by Daniel Miller (Durham, NC: Duke University Press, 2005a), 141.

28 Maurer, "Does Money Matter?" 141.

29 David Graeber, "Beads and Money: Notes Toward a Theory of Wealth and Power," *American Ethnologist* 23, no. 1 (1996): 4–24. Alexander also knew about David Graeber's work and cited his book *Debt: The First 5,000 Years*, specifically referring to his point about how credit arrangements have been part of commercial transactions for millennia, usually denominated in commodities like cattle and grain. These commodities were eventually formalized as currency. David Graeber, *Debt: The First 5,000 Years* (Brooklyn, NY: Melville House, 2011).

30 See Howard Scott, *Introduction to Technocracy* (New York: John Day, 1933).

31 William E. Akin, *Technocracy and the American Dream: The Technocrat Movement, 1900–1941* (Berkeley: University of California Press, 1977), 84.

32 As Akin states, "In the minds of the technocratic planners, the rationality of science and the harmony of the machine, not utopian virtues, would dictate organizational forms." However, the rationality of science and the harmony of the machine could only be achieved through specific social and psychological transformations. First of all, humans would have to accept that they are machines through precise conditioning methods. Akin writes, "Since the basic need of society was technical expertise, their education system would abolish the liberal arts, which stressed outmoded moralistic solutions to human problems. It would essentially replace the humanities with the machine shop. In the process, members of society would be conditioned to think in terms of engineering rationality and efficiency. Man, in short, would then be conditioned to assume the character of machines, to accept 'a reality understood in terms of machine-like functions.' In this way, the technocrats would eliminate religion, fine arts, and humanities along with all other possible kinds of intellectual activity. For them, these nonproductive acts had no function within the upcoming era of technical rationality, organized around an energy theory of value." Akin, *Technocracy and the American Dream*, 84, 142.

33 Mirowski, *More Heat Than Light*, 812.

34 For a history of energetics, from which neo-energetics derives its name, please see Mirowski, *More Heat Than Light*, 53–59.

35 Anthropology has also been one of the disciplines to underline the significance of energy theories of value, while providing an interpretation of its own. Mirowski highlights how, writing in *American Anthropologist* in 1943, Leslie White "proposed that all culture be conceptualized as a manifestation of "the amount of energy per capita per year harnessed and put to work." He continues, "This theme was taken up by many other anthropologists, such as [Leslie White's student, Richard Newbold] Adams." While their frame of analysis remained at the macro level, Leslie White and Richard N. Adams are commonly perceived as the first scholars to make energy a matter of concern in anthropology. White, "Energy and the Evolution of Culture."

36 Ernst R. Berndt, "From Technocracy to Net Energy Analysis: Engineers, Economists, and Recurring Energy Theories of Value," In *Progress in Natural Resource Economics*, edited by Anthony Scott, John Heliwel, Tracy Lewis, and P. A. Neher, 337–66 (Oxford: Clarendon Press, 1983), 342.

37 Robert Costanza, as quoted in Herman Daly and Alvaro Umaña, *Energy, Economics and the Environment: Conflicting Views of an Essential Interrelationship* (Boulder, CO: Westview, 1981), 167.

38 Scholarship in the anthropology of value examines the economy by studying the social transformations that take place within spheres of exchange. In doing so, many scholars, perhaps starting with Marcel Mauss's seminal work on the gift, argue that monetary exchange is shaped and defined by varying beliefs, affects, and cultural practices.

39 Rowan Moore wrote, "There is something spooky in the controls [Masdar] employs in the name of the environment—a touch of eco-Orwell or at least eco-Huxley. A hidden brain, for example, knows when you enter your building, so that your flat can be cooled before you arrive, while in public places flat screens broadcast uplifting news on the environmental performance of the complex." See Norman Foster, "Masdar City, Abu Dhabi: The Gulf between Wisdom and Folly," *The Guardian*, December 19, 2010, http://www.guardian.co.uk/artanddesign/2010/dec/19/norman-foster-masdar-city-review, accessed December 21, 2011. While on-site architects suggested that what they called "the intelligent system" would eventually enable such controls to be implemented, specifying that "when you're entering the building the entrance recognizes you and you walk into a room that's 24 degrees Celsius, and when you're out it goes up to 28 again," the system had not yet been put into use when my fieldwork at Masdar City ended at the end of May 2011. For an exploration of the BMS system at Masdar, please see Gökçe Günel, "Masdar City's Hidden Brain: When Monitoring and Modification Collide," *The arpa Journal*, inaugural issue on "Test Subjects," 2014, http://arpajournal.gsapp.org/masdar-citys-hidden-brain/, accessed July 14, 2014.

40 See, for instance, Shengwei Wang, *Intelligent Buildings and Building Automation* (London: Spon, 2010).

41 Catherine Fennell, "'Project Heat' and Sensory Politics in Redeveloping Chicago Public Housing," *Ethnography* 12 (2011): 40–64, 42.

42 Bryan Walsh, "Masdar City: The World's Greenest City?" *Time*, January 25, 2011, http://www.time.com/time/health/article/0,8599,2043934,00.html#ixzz1pGgoZ1Dg, accessed March 14, 2016.

43 "Masdar City—A Glimpse of the Future in the Desert," *The Guardian*, April 26, 2011, http://www.guardian.co.uk/environment/2011/apr/26/masdar-city-desert-future, accessed March 14, 2016.

44 In an article on dummy thermostats, Checket-Hanks argues: "Some HVAC experts acknowledge what millions of office workers have suspected all along. A lot of office thermostats are completely fake—meant to dupe you into thinking you have altered the office weather conditions. Fifty-one of seventy respondents to an informal survey on the *Air Conditioning, Heating and Refrigeration News* web site replied that they had installed 'dummy' thermostats. HVACR engineer Joe Olivieri has compared the fake thermostat to a placebo, a fake pill given by doctors to patients who have imaginary

aches and pains. If a contractor decides that use of a nonfunctioning thermostat is justifiable, it is critical that he tells a decisionmaker such a thermostat is part of the plan. Dan Int-Hout, chief engineer for Krueger, says that placebo thermostats can sometimes satisfy chronic complainers. However, sooner or later, he says, they figure it out." In an editor's note to *Engineered Systems* magazine, Beverly discusses how a fake thermostat positively affects the behavior of people inside a room. Please see B. Checket-Hanks, "Placebo Stats," *Air Conditioning, Heating and Refrigeration News* 218, no. 13 (2003), https://www.achrnews.com/articles/92414-placebo-stats, and R. Beverly, "Editor's Note: Your Thermostat: Trusty Friend or Two-Faced Double Agent?" *Engineered Systems* 20, no. 4: 8.

45 Michelle Murphy, *Sick Building Syndrome and the Problem of Uncertainty: Environmental Politics, Technoscience, and Women Workers* (Durham, NC: Duke University Press, 2006).

46 Beverly, "Editor's Note."

Chapter 4: An Expensive Toy

1 "Masdar City: The World's Greenest City?" *Time*, January 25, 2011, http://www.time.com/time/health/article/0,8599,2043934,00.html#ixzz1pGgoZ1Dg, accessed March 14, 2016.

2 This was the 2010 sequel to the original *tron* movie of 1982. The desire to remake a movie from 1982 in 2010 speaks for the hold of these sci-fi scenarios in the imagination—they continue to have a grip on the imagination because their worlds are, as "science fiction," never realized.

3 A consultant from Systematica told me that decision-making regarding the PRT project usually depended on the number of people a company was able to send to the meetings. For instance, Foster + Partners would send five to twelve architects to each meeting, depending on the importance of the issue, in order to have the power to enforce their demands. Systematica was able to appoint one or two people to each meeting, putting them in a minority position, and therefore had trouble convincing the client regarding their perspectives.

4 Initially, the PRT consultants at Systematica proposed a system of stations that could be reached within 250 meters of maximum walking distance from any point in the city. This meant about three minutes' walk, at a relaxed pace. Based on this measure, there would be about fifty to fifty-two stations in the city. However, Masdar executives requested that the maximum walking distance be reduced to 150 m (2 min), claiming that 250 meters was unacceptable in the Abu Dhabi climate. This resulted in

nearly doubling the number of stations, adding significant complexity and cost to the design.

5 The existing PRT system between the Masdar Institute building and the parking lot consists of ten passenger and three freight pods, which are stationed at two passenger and three freight stations connected by approximately a one-mile track. The system remains in operation eighteen hours a day, seven days a week, serving the Masdar Institute students, faculty, and visitors.

6 Bruno Latour, *Aramis, or the Love of Technology* (Cambridge, MA: Harvard University Press, 1996), ix.

7 One of his critiques regarding the PRT project is about how it is constructed as a "complete object" (1996: 119) by the engineers in charge. *Aramis* underlines that there is rarely a fatal inherent flaw to technological projects. "Such is the heroic narrative of technological innovation," Latour suggests (1996: 119), "a narrative of light and shadow in which the original object is complete and can only be degraded or maintained intact—allowing, of course, for a few minor adjustments."

8 There has been other scholarship focusing on the study of how grand projects fail, pointing out the role of incompleteness and potentiality. James Holston's great book *Modernist City*, which studies the design and construction of Brazil's capital city Brasília, shows how city dwellers in Brasilia materialized and enacted the incompleteness of the plan through their various interventions in the buildings, and eventually by occupying the city in ways that were never intended by the designers. Brasília, like any other city, would always remain an incomplete aggregate, never 'finished' in any way. In his book *Seeing Like a State*, James Scott (1998: 311–41) explores the idea of metis, which encapsulates the dynamic and plastic nature of knowledge practices, where expertise is born out of developing a "feel" for the task at hand, requiring every actor to "complete" the work in his or her own unique way. There is an openness and an incompleteness to metis, which allows for mutuality in the making of these projects, and which indicates perpetual potential. See James Holston, *The Modernist City: An Anthropological Critique of Brasília* (Chicago: University of Chicago Press, 1989), and James C. Scott, *Seeing Like a State: How Certain Schemes to Improve the Human Condition Have Failed* (New Haven, CT: Yale University Press, 1998).

9 For some images of the exhibit see http://www.flickr.com/photos/imresolt/3209978452/in/photostream/, accessed February 1, 2012.

10 Federico Parolotto, "Sustainable Mobility in Action," in *Ecological Urbanism*, edited by Mohsen Mostafavi and Gareth Doherty (Baden, Switzerland: Lars Müller, 2010), 401.

11 Parolotto, "Sustainable Mobility in Action," 401.

12 "Zagato's PRT Pod a Huge Hit at WFES," http://alternate-power.org/zagatos-prt-pod-a-huge-hit-at-wfes/, accessed March 14, 2016.

13 See the brochure for "Highways and Horizons" exhibit, http://ia600308.us.archive.org/12/items/generalmotorshigoogeddrich/generalmotorshigoogeddrich.pdf. Also see "Magic Motorways" by Norman Bel Geddes, the industrial designer who introduced the automated highway concept, which was exhibited at Highways and Horizons: http://ia600208.us.archive.org/10/items/magicmotorwaysoogeddrich/magicmotorwaysoogeddrich.pdf, accessed February 6, 2012.

14 For a discussion of automated transit, also see Keller Easterling, *Enduring Innocence: Global Architecture and Its Political Masquerades* (Cambridge, MA: MIT Press, 2005), 108–13.

15 U.S. Department of Housing and Urban Development, Office of Metropolitan Development, Urban Transportation Administration, *Tomorrow's Transportation: New Systems for the Urban Future* (Washington, DC: U.S. Government Printing Office, 1968), 60–65.

16 Taking inflation into account, in 2012 this amount would roughly translate to $2 billion.

17 William F. Hamilton II and Dana K. Nance, "Systems Analysis of Urban Transportation," *Scientific American* 221, no. 1 (1969): 19–27.

18 See more about the Morgantown PRT project at Sean D. Hamill, "City's White Elephant Now Looks Like a Transit Workhorse," *New York Times*, June 11, 2007, http://www.nytimes.com/2007/06/11/us/11tram.html?_r=1&oref=slogin, accessed March 14, 2016.

19 The Aerospace Corporation built a PRT model in 1978: https://www.youtube.com/watch?v=N6wFacwBMZE&ab_channel=sktavdr, accessed January 7, 2016.

20 "America's One and Only Personal Rapid Transit System," http://www.governing.com/topics/transportation-infrastructure/personal-rapid-transit-system-morgantown-west-virginia.html, accessed May 30, 2017.

21 The French PRT network Aramis had also been displayed in a World's Fair in Paris in 1989. See Latour, *Aramis*, 34.

22 For a comparative analysis of intelligent transportation systems in United States, Japan, and Europe, see Hans K. Klein, "Institutions, Innovation, and Information Infrastructure: The Social Construction of Intelligent Transportation Systems in the U.S., Europe, and Japan," PhD diss., Technology, Management, and Policy Program, MIT, 1996.

23 For an overview of the ULTra PRT system, please see http://www.ultraprt.com/heathrow/, accessed February 9, 2012.

24 A *Guardian* article from 2007 argues, for instance: "PRT is good for a closed network such as an airport, but there are indications that it could soon wend its way into our towns and cities. Several local authorities are looking closely at PRT, and the one furthest down the line is Daventry in Northamptonshire. Its population of 23,000 is set to expand to more than 40,000 by 2021 as part of the government's strategy to build lots of new houses within striking distance of London." "Welcome to the Transport of Tomorrow," *The Guardian*, October 11, 2007, https://www.theguardian.com/technology/2007/oct/11/guardianweeklytechnologysection.news1, accessed May 30, 2017.

25 "Abu Dhabi to Debut Personal Rapid Transit 'Podcars' Later This Year," http://www.treehugger.com/cars/abu-dhabi-to-debut-personal-rapid-transit-apodcarsa-later-this-year.html, accessed March 14, 2016.

26 "Abu Dhabi to Debut Personal Rapid Transit 'Podcars' Later This Year."

27 Isaac Asimov, "Visit to the World's Fair of 2014," *New York Times*, March 23, 1997, http://www.nytimes.com/books/97/03/23/lifetimes/asi-v-fair.html, accessed May 30, 2017.

28 For work that directly addresses the shift to driverless cars and investigates the technical, legal, and social challenges involved, please see Markus Maurer, J. Christian Gerdes, Barbara Lenz, and Hermann Winner, eds., *Autonomous Driving: Technical, Legal and Social Aspects* (New York: Springer, 2016), and Hod Lipson and Melba Kurman, *Driverless: Intelligent Cars and the Road Ahead* (Cambridge, MA: MIT Press, 2016).

29 In fact, the transportation planners and PRT subcontractors at Masdar did not necessarily understand this lack of speed as a problem. In an exchange in November 2014, one of the PRT consultants explained, "As for speed: one of the reasons that Foster's master plan won the competition is that it was the only one that considered a compact development which did not occupy the entire area of the plot. This was good for us because it reduced dramatically the distances between the points of interest. So we could use a very slow system without the fear that trips would be unacceptably long. Indeed, a higher acceleration and speed would be pleasant to have, but it would also have required much more energy: the relationship between energy and speed is a square curve: if you double the speed the energy required becomes quadruple. So going slow is one of the proper ways to sustainability." For the transport planners, this obsession with speed signaled how humans did not want to let go of the luxuries that the current fossil fuel economy made possible and demanded ways of extending the status quo.

30 For a discussion of "astonished contemplation," please see Ernst Bloch, *The Utopian Function of Art and Literature: Selected Essays* (Cambridge, MA:

MIT Press, 1988), and Jose Esteban Muñoz, *Cruising Utopia: The Then and There of Queer Futurity* (New York: NYU Press, 2009).

31 Nicolai Ouroussoff, "In Arabian Desert, a Sustainable City Rises," *New York Times*, September 26, 2009, http://www.nytimes.com/2010/09/26/arts/design/26masdar.html, accessed April 22, 2015.

32 For more details on the event, please see http://masdarcity.ae/en/75/resource-centre/press-releases/?view=details&id=84, accessed May 28, 2014.

33 Michael Taussig, *The Nervous System* (New York: Routledge, 1992), 1–3.

34 Although they did not come up in my conversations with Sylvia, there had been other occasions that seemed to define failure for PRT pods at Masdar City. First, the day when a committee from Switzerland came to visit the institute had been one of those times when the PRT failed. Following their site tour, the committee had been guided to the undercroft to take the pod cars to the parking lot, only to realize that the system was down. They had waited at the station for some time, but then were taken upstairs to take a regular shuttle bus to the parking lot. The tour guides apologized to the committee and explained that this was an experimental system, so it was only natural that it malfunctioned sometimes. Second, when Hillary Clinton paid a visit to the new Masdar Institute campus, Masdar authorities prepared for her to enter the building by taking the PRT. Clinton's security guards studied the PRT pods carefully and reported that she could not ride the experimental transit system. Eventually, she was taken to the institute by car. The security guards had not been able to figure out what it would mean for the emergent transit system to be safe and accordingly preempt its possible risks and uncertainties. In this case, it had proved more logical for the secretary of state to travel by car, a means of transport that the security guards were more familiar with. However, the Hillary Clinton story at times became bundled up with other stories of failure and became interpreted as one such incident.

35 According to Luca Guala, however, total breakdown was inevitable. Given its connectedness, the system was vulnerable and fragile. He continued, "Once again, the inflexibility of the 'complete object' renders it unable to cope with unexpected (yet not so tragic) environmental and social difficulties, and makes it easier to eliminate them rather than adapt the system to cope with them."

36 For more information on EPCOT, please see Steve Mannheim, *Walt Disney and the Quest for Community* (New York: Routledge, 2002).

37 "Masdar City Abandons Transportation System of the Future," http://singularityhub.com/2011/03/01/masdar-city-abandons-public-transportation-system-of-the-future/, accessed March 14, 2016.

38 The quote referred to the science fiction movie *Fifth Element*. Please see "Why Masdar's Personal Rapid Transport Would Have Been Great," https://

www.greenprophet.com/2011/03/masdar-personal-rapid-transport/, accessed May 22, 2017.

39 Also see Latour, *Aramis*, 218.

40 Also see Paul Rabinow, *Designs for an Anthropology of the Contemporary* (Durham, NC: Duke University Press, 2008), 59.

41 Latour, *Aramis*, 122.

42 "Review: Masdar City Personal Rapid Transit," http://everythingexpress.wordpress.com/2011/12/29/review-masdar-city-personal-rapid-transit/, accessed March 14, 2016.

43 "Masdar and Heathrow PRT Still Not Happening," http://prtboondoggle.blogspot.com/2010/12/masdar-and-heathrow-prt-still-not.html, accessed February 9, 2012.

44 See, for instance, Richard Gilbert and Anthony Perl, *Transport Revolutions: Moving People and Freight without Oil* (London: Earthscan, 2008).

45 Vukan R. Vuchic, *Urban Transit Systems and Technology* (New York: John Wiley, 2007), 474.

Chapter 5: Subsurface Workings

1 CDM is a market-based "flexibility mechanism" that was initiated under the Kyoto Protocol with the intention of encouraging industrialized countries to invest in greenhouse gas emission reduction programs in developing countries, such as hydropower, wind energy, or solar energy projects. In this way, industrialized countries could meet their own emission reduction commitments while fostering sustainable development within host countries. Yet CDM projects had to satisfy the so-called additionality requirement, meaning the project proponents had to prove that the given project would not have been initiated without the additional CDM incentive from the UNFCCC. As such, the first step for starting a CDM application to the UNFCCC consisted of proving that the project would not have happened without this additional push. These project proposals would then be evaluated by third-party designated operational entities (DOEs) to guarantee that the project would instigate valid emission reductions. If the DOE gave approval to the project, the proposal would be submitted to the CDM Executive Board within the UNFCCC, waiting to be registered. "But the registration of hundreds of Clean Development Mechanism (CDM) projects at the United Nations Framework Convention for Climate Change (UNFCCC) only shows how successful the consultants that work within these procedures are, rather than proving the success of CDM as a program," a senior environmental consultant I worked with told me, thereby questioning the legitimacy of their policy infrastructure. Upon registration with the UNFCCC, the project

would start to produce carbon credits for the involved entities, based on the supposed emissions reduced by its implementation. In this framework, if China, a developing country under the UNFCCC guidelines, decided to build a solar power station with technology or expertise from a German company, rather than relying on lower-cost energy from coal plants, the reduced carbon emissions attributed to this investment could be credited toward the German company's emission reduction commitment, set by the Kyoto Protocol. The development of a solar power station would also contribute to sustainable development in China, or at least this is what CDM proposed. However, if carbon capture and storage were to be included under the CDM, China could build a coal-powered plant, provided that it is equipped with CCS technology, and still receive carbon credits for it. Accordingly, the inclusion of CCS in the CDM would mean that carbon credits would be issued for carbon dioxide sequestered through future carbon capture and storage projects undertaken in so-called developing countries, providing incentives for further investments in this technology.

2 A carbon credit is a permit that allows a country or organization to produce one ton of carbon emissions. In a cap-and-trade system, if a country's emissions fall below the permitted volume, that country can sell their remaining permits in a carbon market, in the form of carbon credits to others that have gone above their limits. The Kyoto Protocol, an international treaty signed in 1997 and entering into force in 2005, committed its signatories to internationally binding emission reduction targets, and set these carbon emission limits. The countries that have signed the protocol have trade carbon credits.

3 For a list of Non-Annex I countries, see http://unfccc.int/parties_and_observers/parties/non_annex_i/items/2833.php, accessed October 1, 2011. Please note that the United Arab Emirates is one of many other oil-producing countries included within the list.

4 These issues had been identified in United Nations Framework for Climate Change (UNFCCC) Decision 2/CMP.5, paragraph 29. Paragraph 29 specifically stated that the United Nations "*Recognizes* the importance of carbon dioxide capture and storage in geological formations as a possible mitigation technology, bearing in mind the concerns related to the following outstanding issues, inter alia: (a) Non-permanence, including long-term permanence, (b) Measuring, reporting and verification, (c) Environmental impacts, (d) Project activity boundaries, (e) International law, (f) Liability, (g) The potential for perverse outcomes, (h) Safety, (i) Insurance coverage and compensation for damages caused due to seepage or leakage."

5 The environmental consultants at Masdar, as well as the other participants in the preparation of the modalities and procedures submission, had

advanced engineering degrees. They came from various countries around the world, and mostly were in the UAE for temporary periods. The individuals who informed this chapter, through meetings, interviews, or informal conversations, specifically originated from Algeria, Germany, India, Iran, Lebanon, the United Arab Emirates, and the United Kingdom.

6 For another examination of CCS technologies, please see Gökçe Günel, "What Is Carbon Dioxide? When Is Carbon Dioxide?" *PoLAR: Political and Legal Anthropology Review* 39, no. 1 (2016): 33–45.

7 In addition to oil producers, technology developers, such as Japan's Mitsubishi, promoted the inclusion of CCS-EOR as a mitigation strategy. I will not engage more with this point here, but would like to suggest that these technology developers were perceived to be largely responsible for the positions that their governments held in the negotiations with the UNFCCC.

8 See Michael M. J. Fischer, *Emergent Forms of Life and the Anthropological Voice* (Durham, NC: Duke University Press, 2003).

9 Annelise Riles, *The Network Inside Out* (Ann Arbor: University of Michigan Press, 2000), 91.

10 Please see submission document, "Submission of Views from the United Arab Emirates on Addressing the Issues referred to in Paragraph 3 of FCCC/CMP/2010/L.10 in the Modalities and Procedures for the Inclusion of Carbon Dioxide Capture and Storage (CCS) in Geological Formations as Clean Development Mechanism Project Activities," 24, https://unfccc.int/files/methods/application/pdf/uae_submission_on_ccs_in_cdm_20110221.pdf, accessed May 2, 2017.

11 Later in the negotiations this provision would continue to be controversial, as government representatives would be reluctant to take over liability for carbon dioxide.

12 Here, the chemical behavior and porosity and permeability levels of carbonate and sandstone rock formations are argued to be different from each other, which may require differing levels of risk and uncertainty, as well as customized monitoring criteria. For more information on the differences between two types of reservoirs, please see S. N. Ehrenberg and P. H. Nadeau, "Sandstone vs. Carbonate Petroleum Reservoirs: A Global Perspective on Porosity-Depth and Porosity-Permeability Relationships," AAPG *Bulletin* 89, no. 4 (2005): 435–45.

13 Timothy Luke, "On Environmentality: Geo-Power and Eco-Knowledge in the Discourses of Contemporary Environmentalism," *Cultural Critique* 31 (1995): 57–81.

14 See Timothy Choy, *Ecologies of Comparison: An Ethnography of Endangerment in Hong Kong* (Durham, NC: Duke University Press, 2011), 84.

15 Geoffrey Bowker, *Science on the Run: Information Management and Industrial Geophysics at Schlumberger, 1920–1940* (Cambridge: Cambridge University Press, 1994), 32–33.

16 Spelled as Ain Salah in other transliterations, the name of this oasis town translates as "good well" or "good spring."

17 Other participants to the project are Lawrence Livermore National Laboratory, Lawrence Berkeley National Laboratory, Institut Française du Pétrole, European Commission, U.S. Department of Energy (DOE), Carbon Sequestration Leadership Forum (CSLF), and CO2ReMoVe. For an analysis of the project, conducted by Lawrence Livermore National Laboratory, please see S. J. Friedmann, *The Scientific Case for Large* CO_2 *Storage Projects Worldwide: Where They Should Go, What They Should Look Like, and How Much They Should Cost* (Washington, DC: U.S. Department of Energy, 2006).

18 My interlocutors comfortably used phrases such as "saving the environment" or being "good for the environment." Although it is necessary to deconstruct what the circulation of these phrases implies for larger issues around climate change mitigation, I will not engage with these problems in the scope of this chapter.

19 According to a Global CCS Institute report, "at the end of 2010, a total of 234 active or planned CCS projects [were] identified across a range of technologies, project types and sectors," and indicated that twenty-one new CCS projects had been started in the year 2010. In many of these projects, major oil companies served as stakeholders. Please see report, "The Global Status of CCS 2010, http://hub.globalccsinstitute.com/sites/default/files/publications/12776/global-status-ccs-2010.pdf, accessed May 19, 2017.

20 For more information on the negotiation process at climate summits, please see Gökçe Günel, "A Dark Art: Field Notes on Carbon Capture and Storage Negotiations at COP 17, Durban," *Ephemera* 12, no. 1 (2012): 33–41.

21 Larry Lohmann, "Climate as Investment," *Development and Change* 40 (2009): 1063–83, 1078–79.

22 Lohmann, "Climate as Investment," 1078–79.

23 Elaine Shanklin writes: "In the night of 21 August 1986 Lake Nyos exploded. The 'good' lake, as the locals called it, the most beautiful crater lake in Cameroon's North West Province, exploded and sent down to the valley beneath a deadly cloud of carbon dioxide that killed most of the living things it touched—1746 men, women and children, more than 3,000 cattle, plus countless numbers of sheep, goats, birds and insects. Little or no damage was done to plants, crops or inanimate property. Houses, market stalls, village ovens and motorcycles stood untouched, while their owners lay dead nearby." Elaine Shanklin, "Beautiful Deadly Lake Nyos: The Explosion and Its Aftermath," *Anthropology Today* 4, no. 1 (1988): 12–14.

24 International Energy Agency, "Carbon Capture and Storage: Legal and Regulatory Review," 2011, www.iea.org/Papers/2011/ccs_legal.pdf, accessed September 28, 2011.

25 For a report on German CCS legislations, please see https://hub.globalccs institute.com/publications/dedicated-ccs-legislation-current-and-proposed /german-ccs-legislation, accessed May 5, 2017.

Epilogue: The Potential Futures of Abu Dhabi's Masdar

1 Suzanne Goldenberg, "Masdar's Zero-Carbon Dream Could Become World's First Green Ghost Town," *The Guardian*, February 16, 2016, http:// www.theguardian.com/environment/2016/feb/16/masdars-zero-carbon -dream-could-become-worlds-first-green-ghost-town, accessed February 19, 2016.

2 "Eerie Video Shows Masdar City—The Sustainable City of the Future—Has No One in It," http://www.fastcoexist.com/3035446/eerie-video-shows -masdar-city-the-sustainable-city-of-the-future-has-no-one-in-it, accessed January 15, 2016.

3 This was perceived to be in contrast to the South Korean smart city Songdo, which relied on public institutions to ensure its growth.

4 See the HERM website, http://theherm.org/, accessed July 15, 2014. Also see http://ourstreamingplanet.com/tag/herm/, accessed July 15, 2014.

5 The modalities and procedures draft text that started the discussions in Durban is available at http://unfccc.int/resource/docs/2011/sbsta/eng/04 .pdf, accessed December 8, 2011.

6 See Annelise Riles, *The Network Inside Out* (Ann Arbor: University of Michigan Press, 2000).

7 Perhaps the best-known instance of "constructive ambiguity" is the UN Security Council's Resolution 242 of November 1967. Referring to the six-day Arab-Israeli war of June 1967, it required the "[w]ithdrawal of Israeli armed forces from territories occupied in the recent conflict." It left unclear the question of whether Israel was obliged to engage in a complete or only partial withdrawal.

8 G. R. Berridge and Lorna Lloyd, *The Palgrave Macmillan Dictionary of Diplomacy* (Houndmills, UK: Palgrave Macmillan, 2012), 73.

9 Berridge and Lloyd, *The Palgrave Macmillan Dictionary of Diplomacy*, 73.

10 The London Protocol suggests: "disposal or storage of wastes or other matter directly arising from, or related to the exploration, exploitation and associated off-shore processing of seabed mineral resources is not covered by the provisions of this Protocol," and thereby does not provide any regulations regarding the transboundary flow of carbon dioxide for enhanced oil

recovery (EOR) purposes. For more information on the London Convention and CCS, please see the International Energy Agency (IEA) working paper entitled "Carbon Capture and Storage and the London Protocol: Options for Enabling Transboundary CO_2 Transfer," https://www.iea.org/publications/freepublications/publication/CCS_London_Protocol.pdf, accessed December 6, 2013.

11 "Majid Al Futtaim Plans to Open Masdar City Mall in 2018," http://www.thenational.ae/business/retail/majid-al-futtaim-plans-to-open-masdar-city-mall-in-2018, accessed January 25, 2017.

12 "Eco-Villa Prototype Opens Its Doors at Masdar City," http://www.masdar.ae/en/media/detail/eco-villa-prototype-opens-its-doors-at-masdar-city, accessed May 8, 2017.

13 "If the Foster + Partners–designed first generation of Masdar's vision was the architectural equivalent of a temperamental but finely tuned F1 car, with the Eco-Villa, Masdar appears to be aiming for the architectural equivalent of the Volkswagen, a national project that can be rolled out quickly, economically and en masse." "Masdar City's New Eco-Villa: Abu Dhabi's Residential Future?" http://www.thenational.ae/arts-life/home-garden/masdar-citys-new-eco-villa-abu-dhabis-residential-future#full, accessed January 25, 2017.

14 "Masdar City Free Zone," http://www.masdarcityfreezone.com/en/, accessed May 14, 2017.

References

Abdelal, Rawi. 2009. "Sovereign Wealth in Abu Dhabi." *Geopolitics* 14, no. 2: 317–27.

Abu-Lughod, Janet. 1987. "The Islamic City—Historical Myth, Islamic Essence, and Contemporary Relevance." *International Journal of Middle East Studies* 19: 155–76.

Agamben, Giorgio. 2000. *Potentialities: Collected Essays in Philosophy*. Palo Alto, CA: Stanford University Press.

Ahmad, Attiya. 2017. *Everyday Conversions: Islam, Domestic Work, and South Asian Migrant Women in Kuwait*. Durham, NC: Duke University Press.

Akin, William E. 1977. *Technocracy and the American Dream: The Technocrat Movement, 1900–1941*. Berkeley: University of California Press.

Al-Gurg, Easa Saleh. 1998. *The Wells of Memory: An Autobiography*. London: J. Murray.

Al-Nakib, Farah. 2016. *Kuwait Transformed: A History of Oil and Urban Life*. Palo Alto, CA: Stanford University Press.

Altan-Olcay, Özlem. 2008. "Defining 'America' from a Distance: Local Strategies of the Global in the Middle East." *Middle Eastern Studies* 44, no. 1: 29–52.

Anker, Peder. 2010. *From Bauhaus to Ecohouse: A History of Ecological Design*. Baton Rouge: Louisiana State University Press.

Appel, Hannah. 2012. "Offshore Work: Oil, Modularity, and the How of Capitalism in Equatorial Guinea." *American Ethnologist* 39, no. 4: 692–709.

Barnes, Jessica. 2014. *Cultivating the Nile: the Everyday Politics of Water in Egypt*. Durham, NC: Duke University Press.

Bendell, Jem, and Ian Doyle. 2014. *Healing Capitalism: Five Years in the Life of Business, Finance and Corporate Responsibility*. London: Greenleaf.

Berndt, Ernst R. 1983. "From Technocracy to Net Energy Analysis: Engineers, Economists, and Recurring Energy Theories of Value." In *Progress in Natural Resource Economics*, edited by Anthony Scott, John Heliwel, Tracy Lewis, and P. A. Neher, 337–66. Oxford: Clarendon Press.

Berridge, G. R., and Lorna Lloyd. 2012. *The Palgrave Macmillan Dictionary of Diplomacy*. Houndmills, UK: Palgrave Macmillan.

Beverly, R. 2003. "Editor's Note: Your Thermostat: Trusty Friend or Two-Faced Double Agent?" *Engineered Systems* 20, no. 4: 8.

Bloch, Ernst. 1988. *The Utopian Function of Art and Literature: Selected Essays*. Cambridge, MA: MIT Press.

Blumenberg, Hans. 1996. *Shipwreck with Spectator: Paradigm of a Metaphor for Existence*. Cambridge, MA: MIT Press.

Bowden, Gary. 1985. "The Social Construction of Validity Estimates of US Crude Oil Reserves." *Social Studies of Science* 15, no. 2: 207–40.

Bowker, Geoffrey. 1994. *Science on the Run: Information Management and Industrial Geophysics at Schlumberger, 1920–1940*. Cambridge: Cambridge University Press.

Boyer, Dominic. 2014. "Energopolitics: An Introduction." *Anthropological Quarterly* 87, no. 2: 309–33.

Boyer, Dominic, and Cymene Howe. 2016. "Aeolian Infrastructures, Aeolian Publics." *Limn* 7 (July): 4598.

Brand, Laurie. 2001. "Development in Wadi Rum? State Bureaucracy, External Funders, and Civil Society." *International Journal of Middle East Studies* 33, no. 4: 571–90.

Bridge, Gavin. 2010. "Geographies of Peak Oil: The Other Carbon Problem." *Geoforum* 41, no. 4: 523–30.

Burger, Scott. 2012. "Desertec: A Fata Morgana?" *Africa Policy Journal* 8: 52–53.

Callon, Michel. 2007. "An Essay on the Growing Contribution of Economic Markets to the Proliferation of the Social." *Theory, Culture and Society* 24, nos. 7–8: 139–63.

Carlson, W. Bernard. 2013. *Tesla: Inventor of the Electrical Age*. Princeton, NJ: Princeton University Press.

Castañeda, Carlos. 1968. *The Teachings of Don Juan: A Yaqui Way of Knowledge*. Berkeley: University of California Press.

Chatters, C. H. 1933. "Appendix E: Is Municipal Scrip a Panacea?" *Annals of Public and Cooperative Economics* 9, no. 2: 323–25.

Chatty, Dawn. 1996. *Mobile Pastoralists: Development Planning and Social Change in Oman*. New York: Columbia University Press.

Chatty, Dawn. 2009. "Rituals of Royalty and the Elaboration of Ceremony in Oman: View from the Edge." *International Journal of Middle East Studies* 41, no. 1: 39–58.

Checket-Hanks, B. 2003. "Placebo Stats." *Air Conditioning, Heating and Refrigeration News* 218, no. 13. https://www.achrnews.com/articles/92414-placebo-stats.

Choucri, N., D. Goldsmith, and T. Mezher. 2010. "Renewable Energy Policy in an Oil-Exporting Country: The Case of the United Arab Emirates." *Renewable Energy Law and Policy Review* 1, no. 1: 77–86.

Choy, Timothy. 2011. *Ecologies of Comparison: An Ethnography of Endangerment in Hong Kong*. Durham, NC: Duke University Press.

Collins, James, Jr. 1999. "The Design Process for the Human Workplace." In *Architecture of Science*, edited by Peter Galison and Emily Ann Thompson, 399–413. Cambridge, MA: MIT Press.

Cross, Jamie. 2013. "The 100th Object: Solar Lighting Technology and Humanitarian Goods." *Journal of Material Culture* 18, no. 4: 367–87.

Daly, Herman, and Alvaro Umaña. 1981. *Energy, Economics, and the Environment: Conflicting Views of an Essential Interrelationship*. Boulder, CO: Westview.

Davidson, Christopher M. 2006. "After Shaikh Zayed: The Politics of Succession in Abu Dhabi and the UAE." *Middle East Policy* 13, no. 1: 42–59.

Davidson, Christopher M. 2009a. *Abu Dhabi: Oil and Beyond*. New York: Columbia University Press.

Davidson, Christopher M. 2009b. "Abu Dhabi's New Economy: Oil, Investment and Domestic Development." *Middle East Policy* 16, no. 2: 59–79.

Deeb, Lara, and Jessica Winegar. 2012. "Anthropologies of Arab-Majority Societies." *Annual Review of Anthropology* 41, no. 41: 537–58.

Dennis, Michael Aaron. 1985. "Drilling for Dollars: The Making of US Petroleum Reserve Estimates, 1921–25." *Social Studies of Science* 15, no. 2: 241–65.

Doherty, Gareth. 2017. *Paradoxes of Green: Landscapes of a City-State*. Berkeley: University of California Press.

Douthwaite, R. J. 1999. *The Ecology of Money*. Totnes, UK: Green.

Easterling, Keller. 2005. *Enduring Innocence: Global Architecture and Its Political Masquerades*. Cambridge, MA: MIT Press.

Ehrenberg, S. N., and P. H. Nadeau. 2005. "Sandstone vs. Carbonate Petroleum Reservoirs: A Global Perspective on Porosity-Depth and Porosity-Permeability Relationships." *AAPG Bulletin* 89, no. 4: 435–45.

Ehteshami, Anoushiravan, Neil Quilliam, and Gawdat Bahgat. 2017. *Security and Bilateral Issues between Iran and Its Arab Neighbors*. London: Springer.

Eichengreen, Barry J. [1985] 1997. *The Gold Standard in Theory and History.* New York: Methuen.

Elsheshtawy, Yasser. 2008. *The Evolving Arab City: Tradition, Modernity and Urban Development.* London: Routledge.

Elvins, Sarah. 2010. "Scrip, Stores, and Cash-Strapped Cities: American Retailers and Alternative Currency during the Great Depression." *Journal of Historical Research in Marketing* 2, no. 1: 86–107.

Erken, Ali. 2016. "The Making of Politics and Trained Intelligence in the Near East: Robert College of Istanbul." *European Review of History: Revue européenne d'histoire* 23, no. 3: 554–71.

Ewald, François. 1993. "Two Infinities of Risk." In *The Politics of Everyday Fear,* edited by Brian Massumi, 221–28. Minneapolis: University of Minnesota Press.

Fennell, Catherine. 2011. "'Project Heat' and Sensory Politics in Redeveloping Chicago Public Housing." *Ethnography* 12:40–64.

Ferguson, James. 1994. *Anti-Politics Machine: Development, Depoliticization, and Bureaucratic Power in Lesotho.* Minneapolis: University of Minnesota Press.

Ferguson, James. 1999. *Expectations of Modernity: Myths and Meanings of Urban Life on the Zambian Copperbelt.* Berkeley: University of California Press.

Fields, Gary. 2010. "Landscaping Palestine: Reflections of Enclosure in a Historical Mirror." *International Journal of Middle East Studies* 42, no. 1: 63–82.

Fischer, Michael M. J. 2003. *Emergent Forms of Life and the Anthropological Voice.* Durham, NC: Duke University Press.

Fortun, Michael. 2008. *Promising Genomics: Iceland and deCODE Genetics in a World of Speculation.* Berkeley: University of California Press.

Fuller, Buckminster. [1969] 2008. *Operating Manual for Spaceship Earth.* Rotterdam: Lars Müller.

Gardiner, Stephen. 2011. *A Perfect Moral Storm: The Ethical Tragedy of Climate Change.* Oxford: Oxford University Press.

Gardner, Andrew. 2010. *City of Strangers: Gulf Migration and the Indian Community in Bahrain.* Ithaca, NY: Cornell University Press.

Gatch, Loren. 2008. "Local Money in the United States during the Great Depression." *Essays in Economic and Business History* 26: 47–61.

Gatch, Loren. 2012. "Tax Anticipation Scrip as a Form of Local Currency in the USA during the 1930s." *International Journal of Community Currency Research* 16 (D): 22–35.

Gilbert, Richard, and Anthony Perl. 2008. *Transport Revolutions: Moving People and Freight without Oil.* London: Earthscan.

Graeber, David. 1996. "Beads and Money: Notes toward a Theory of Wealth and Power." *American Ethnologist* 23, no. 1: 4–24.

Graeber, David. 2011. *Debt: The First 5,000 Years*. Brooklyn, NY: Melville House.

Guarasci, Bridget. 2015. "The National Park: Reviving Eden in Iraq's Marshes." *Arab Studies Journal* 23, no. 1. https://www.questia.com/library/journal/1P3-4066730961/the-national-park-reviving-eden-in-iraq-s-marshes.

Günel, Gökçe. 2012. "A Dark Art: Field Notes on Carbon Capture and Storage Negotiations at COP 17, Durban." *Ephemera* 12, no. 1: 33–41.

Günel, Gökçe. 2014. "Masdar City's Hidden Brain." *The arpa Journal*. Accessed September 25, 2014. http://arpajournal.gsapp.org/masdar-citys-hidden-brain/.

Günel, Gökçe. 2016a. "The Infinity of Water: Climate Change Adaptation in the Arabian Peninsula." *Public Culture* 28, no. 2: 291–315.

Günel, Gökçe. 2016b. "What Is Carbon Dioxide? When Is Carbon Dioxide?" *PoLAR: Political and Legal Anthropology Review* 39, no. 1: 33–45.

Gupta, Akhil. 2015. "An Anthropology of Electricity from the Global South." *Cultural Anthropology* 30, no. 4: 555–68.

Guyer, Jane. 2004. *Marginal Gains: Monetary Transactions in Atlantic Africa*. Chicago: University of Chicago Press.

Guyer, Jane. 2009. "Composites, Fictions, and Risks: Toward an Ethnography of Price." In *Market and Society: The Great Transformation Today*, edited by C. Hann and K. Hart, 203–20. Cambridge: Cambridge University Press.

Guyer, Jane. 2011. "Blueprints, Judgment, and Perseverance in a Corporate Context." *Current Anthropology* 52, no. 3: S17–S27.

Guyer, Jane. 2015. "Oil Assemblages and the Production of Confusion: Price Fluctuations in Two West African Oil-Producing Economies." In *Subterranean Estates: Life Worlds of Oil and Gas*, edited by Hannah Appel, Arthur Mason, and Michael Watts, 237–52. Ithaca, NY: Cornell University Press.

Haberly, Daniel. 2011. "Strategic Sovereign Wealth Fund Investment and the New Alliance Capitalism: A Network Mapping Investigation." *Environment and Planning A* 43, no. 8: 1833–52.

Haberly, Daniel. 2014. "White Knights from the Gulf: Sovereign Wealth Fund Investment and the Evolution of German Industrial Finance." *Economic Geography* 90, no. 3: 293–320.

Halpern, Orit. 2015. *Beautiful Data: A History of Vision and Reason since 1945*. Durham, NC: Duke University Press.

Halpern, Orit, J. LeCavalier, N. Calvillo, and W. Pietsch. 2013. "Test-Bed Urbanism." *Public Culture* 25, no. 2: 273–305.

Hamdy, Shirine. 2012. *Our Bodies Belong to God: Organ Transplants, Islam, and the Struggle for Human Dignity in Egypt*. Berkeley: University of California Press.

Hamilton, William F., II, and Dana K. Nance. 1969. "Systems Analysis of Urban Transportation." *Scientific American* 221, no. 1: 19–27.

Hanieh, Adam. 2011. *Capitalism and Class in the Gulf Arab States*. London: Palgrave Macmillan.

Hart, Keith. 2000. "Money in an Unequal World." *The Memory Bank*. Accessed December 22, 2014. http://thememorybank.co.uk/papers/money-in-an-unequal-world/.

Helmreich, Stefan. 2009. *Alien Ocean: Anthropological Voyages in Microbial Seas*. Berkeley: University of California Press.

Höhler, Sabine. 2010. "The Environment as a Life Support System: The Case of Biosphere 2." *History and Technology* 26, no. 1: 39–58.

Höhler, Sabine. 2015. *Spaceship Earth in the Environmental Age, 1960–1990*. London: Pickering and Chatto.

Holston, James. 1989. *The Modernist City: An Anthropological Critique of Brasília*. Chicago: University of Chicago Press.

Inhorn, Marcia. 2015. *Cosmopolitan Conceptions: IVF Sojourns in Global Dubai*. Durham, NC: Duke University Press.

Jamieson, Dale. 1992. "Ethics, Public Policy, and Global Warming." *Science, Technology, and Human Values* 17, no. 2: 139–53.

Jones, Toby Craig. 2010. *Desert Kingdom: How Oil and Water Forged Modern Saudi Arabia*. Cambridge, MA: Harvard University Press.

Kanna, Ahmed. 2011. *Dubai, the City as Corporation*. Minneapolis: University of Minnesota Press.

Keane, David, and Nicholas McGeehan. 2008. "Enforcing Migrant Workers' Rights in the United Arab Emirates." *International Journal on Minority and Group Rights* 15, no. 1: 81–115.

Khalaf, Sulayman, and Saad Alkobaisi. 1999. "Migrants' Strategies of Coping and Patterns of Accommodation in the Oil-Rich Gulf Societies: Evidence from the UAE." *British Journal of Middle Eastern Studies* 26, no. 2: 271–98.

Kirk, D., and D. Napier. 2009. "The Transformation of Higher Education in the United Arab Emirates: Issues, Implications, and Intercultural Dimensions." In *Nation-Building, Identity and Citizenship Education: Cross Cultural Perspectives*, edited by J. Zajda, H. Daun, and L. J. Saha, 131–42. Dordrecht, Netherlands: Springer Science + Business Media B.V.

Klein, Hans K. 1996. "Institutions, Innovation, and Information Infrastructure: The Social Construction of Intelligent Transportation Systems in the U.S., Europe, and Japan." PhD diss., Technology, Management, and Policy Program, MIT.

Klein, Naomi. 2014. *This Changes Everything: Capitalism vs. the Climate*. New York: Verso.

Larkin, Brian. 2013. "The Politics and Poetics of Infrastructure." *Annual Review of Anthropology* 42: 327–43.

Latour, Bruno. 1996. *Aramis, or the Love of Technology*. Cambridge, MA: Harvard University Press.

Limbert, Mandana. 2010. *In the Time of Oil: Piety, Memory, and Social Life in an Omani Town*. Stanford, CA: Stanford University Press.

Limbert, Mandana. 2015. "Reserves, Secrecy and the Science of Oil Prognostication in Southern Arabia." In *Subterranean Estates: Life Worlds of Oil and Gas*, edited by Arthur Mason, Hannah Appel, and Michael Watts. Ithaca, NY: Cornell University Press.

Lipson, Hod, and Melba Kurman. 2016. *Driverless: Intelligent Cars and the Road Ahead*. Cambridge, MA: MIT Press.

Lohmann, Larry. 2009. "Climate as Investment." *Development and Change* 40: 1063–83.

Longva, Anh Nga. 1997. *Walls Built on Sand: Migration, Exclusion, and Society in Kuwait*. Boulder, CO: Westview.

Looser, Tom. 2012. "The Global University, Area Studies, and the World Citizen: Neoliberal Geography's Redistribution of the 'World.'" *Cultural Anthropology* 27, no. 1: 97–117.

Lorin, Ritchie, and Kathlin Ray. 2008. "Incorporating Information Literacy into the Building Plan: The American University of Sharjah Experience." *Reference Services Review* 36, no. 2: 167–79.

Luke, Timothy. 1995. "On Environmentality: Geo-Power and Eco-Knowledge in the Discourses of Contemporary Environmentalism." *Cultural Critique* 31: 57–81.

Makdisi, Karim. 2013. "The Rise and Decline of Environmentalism in Lebanon." In *Water on Sand: Environmental Histories of the Middle East and North Africa*, edited by Alan Mikhail, 207–29. Oxford: Oxford University Press.

Mannheim, Steve. 2002. *Walt Disney and the Quest for Community*. New York: Routledge.

Maurer, Bill. 2005a. "Does Money Matter? Abstraction and Substitution in Alternative Financial Forms." In *Materiality*, edited by Daniel Miller. Durham, NC: Duke University Press.

Maurer, Bill. 2005b. *Mutual Life, Limited: Islamic Banking, Alternative Currencies, Lateral Reason*. Princeton, NJ: Princeton University Press.

Maurer, Markus, J. Christian Gerdes, Barbara Lenz, and Hermann Winner, eds. 2016. *Autonomous Driving: Technical, Legal and Social Aspects*. New York: Springer.

May, Shannon. 2008. "Ecological Citizenship and a Plan for Sustainable Development." *City* 12, no. 2: 237–44.

Mazzarella, William. 2010. "Beautiful Balloon: The Digital Divide and the Charisma of New Media in India." *American Ethnologist* 37, no. 4: 783–804.

McCarthy, Tom. 2007. *Remainder*. New York: Vintage.

Menoret, Pascal. 2014. *Joyriding in Riyadh: Oil, Urbanism, and Road Revolt*. Cambridge: Cambridge University Press.

Mikhail, Alan. 2014. *The Animal in Ottoman Egypt*. Oxford: Oxford University Press.

Miller-Idriss, Cynthia, and Elizabeth Hanauer. 2011. "Transnational Higher Education: Offshore Campuses in the Middle East." *Comparative Education* 47, no. 2: 181–207.

Mindell, David A. 2008. *Digital Apollo: Human and Machine in Spaceflight*. Cambridge, MA: MIT Press.

Mirowski, Philip. 1989. *More Heat Than Light: Economics as Social Physics, Physics as Nature's Economics*. Cambridge: Cambridge University Press.

Mitchell, Kevin. 2015. "Design for the Future: Educational Institutions in the Gulf." *Architectural Design* 85, no. 1: 38–45.

Mitchell, Timothy. 2002. *Rule of Experts: Egypt, Techno-Politics, Modernity*. Berkeley: University of California Press.

Mitchell, Timothy. 2012. *Carbon Democracy*. New York: Verso.

Mostafavi, Mohsen, and Gareth Doherty. 2010. *Ecological Urbanism*. Baden, Switzerland: Lars Müller.

Muñoz, Jose Esteban. 2009. *Cruising Utopia: The Then and There of Queer Futurity*. New York: NYU Press.

Murphy, Michelle. 2006. *Sick Building Syndrome and the Problem of Uncertainty: Environmental Politics, Technoscience, and Women Workers*. Durham, NC: Duke University Press.

Nagy, Sharon. 2000. "Dressing Up Downtown: Urban Development and Government Public Image in Qatar." *City and Society* 12, no. 1: 125–47.

Orwell, George. 1950. *Nineteen Eighty-Four*. New York: Signet Classic.

Parry, Jonathan, and Maurice Bloch. 1989. *Money and the Morality of Exchange*. Cambridge: Cambridge University Press.

Peattie, Lisa Redfield. 1987. *Planning, Rethinking Ciudad Guayana*. Ann Arbor: University of Michigan Press.

Peebles, Gustav. 2008. "Inverting the Panopticon: Money and the Nationalization of the Future." *Public Culture* 20, no. 2: 233–65.

Pinkus, Karen. 2016. *Fuel: A Speculative Dictionary*. Minneapolis: University of Minnesota Press.

Polich, Judith Bluestone. 2001. *Return of the Children of the Light: Incan and Mayan Prophecies for a New World*. Rochester: Bear and Company.

Povinelli, Elizabeth. 2016. *Geontologies: A Requiem to Late Liberalism*. Durham, NC: Duke University Press.

Rabinow, Paul. 2008. *Designs for an Anthropology of the Contemporary*. Durham, NC: Duke University Press.

Rademacher, Anne. 2017. *Building Green: Environmental Architects and the Struggle for Sustainability in Mumbai*. Berkeley: University of California Press.

Rajan, Kaushik Sunder. 2005. "Subjects of Speculation: Emergent Life Sciences and Market Logics in the United States and India." *American Anthropologist* 107, no. 1: 19–30.

Ramos, Stephen J. 2010. *Dubai Amplified: The Engineering of a Port Geography*. London: Ashgate.

Reisz, Todd. 2008. "As a Matter of Fact: The Legend of Dubai." *Log* 13–14: 127–37.

Riles, Annelise. 2000. *The Network Inside Out*. Ann Arbor: University of Michigan Press.

Rogers, Douglas. 2015. "Oil and Anthropology." *Annual Review of Anthropology* 44: 365–80.

Sanal, Aslıhan. 2011. *New Organs within Us*. Durham, NC: Duke University Press.

Schumacher, E. F. 1973. *Small Is Beautiful: A Study of Economics as If People Mattered*. New York: Blond and Briggs.

Scott, James C. 1998. *Seeing Like a State: How Certain Schemes to Improve the Human Condition Have Failed*. New Haven, CT: Yale University Press.

Shanklin, Elaine. 1988. "Beautiful Deadly Lake Nyos: The Explosion and Its Aftermath." *Anthropology Today* 4, no. 1: 12–14.

Shell, Marc. [1978] 1993. *The Economy of Literature*. Baltimore: Johns Hopkins University Press.

Sieden, Steven. 2000. *Buckminster Fuller's Universe: His Life and Work*. New York: Basic Books.

Slayton, Rebecca. 2013. "Efficient, Secure Green: Digital Utopianism and the Challenge of a 'Smart' Grid." *Information and Culture* 48, no. 4: 448–78.

Sloterdijk, Peter. 2014. *Globes: Spheres 2*. South Pasadena, CA: Semiotext(e).

Stamatopoulou-Robbins, Sophia. 2014. "Occupational Hazards." *Comparative Studies of South Asia, Africa and the Middle East* 34, no. 3: 476–96.

Stanek, Łukasz. 2015. "Mobilities of Architecture in the Global Cold War: From Socialist Poland to Kuwait and Back." *International Journal of Islamic Architecture* 4, no. 2: 365–98.

Star, Susan Leigh. 1999. "The Ethnography of Infrastructure." *American Behavioral Scientist* 43, no. 3: 377–91.

Stark, Laura. 2012. *Behind Closed Doors: IRBs and the Making of Ethical Research*. Chicago: University of Chicago Press.

Stein, Rebecca. 2009. "Traveling Zion: Hiking and Settler Nationalism in Pre-1948 Palestine." *Interventions: International Journal of Postcolonial Studies* 11, no. 3: 334–51.

Strathern, Marilyn. 1996. "Cutting the Network." *Journal of the Royal Anthropological Institute* 2, no. 3: 517–35.

Svendsen, Mette N. 2011. "Articulating Potentiality: Notes on the Delineation of the Blank Figure in Human Embryonic Stem Cell Research." *Cultural Anthropology* 26, no. 3: 414–37.

Sze, Julie. 2014. *Fantasy Islands: Chinese Dreams and Ecological Fears in an Age of Climate Crisis*. Palo Alto, CA: University of California Press.

Taussig, Michael. 1992. *The Nervous System*. New York: Routledge.

Thrift, Nigel. 2000. "Performing Cultures in the New Economy." *Annals of the Association of American Geographers* 90, no. 4: 674–92.

Thrift, Nigel. 2005. *Knowing Capitalism*. London: SAGE.

Thrift, Nigel. 2006. "Re-Inventing Invention: New Tendencies in Capitalist Commodification." *Economy and Society* 35, no. 2: 279–306.

Tse Kwai Zung, Thomas. 2002. *Buckminster Fuller: Anthology for a New Millennium*. New York: St. Martin's.

Tsing, Anna. 2015. *The Mushroom at the End of the World: On the Possibility of Life in Capitalist Ruins*. Princeton, NJ: Princeton University Press.

Valentine, David. 2016. "Atmosphere: Context, Detachment, and the View from above Earth." *American Ethnologist* 43, no. 3: 511–24.

Veblen, Thorstein. 1898. "Why Is Economics Not an Evolutionary Science?" *Quarterly Journal of Economics* 12, no. 4: 373–97.

Virilio, Paul. 2007. *The Original Accident*. Translated by Julie Rose. Malden, MA: Polity.

Virno, Paolo. 2015. *Déjà Vu and the End of History*. New York: Verso.

Vitalis, Robert. 2006. *America's Kingdom: Mythmaking on the Saudi Oil Frontier*. Stanford, CA: Stanford University Press.

von Meijenfeldt, Ernst, and Marit Geluk. 2003. *Below Ground Level: Creating New Spaces for Contemporary Architecture*. Basel: Birkhäuser.

von Schnitzler, Antina. 2016. *Democracy's Infrastructure: Techno-Politics and Protest after Apartheid*. Princeton, NJ: Princeton University Press.

Vora, Neha. 2013. *Impossible Citizens: Dubai's Indian Diaspora*. Durham, NC: Duke University Press.

Vora, Neha. 2014. "Between Global Citizenship and Qatarization: Negotiating Qatar's New Knowledge Economy within American Branch Campuses." *Ethnic and Racial Studies* 37, no. 12: 2243–60.

Vora, Neha. 2015. "Is the University Universal? Mobile (Re)Constitutions of American Academia in the Gulf Arab States." *Anthropology and Education Quarterly* 46, no. 1: 19–36.

Vora, Neha. 2018. *Teach for Arabia: American Universities, Liberalism, and Transnational Qatar*. Stanford, CA: Stanford University Press.

Vuchic, Vukan R. 2007. *Urban Transit Systems and Technology*. New York: John Wiley and Sons.

Wang, Shengwei. 2010. *Intelligent Buildings and Building Automation*. London: Spon.

Weszkalnys, Gisa. 2015. "Geology, Potentiality, Speculation: On the Indeterminacy of First Oil." *Cultural Anthropology* 30, no. 4: 611–39.

White, Leslie. 1943. "Energy and the Evolution of Culture." *American Anthropologist* 45, no. 3: 335–56.

Wilkins, Stephen. 2010. "Higher Education in the United Arab Emirates: An Analysis of the Outcomes of Significant Increases in Supply and Competition." *Journal of Higher Education Policy and Management* 32, no. 4: 389–400.

Williams, Rosalind. [1990] 2008. *Notes on the Underground: An Essay on Technology, Society, and the Imagination*. Cambridge, MA: MIT Press.

Yalman, Nur. 2016. "The Rashomon Effect: Considerations for Existential Anthropology." In *Rashomon Effects: Kurosawa, Rashomon and Their Legacies*, edited by Blair Davis, Robert Anderson, and Jan Walls. New York: Routledge.

Yergin, Daniel. 1990. *The Prize: The Epic Quest for Oil, Money, and Power*. New York: Free Press.

Zahlan, Rosemarie Said. 1978. *The Origins of the United Arab Emirates: A Political and Social History of the Trucial States*. New York: St. Martin's.

Index

Page numbers followed by f indicate illustrations.